CULTURE AND RESOURCE CONFLICT

CULTURE AND RESOURCE CONFLICT

Why Meanings Matter

Douglas L. Medin
Norbert O. Ross
Douglas G. Cox

Russell Sage Foundation
New York

Library of Congress Cataloging-in-Publication Data
Medin, Douglas L.
   Culture and resource conflict : why meanings matter / Douglas L. Medin, Norbert O. Ross, Douglas G. Cox.
     p. cm.
   ISBN 10: 0-87154-570-5   ISBN 13: 978-0-87154-570-1
   1. Menominee Indians—Wisconsin—Fishing.   2. Menominee Indians—Wisconsin—Hunting.   3. Human ecology—Wisconsin.   4. Nature—Effect of human beings on—Wisconsin.   5. Culture conflict—Wisconsin.   6. Wisconsin—Social life and customs.   7. Wisconsin—Ethnic relations.   I. Ross, Norbert (Norbert O.)   II. Cox, Douglas G..   III. Title.

E99.M44.M32   2006
304.2089'009775—dc22   2006040900

The paper used in this publication meets the minimum requirements of American National Standard for Information Sciences—Permanence of Paper for Printed Library Materials. ANSI Z39.48–1992.

Photograph: The cover is a photograph of a pastel by Santa Fe artist Carole LaRoche, entitled *Protector*. We thank her for her permission to use it. One factor motivating her exploration of this ecological and environmental theme is the Exxon Valdez oil spill in Prudhoe Bay, Alaska, and the slow, begrudging cleanup that followed it. The black coat of the wolf may represent the oil spilled. Perhaps the artist is using the wolf as a symbolic pointer to humans to both remind us that we are a part of nature and that we have an important role to play.

Text design by Genna Patacsil.

RUSSELL SAGE FOUNDATION
112 East 64th Street, New York, New York 10021
10 9 8 7 6 5 4 3 2 1

Norbert Ross
To my family for allowing me to spend time—that should have been yours—to conduct research and write another book.

Douglas Cox
To my wife, Jean, I would like to thank you for all your patience, understanding, and most importantly your willingness to stand by me through the hard times as well as the good times. You are my best friend and my favorite fishing partner.

Douglas Medin
To my wife, Linda, for her limitless patience and support—a weekend fishing trip is one thing—eight years of constant time away is quite another. And to Samuel Medin, naturalist.

Contents |

About the Authors |

Douglas L. Medin is professor of psychology and education and social policy at Northwestern University.

Norbert O. Ross is assistant professor of anthropology at Vanderbilt University.

Douglas G. Cox is an environmental specialist at the Hilary J. Waukau Environmental Services Center on the Menominee reservation in Wisconsin.

Preface |

When the wind is in the north fishermen go forth,
When the wind is in the east fishing is the least,
When the wind is in the south it blows the hook in their mouth,
When the wind is in the west, fishing is best.

THE PROPER ATTRIBUTION for the above verse is probably lost to history—it has been widespread in the Midwest since at least the early twentieth century. It seems to echo another, much more ancient and widespread, set of ideas based on the four directions: Native American notions of the circle of life, in which the directions correspond to the seasons. East is spring, south is summer, west is fall, and north is winter. For Native Americans, the circle of life is also the cycle of life, from emergence and growth to decay and regeneration. This pattern is believed to hold for both plants and animals in general and in the lives of individuals in particular.

Sometimes it seems as if the primary metaphor for mainstream European-American culture—what we call majority culture in our studies—is more linear than cyclic: theoretically we progress in a more or less straight line in our educational attainment and in our accumulation of wealth, and our experience expands in a variety of linear ways. But the cycle image also fits with many aspects of our lives.

Virtually every aspect of this project reflects a close collaboration between its three authors, and we all share core convictions—yet we three also bring very personal, local, meanings and viewpoints to our work, which we here convey to our readers.

DOUGLAS MEDIN

The circle metaphor seems especially apt with respect to this book, for the experiences of my childhood and early adulthood opened circles that have been completed by my academic work. I grew up in the Midwest, and hunting, fishing, and trapping were significant components of my childhood and adolescence. Particularly memorable were the summers I would spend at my grandparents' cottage in northern Minnesota on Woman Lake. My grandmother's fishing expertise was legendary and some called her "the lady of the lake." Resort owners would advise people to fish wherever they saw her fishing, sometimes to my annoyance. My grandmother would take me out fishing every late afternoon until the mosquitoes forced us to go in at dusk. Fishing was always accompanied by stories from my grandmother, with additional entertainment provided by families of loons and the occasional eagle.

My grandfather didn't like to sit for long periods of time, so for him, fishing was out. He was always out working on the property, trying to keep the chipmunks from his strawberries, and splitting logs for firewood. Although he was burdened with just a sixth-grade school education, he was intellectually curious. He would often read the dictionary at night. And he was a naturalist. He loved birds; I think the cedar waxwing would be close to the top of his list of favorites, though he maintained a martin house, so they would be up there as well.

Two more circles that would lead back to folkbiology were begun around this time, one in my wife's childhood and one from mine. Linda spent significant portions of her childhood on her grandparents' farm in Upstate New York, where her favorite activities were collecting frogs and newts and watching her grandmother's garden.

My family lived in Klemme, Iowa (population 411), on the edge of town, a location where we could have a barn—we were among the very few townspeople to have one. This barn contained the results of Boy Scout paper drives: newspapers, wallpaper, and mainly books. Our community had its share of German immigrants, and my sisters and I pored over books written in German, especially those that used the ornamental type with curlicues that is called Fraktur. Perhaps this early exposure to such a foreign way of expressing familiar ideas (several of the Fraktur-script books were bibles) planted the seeds of my later interest in cultural differences, of which this book is a product. We did some gardening, too, but I recall helping as little as possible.

After graduate school I left the Midwest and relegated these activities to childhood memories. The next decade was in New York City, where "culture" never had "agri" in front of it. During this period I was on the faculty at Rockefeller University, where I was strongly influenced by Michael Cole and Sylvia Scribner and their culture and cognition working group. At that time, my own research was completely laboratory-based, and the group's influence was not reflected in a change in my own behavior.

A decade later Linda and I returned to the Midwest, and were able to afford our first house, where Linda first took up gardening and soon cultivated my interest in plants. My first research commitment to biology came when I was searching for an excuse to learn the names of those big woody plants that were everywhere. The fact that undergraduates in Illinois were ignorant about the names of trees led me to shift my research interest to people who did know about trees, people like landscapers and park maintenance workers. My wife and I would often take summer walks, she supplying the names of the small plants and I the names of the really big ones. For each of us it was a return to childhood but also a shift to something new. Soon our interest in biology focused on birds, and we installed a martin house in our own backyard.

Another impetus for our project was the evidence that emerged when Scott Atran and I and our dedicated team started studying the sustainability of the agroforestry practices of three cultural groups in Guatemala (agroforestry is, basically, farming on land that is or was forested with varying degrees of success for both the forest and the cultivated area). In the mid-1990s, some Internet browsing revealed to me the existence of a Native American group in Wisconsin, the Menominee, with an excellent record of sustainable forestry; further research produced information about a population of fish experts in the same area, and our group's interests thus expanded to north-central Wisconsin. As a consequence, almost two decades after coming back to the Midwest I returned to hunting and fishing, this time undertaking research on how people's conceptions of nature affect how they act in nature and the impact they have on it. Sitting and listening to Menominee elders talking about fishing brought me back to my grandmother and completed one circle. Our comparative study of Menominee and majority-culture understandings of nature completed another.

When I think about the way my early experiences in nature have come full circle to a deeper intellectual and personal understanding of both nature and culture, I am reminded of the life of my ancestor, Daniel Boone. His early activities in and around Kentucky showed little respect for nature. For example, he would often shoot deer for their hides and leave the meat to rot, a practice that was very upsetting to Native Americans in that area. At one point Boone was captured by Shawnee Indians, who adopted him into the tribe. Boone eventually escaped and returned to establish his fame as a frontiersman, but not before he had learned lasting lessons from the Shawnee about showing respect for nature. His Shawnee kinsmen continued to visit him throughout his life and in his old age Boone's closest friends were Shawnee.

Possibly like Boone himself, I grew up wanting to trap the most valuable pelts, shoot the most pheasants, and catch the largest walleyes and northerns (pike). I memorized the Minnesota state records for size for most species of fish and dreamed about getting my name into the record book. We ate what we caught, but I could hardly be accused of having great respect for nature. Just as Daniel Boone learned from the Shawnee, I have learned from the Menominee. (I have also learned a great deal from majority-culture hunters and fishermen and their respect for nature is also unquestionable.) The Menominees had no particular reason to welcome me and take me into their homes, but nonetheless that's what they did. So, another circle closed.

A final word on Boone. There is an official "Boone and Crockett scoring system" for measuring the attributes of trophy-quality game. As a relative of Boone, I have to protest. By the end of his life and perhaps even throughout it, I'm sure Boone would have found the focus on trophy qualities to be repugnant. Maybe there should be a Boone and Crockett scoring system for ecosystem balance and sustainability.

NORBERT ROSS

In this book we talk a lot about cultural differences as the result of distributed cognition. One way of looking at this issue is by thinking of cultural contact and constantly changing individual ideas and models emerging from this contact. In other studies we have painted a slightly positive picture, with groups actually learning from one another as a result of contact.

Although the bottom line of this book is less positive, I am hopeful that it is not the whole story, but is just a snapshot within the larger circle of life. In a sense my own life is illustrative of this idea. Having grown up in Germany and having lived extensively in Mexico and the United States, I find that my ideas and models are certainly idiosyncratic while simultaneously they are also the result of innumerable encounters with other people. As an anthropologist I made a profession out of meeting strangers and learning from them, and countless times I have been baffled by how wrong my expectations have been . . . just like many of the majority-culture participants in our studies described in this book. I'd like to expand the circle metaphor: I think of life as a circle, yet an elliptical one with a slight orientation upward. People can learn and do improve, and we sure can use a good deal of both!

Before starting to work on this book, or rather the research that led to it, I had never fished in my life, other than catching fingerlings by hand as a young kid. I have not become an expert at fishing, but I appreciated the time spent wading in the Wisconsin rivers, and listening to what I hope (for my self-esteem) were outrageously exaggerated tales about fish caught previously by my fishing buddies, both Menominee and majority-culture. Still, despite the big-fish stories, one thing was obvious: the values that animated a good fishing day on a river in Wisconsin were strikingly similar to basic values and attitudes I was taught by my dad when we were mountaineering in the Alps. I'll take this as a good sign for the future!

DOUGLAS COX

Catch and release is a term that is widely used in modern fishing experience. Admittedly, today I occasionally practice catch-and-release fishing, which is very different from how I fished as a boy and young man with my father and brothers, who taught me everything I know about fishing. Growing up a Menominee Indian and living on the Menominee Reservation in Northeast Wisconsin, how would I ever know what catch and release is, much less know how the majority culture of fisherman practice it? At a very young age I started fishing with my father and brothers, as well as other members of the family. We fished often and everywhere, including off the reservation in places like Door County, Oconto County, the lower Wolf River, and even as far as upper Michigan and Canada. Did this experience teach me to catch and release? Not by any means, especially in those years when Dad was still around (up to my twentieth year). In those days, fishing was about bringing food home. This was an important part of my life, and it meant everything to bring the food home (as much as the thrill of the catch), even though it never seemed like we were in need of a lot. In most years, the majority of the wild game that went in the freezer was venison and bear.

I will always remember Dad's advice whenever we fished: "Do not keep more than we can eat and never, ever waste anything you catch." My parents always stressed that to waste food was greatly disrespectful to the Creator, who offered gifts to us in the form of fish and game. It seems that there was always room in the freezer at the beginning of each spring, as the winters seemed to be longer in those days, and the fish and game that was gathered over the previous season had been well utilized. Usually the fish were the first to go, as they did not last long, so the smoker was rarely cool from spring until fall. The fish that did make it to the freezer were always the first to come out for family or community feasts, which usually happen in midsummer and early fall.

Although the Menominee are well known for our practices to sustain the natural resources, which is exemplified by our outstanding Forest Resource, it never seemed like this was something that was actually "taught" to me in my youth. But looking back at those years it is quite evident that my family was well aware of the need to practice our Menominee cultural values and to make sure that I passed this knowledge along to my own children in their teachings.

Today in my mid-forties I still fish as much as possible. I hunt actively, but probably not as much as I pursue trout, salmon, walleye, bass and panfish on the water alongside my wife Jean, who enjoys the outdoors as much as I do. My approach has not changed in relation to the respect, gratitude, care, and importance of passing along those lessons to my younger Menominees, including my own children. Getting back to the question, where did I learn catch and release? To me, it is very simple: on television, in books, and in fishing magazines. How do I practice catch and release? Only after my family is cared for, and if I am fishing off the Menominee Reservation in waters that have been disrespected with pollutants like PCBs, dioxins, and heavy metals. And even in those faraway places, where my dad first took me off the reservation to fish, there are still waters from which I am able to proudly bring home food that is so appreciated after a long winter. These things would not be important to me if fishing were merely a sport.

The Menominee Reservation is and always will be my home. It also will always be a home to the Menominee for perpetuity. My goals are to ensure that the tribal resource is protected and will be available for future Menominee generations to utilize as I have been able to over the years.

Douglas L. Medin
Norbert O. Ross
Douglas G. Cox

Acknowledgments |

THIS PROJECT BENEFITED from a variety of forms of help at every step of the way. Paula Huff and Lisa James provided important initial introductions on the Menominee reservation, and Gahrwood Barr, Richard Barr, and Duane Henning played the same role for Shawano County. The College of the Menominee Nation (especially the director of the Sustainable Development Insititute, Dr. Holly Youngbear-Tibbets) and NAES College (now East-West University), Keshena campus (especially Dean Karen Washinawatok), provided opportunities for teaching, meeting community members, and becoming better acquainted with Menominee history and values. We are also grateful to Menominee elders Steve Askinette, Earl Deer, Carl Maskewit, George Vigue, Richard Vigue, Sara Skubbitz, Irene Pywasit, and Vyron Dixon Sr. for their wisdom and experience.

Research team members who have contributed importantly to this project include Scott Atran, Beth Proffitt, Hillarie Schwartz, John Coley, Sergey Blok, Russ Burnett, Beth Lynch, Dan Bartels, and Stephanie Schmidt. Will Bennis, Sonya Sachdeva, Rumen Iliev, and Sara Unsworth also helped in various ways. Katya Otis was responsible for a wide range of editorial and management functions but she also performed some very thoughtful background analyses, so her contributions fall into a number of categories.

Dick Nisbett provided valuable encouragement and advice at virtually every stage of this project. He and Eugene Hunn also read an earlier draft of this manuscript and offered insightful suggestions for improving it.

The research itself was supported by the Russell Sage Foundation and the National Science Foundation. We thank Suzanne Nichols of the Russell Sage Foundation for her technical assistance and advice throughout the project, and Genna Patacsil for improving the readability of the manuscript. Preparation of the book was supported by a Guggenheim Fellowship to DLM. The Menominee Language and Culture Commission also gave very generously of their time and attention in reading and approving our manuscript.

Finally, we owe a special thinks to each and every hunter and fisherman we interviewed. Their respect for nature is impossible to ignore and, like nature itself, concrete.

Chapter One | Contexts

"Once I used a rock to kill a goose that was flying by. It came down in a muddy area of the millpond. I hated wading in after it, but I couldn't let it go to waste."

—A middle-aged Menominee hunter

PRETTY MUCH EVERYONE is an environmentalist. One fairly recent survey of lay people in the United States indicated that virtually 100 percent of those polled agreed with the statement "We have a moral duty to leave the Earth in as good or better shape than we found it." One might expect this figure to be lower for two industry groups whose members have been involved in controversies over protecting the environment, dry cleaners and sawmill workers, but even among these groups 96 percent agree with the statement (Kempton, Boster, and Hartley 1995).

This apparent consensus starts to break down when one value is placed into conflict with another. For the statement "It's unfortunate but acceptable if some people lose their jobs and have to change their line of work for the sake of the environment," agreement ranges from 89 percent for Sierra Club members to 73 percent for the general public to 56 percent for sawmill workers. For the statement "There are too many environmental regulations right now," 11 percent the Sierra Club members, 20 percent of the general public, and 48 percent of sawmill workers agree (Kempton, Boster, and Hartley 1995). In short, disputes—for example, between Greenpeace and the whaling industry—may readily arise when competing values are in play.

But disputes about the environment and its resources can arise even in the presence of shared conservation values and goals. This book focuses on one such controversy between two groups. Both groups are strong supporters of hunting and fishing and both hold respect for nature and

1

resource conservation as deep values. Yet they differ how they think about nature—in the framework theories they use to understand nature and act on it. The groups consist of Native American Menominee and majority-culture hunters and fishermen living in Wisconsin.

Technically we should call majority-culture people "European Americans," a term analogous to Native American. A further reason to do so is that, in all likelihood, European Americans will not constitute a numerical majority in the United States in a few decades but will in fact be a "minority group." Still, the term sounds a bit stilted and is not in common use, so we will avoid it. Occasionally we may lapse into calling majority-culture people whites and to Native Americans as Indians, since that is what they often call themselves. Most often, however, we will refer to a specific tribe, the Menominee. Our research focuses on the Menominee and we do not claim that our results apply equally or at all to other tribes.

Similarly, we cannot assume that our findings with Wisconsin majority-culture hunters and fishermen generalize to all European Americans. The majority-culture sportsmen we are talking about are sportsmen in Shawano County in north-central Wisconsin. The guys in our sample are local, and very likely are different from sportsmen who come up to this area from urban areas like Chicago and Milwaukee. Our primary focus is on very experienced hunters and fishermen, the sort of people that others look to as experts. We've done some work with less expert fishermen but even our less expert fishermen have decades of experience and know far more than the average person about fish and game. These factors should work to reduce differences within and across groups.

THE CONFLICT

Native American hunting and fishing rights have been a conflicted issue since tribes started negotiating treaties with the U.S. government, but they are still a source of discord now, perhaps especially in the last thirty years. We think that cultural differences in mental models of nature are at the heart of it, and the purpose of this book is to examine these models and this hypothesis. Majority-culture individuals object to Native American hunting and fishing practices and they think that Indians are depleting fish and game. For example, several majority-culture hunters interviewed commented, "You can drive through the reservation and not see a single deer, because they kill them all."

Like turtle meat, which is said to have at least seven distinct flavors, our story doesn't fit neatly into any one social- or behavioral-science discipline. It has a heavy flavor of anthropology, but the fact that we conduct formal experiments makes us atypical of that discipline. Our experiments lend a strong flavor of cognitive and social psychology, but many of our observations are correlational and our use of ethnography and anecdote make us suspect to experimentalists. Our interest in how beliefs relate to actions is highly relevant to the emerging field of decisionmaking, which has never been owned or operated by any single discipline. Our approach reflects our belief that there is a need to overcome traditional academic boundaries.

There may be seven tastes, but there's only one turtle. Our turtle consists of a focus on how cultural differences in understandings of nature lead to misperceptions of other groups and to intergroup conflict over natural resources. This project represents a case study of culture and environmental decisionmaking and it is relevant to both theory and application. Our study also addresses basic issues in folkbiology, the study of how people conceptualize the world of plants and animals, and the cognitive science of concepts.

A "MEANINGS MATTER" VERSUS A "VALUES-ONLY" APPROACH

The essence of our research perspective is that "meanings matter." In order to explain our motivation for taking this perspective, let's consider the opposite, utilitarian, view. Many models of decisionmaking incorporate the assumption that principles of economic decisionmaking carry over to decisions involving nonmonetary values. Maybe you can't buy love, but you might be able to assign some utility, or value, to it. This may be necessary in order to consider a situation where one must make a tradeoff between two incompatible things, reducing their inherent meaning but gaining a quantitative "scale" that can make decisions much simpler.

How well does this utilitarian perspective work for environmental decisionmaking? There are reasons to think: not very well. Ann Tenbrunsel and David Messick (1999) asked participants in their study, who were business school students, to imagine that they were running a company that was faced with the choice of whether or not to save money by releasing pollutants into the air. In one scenario there were no fines for doing so and in another scenario there were modest fines for polluting. Their counterintuitive finding was that modest fines led to decisions to pollute much more often than when there were no fines. Tenbrunsel and Messick also found that when there were no fines the participants viewed the question of releasing pollutants as an ethical decision, but that when fines were in place participants conceptualized the choice as a business decision, and concluded that paying the fine gave them the right to pollute.

There have been numerous attempts by researchers to determine how much value people assign to various environmental resources. This question is relevant to a variety of policy issues such as how much a company that breaks the law by polluting should be fined. The standard paradigm for this research is called "contingent valuation" and almost always involves judgments of willingness to pay or willingness to accept. Willingness to pay means: How much are people willing to pay to protect a particular resource (such as a lake in Ontario)? Willingness to accept means: How much compensation would people need to accept the loss of some environmental good? These measures should yield comparable and coherent values. Yet decades of research (see Ritov and Kahneman 1997 for one review) show that these two measures typically give dramatically different results and do not have the properties one would expect from an underlying value scale. For example, people are not willing to pay any more to save all the lakes in Ontario than they are to save one lake in Ontario,[1] and they often say that no amount of money would be adequate compensation for a loss. Researchers find themselves caught between the intuition that people attach value to resources and their inability to assign a number to them.

Our third example of how a utility model may fail to capture people's decisionmaking is drawn from our own experience. For more than a decade we have been part of a research team that has studied three cultural groups who live in the rain forest of northern Guatemala and practice slash-and-burn agriculture. One of the groups does this on a sustainable basis, one group is somewhat destructive, and the third group is very destructive. How might one analyze these group differences from a utilitarian perspective?

One idea is that the groups differ in how much they value the land. Note, however, that this analysis is essentially circular. People take care of what they value and we know they value it because they take care of it.

One might further one's analysis if there were some competing land-use practices that affected valuation. For example, if there were independent evidence that the group that is most destructive (and not the group that operates sustainably) values pastureland more than forest, one might begin to understand the group differences. But in the absence of group differences in potential competing uses, it is not clear how one should proceed. Our research team took an alternative, meaning-based approach to understanding differences in agroforestry practices and we describe this research in chapter 2 to explain our decision to use the same strategy in Wisconsin. This approach involves looking for a difference in the interpretation of uses and behaviors by both groups, with an eye to discerning whether their framework theories differed in ways that would predict the difference in use or the apparent "conflict of values."

We don't deny the importance of values, but we also think that they are bound up with framework theories and conceptual understandings in a way that makes it difficult to assess values in isolation. In the remainder of this chapter we will describe the conflict over hunting and fishing practices in Wisconsin in more detail. In chapter 2 we develop our thesis that meanings matter; in chapters 3 and 4 we present our approach to studying culture and cultural differences and on the cognitive science of concepts. In chapters 5 and 6 we give important background information on our Native American and majority-culture study groups and the research setting. Later chapters describe the main body of our project.

NATIVE AMERICAN VERSUS MAJORITY-CULTURE UNDERSTANDINGS OF NATURE

There are significant differences in the ways Native American and majority-culture hunters and fishermen see nature. The view of members of the latter group is heavily influenced by their goals. These goals are organized around a sportsman's model, which often emphasizes "fair chase" and a competition to obtain "trophy" game. Native Americans, in contrast, approach nature from an ecological perspective, hunt and fish for food, and in general interact with nature in terms of multiple goals. Majority-culture sportsmen achieve conservation goals by "catch and release" and selective harvest; Native Americans are guided primarily by a "do not waste" ethic.[2] These differences place the two groups in a conflict over practices. From a majority-culture perspective, Indians use methods that are unethical and very likely resource depleting. From a Native American perspective, majority-culture sportsmen focus on trophy-sized game to the exclusion of all else, and many Indians find disrespectful of nature the idea of dragging a fish around for fun, only to release it. These competing models of nature lead to misperceptions and conflict over conservation.[3]

This is not to say that there are no similarities and overlapping areas in the Menominee and majority-culture views of fish and game. Majority-culture fishermen shoot antlerless deer (which are not trophies) and eat plenty of fish and are not solely preoccupied with catching the largest fish or shooting the biggest buck. By the same token many Menominees are not indifferent to the number of points and the spread of the antlers

on the bucks they shoot. They are also happy to regale others with stories about the huge brown trout or northern pike or walleye that they
caught. In fact, Menominee and white hunters and fishermen in this part
of Wisconsin are so similar in so many respects that their failure to understand each other is a mystery.

CONTEXT: NATIVE AMERICANS

People who have had little experience with Native American communities may have two related misperceptions or tendencies. One is to think
of Indians as a people who basically are from the past, who are part of
history but not of current events. Mahzarin Banaji, a social psychologist
at Harvard University, set up a experiment where people were given the
task of differentiating between two categories of stimuli by pressing one
button for one category and another button for the second category. In
one test the first category contained Indian names and words referring to
the past, such as "ancient," and the second category contained names associated with Caucasians and words referring to the present, such as
"contemporary." In the second test the first category contained both Indian names and present-suggestive words and the second category contained Caucasian names and past-oriented words. Harvard students
found the task of differentiating between the categories easier and responded faster when the Indian names shared a category with past-
suggestive words.[4]

Not present in time can also suggest not present in numbers. A specialist in Indian education told of doing a seminar for Chicago-area
teachers on the topic of Native American history. She asked the teachers
to estimate the total number of tribes and the total Indian population in
the United States. She was shocked to find that the median estimate was
seven tribes and about 35,000 Indians. In fact, there are around seven
hundred tribes, more than five hundred of them federally recognized,
and the 2000 census estimate is that there are more than 4 million Native
Americans in the United States.

Many majority-culture people may also tend to think of Native
Americans as being very spiritual and also very artistic; Navajo rugs and
jewelry, Pueblo pottery, and Hopi kachina dolls reinforce this image.
They also may have a stereotype of the "ecological Indian," an idea that
Native Americans more or less automatically have a close connection
with the earth and never do anything to harm the environment (see
Krech 1999 for a historical analysis that challenges this simplistic view).
This may leave them unprepared for the fairly overt negative attitudes
toward Indians expressed by a significant minority of whites in Wiscon-

sin (and elsewhere) in the context of hunting and fishing. Our goal is to explain at least one major source of that prejudice.

CONTEXT: MAJORITY-CULTURE SPORTSMEN

It may be easy to fall into thinking that the Native Americans in our study are the good guys and the majority-culture folks are the bad guys. That would be wrong. The majority-culture hunters and fishermen we interviewed have a deep love for nature and are dedicated to passing on traditions to future generations. They believe that intimate contact with nature is the key to respecting it. They fear, too, that people who hold the "right" attitudes toward nature, but in the absence of a genuine love for the outdoors and knowledge about it, will only hold these attitudes superficially.

This is related to the reasons that many hunters and fishermen have little regard for environmentalists. In part, this is because they associate environmentalists with extremists in the animal rights movement who have the goal of eliminating hunting and fishing. More important, there is the perception among many sportsmen that environmentalists don't put their money where their mouth is.

Sometimes there is also the sense that environmentalists don't know what they are talking about. Our experience in Petén, Guatemala, suggests that local knowledge is important and that top-down environmental planning based on superficial knowledge may be misguided, no matter how good the intentions. We attended a conference on the future of Petén that was held in its capital, Flores. Our first surprise was that no local farmers had been invited. The second came when more than one governmental official from Guatemala City proclaimed that the abono bean (Mucuna pruriens, also known as the velvet bean), whose roots help fix nitrogen in the soil, is the key to the economic development in the area. However, any Petenero would have told anyone willing to listen that no farmer is his right mind would grow the abono bean. Why? First and foremost because abono bean plants are a haven for snakes and Petén has a lot of poisonous snakes. Second, the dried beanstalks are fuel for potential wildfires.[5]

The majority-culture sportsmen of Shawano County, Wisconsin, are a small segment of a large nationwide community of hunters and fishermen. In 1990 hunters purchased about 30 million and sports fishermen about 37 million licenses (Hummel 1994). A good part of this money supports state departments of natural resources and associated conservation activities. In addition, hunters and fishermen support organizations such as Ducks Unlimited, Pheasants Forever, and local clubs that purchase fingerlings and fry to stock local lakes and rivers. There's no denying that hunters and fishermen have played an essential role in conservation efforts targeted not only at fish and game but also at associated habitats.

Public support for hunting and fishing is widespread. Kellert (1980) conducted a national sampling of public attitudes about hunting and found that 85 percent of people support hunting for food. This figure drops a bit but remains high, 65 percent, when it comes to hunting both for food and as a form of recreation. A 1995 survey by Heberlein and Willebrand show that these approval ratings have gone up by as much as 6 percent since the 1980s. Only 19 percent support hunting for trophies. In fact, public sentiment about hunting and fishing aligns more closely with the ideas of Native American than with those of majority-culture hunters and fishermen.

RELEVANCE TO COGNITIVE SCIENCE

Although the focus of this book is the practical goal of understanding intergroup conflict over natural resources, in it we also present basic research on the psychology of concepts and the role of goals, values, and activities in shaping them. Much of cognitive science has been based on studies whose participants were undergraduates at major research universities—not a very representative group. Studies designed to shed light on concept formation and use often employ stimulus materials such as geometric forms or other materials that are relatively devoid of meaning (though see the work of Gregory Murphy and his colleagues summarized in Murphy 2002 for a notable exception). At least for the domain of biological concepts, we consistently find that results on categorization and reasoning about biological concepts gained through studies using college students do not generalize to the world at large (Medin and Atran 2004). One contribution of this project is to examine conceptual organization for meaningful material in study populations that see these stimuli as relevant to their lives.

College students are a convenient population for researchers to access, but are they the best subjects for this type of study? If cognitive scientists were based in the field and only journeyed to academic institutions to present the results of research, it would be much more natural for them to study local folk in meaningful contexts. There may be particular research questions where undergraduates are the only appropriate population. But, generally speaking, undergraduates are used overwhelmingly simply because they are there. Hence, studies of categorization and reasoning involving other samples are valuable in extending the heretofore extremely narrow empirical base of cognitive studies.

CONCLUSION

This book focuses on cultural differences in understandings of nature and their relationship to intergroup conflict. We argue that differences between Menominee and majority-culture ideas are not based on differential knowledge but rather on different frameworks and approaches to nature that shape meanings and understanding of practices associated with hunting and fishing. Our central thesis is that meanings matter and that we need to consider the interplay of framework theories, conceptual understandings, and values in order to make sense of practices. We will show that this thesis provides insights into intergroup conflict over natural resources and leads to a better understanding of concepts and decisionmaking.

Chapter Two | Why Meanings Matter:
Culture, Concepts,
and Behavior

When I was young my father would always pump some water at night. In the morning he would take a ladleful of water, go outside, greet the sun, toss the water, and let out a whoop. When I asked my father what he was doing, he said that he was giving the chickens a drink of water. When I was older, my mother told me that it was his way of saying thanks to the Creator for the bounty of life. My father lived to be eighty-seven.

—A Menominee elder

IN 1940 THE German-born American anthropologist Franz Boas introduced the notion of cultural relativism to the social sciences. The underlying idea was that we should withhold from judging the behavior of members of other cultures and instead should engage in understanding people's behavior on the basis of their own models of the world, the way they themselves make sense of it.

Taking the perspective of cultural relativism is helpful to our purposes in two ways. First, it allows us to understand the meanings produced by individuals, meanings that guide both an individual's judgments and behavior. Second, it helps us to avoid the mistake of failing to consider other people's point of view, their individual and cultural models of the environment, a mistake that leads to cultural misunderstandings and negative judgments, including conflicts between Native Americans and European Americans.

That meanings matter should not come as a surprise to anthropologists. In fact, one might argue that anthropology is mainly concerned with the process of discerning meanings within specific contexts and the

10

understanding how different cultural groups make sense of their existence. The anthropologist Clifford Geertz viewed culture as a web of meaning within which individuals carry out their daily activities and which they use to make sense of their actions. Though we see some shortcomings of Geertz's view, in general we subscribe to the idea that people's behavior should be understood within the meanings that they themselves ascribe to their actions.

This makes intuitive sense. One does not need to conduct research to know that the value of a great many objects must be measured in meanings and not solely in dollars. Most Americans would condemn the act of burning the U.S. flag, although a flag is easily replaced, because a flag symbolizes many important meanings. A wedding ring does not have the same value at the jewelry store that it has after the wedding, when it has been imbued with meaning. We believe that environments, just like wedding rings and the American flag, have meanings, and these meanings matter for environmental decisionmaking.

As we noted in chapter 1, human decisionmaking often fails to adhere to an economic framework, one in which competing kinds of values can be placed on a common scale and traded off against each other. This fact leaves many policymakers and decision theorists chagrined; they see the unwillingness of people to place a dollar value on a lake in Ontario as a refusal to face the inevitable trade-offs required in resource allocation (see, for example, Baron and Spranca 1997; Tetlock 2003). The lake in Ontario is viewed by these people as a "protected value," that is, one protected from tradeoffs with money or most other goods. How can we have a policy on national parks or selling mining leases on federal lands in the absence of some notion of what these lands and parks are worth?

Although these sorts of protected values have been roundly criticized, we find it hard to imagine that they would have evolved if their consequences were uniformly negative (see Frank 1989 for a nice elaboration of this general point). The phrase "the tragedy of the commons" refers to the notion that, without punitive regulations, resources held in common will be rapidly depleted because each individual will overweight his or her own needs relative to the needs of others. And indeed, when regulation is absent and individual utility is paramount, the commons suffers heavily. This phenomenon suggests that there are contexts where individual rationality (in the sense of each individual maximizing their personal gains) leads to disaster and that it may be possible to do "better than rational."

One such context is represented in the tropical rain forest of northern Guatemala, where we have been studying the forest-management practices of three cultural groups. In chapter 1 we described how one might try to apply an economic approach to understand the differences in their agroforestry practices, but this approach was not very promising. Here we describe an approach based on mental models and meanings. First, we must understand the commons dilemma.

THE TRAGEDY OF THE COMMONS

The earth contains a fixed amount of land and a fixed amount of water. The oceans can support just so many whales, the lakes and rivers just so many trout, and the land just so many cattle. Whales depend on krill for food and the amount of food available sets an upper bound on how many whales there can be; overpopulation is not a problem. In fact, whales are prey for at least one species, Homo sapiens, and as a consequence, several species of whales face extinction.[1] From a human perspective, issues like the whale population are a matter of resource use.

It is natural to think about resource use in terms of a need for balance. If humans are going to harvest whales, then they have to be careful to avoid taking so many of them that whales die out. How do we achieve these sorts of balances? One influential answer to this question came from Adam Smith and boiled down to individuals' rational choices, their cost-benefit analyses. In 1776 Smith suggested that the "invisible hand" of individuals acting in their own self-interest tended to promote the public interest. That is, according to Smith, the best decisions for an entire society will be most effectively achieved when individuals are free to make and act on rational calculations of what is best for themselves. He called this rational-choice theory.

The Dilemma of the Commons

Adam Smith's optimism was severely undermined by observations suggesting that individual rationality may lead to tragic outcomes at the societal level. In an influential article titled "The Tragedy of the Commons," Garrett Hardin (1968) introduced the concept of the commons, which he defined as natural resources viewed and treated as the common property of all. He ascribed the breakdown of environmental resources that are viewed as common property entirely to rational-choice decisionmaking within this conceptual framework. He illustrated his point (131–32) by drawing on a scenario originally developed by Walter Lloyd of Oxford University (1833) that has come to be known as the tragedy of the commons:

Picture a pasture open to all. It is to be expected that each herdsman will try to keep as many cattle as possible on the commons. Such an arrangement may work reasonably satisfactorily for centuries because tribal wars, poaching and disease keep the numbers of both man and beast well below the carrying capacity of the land. Finally, however, comes the day of reckoning, that is, the day when the long-desired goal of social stability becomes a reality. At this point, the inherent logic of the commons remorselessly generates tragedy.

As a rational being, each herdsman seeks to maximize his gain. Explicitly or implicitly, more or less consciously, he asks, "What is the utility to me of adding one more animal to my herd?" This utility has one negative and one positive component.

The positive component is a function of the increment of one animal. Since the herdsman receives all the proceeds from the sale of the additional animal, the positive utility is nearly +1.

The negative component is a function of the additional overgrazing created by one more animal. Since, however, the effects of overgrazing are shared by all the herdsmen, the negative utility for any particular decision-making herdsman is only a fraction of –1.

Adding together the component partial utilities, the rational herdsman concludes that the only sensible course for him to pursue is to add another animal to his herd. And another and another. . . . But this is the conclusion reached by each and every rational herdsman sharing a commons. Therein is the tragedy. Each man is locked into a system that compels him to increase his herd without limit—in a world that is limited. Ruin is the destination toward which all men rush, each pursuing his own best interest in a society that believes in the freedom of commons. Freedom in a commons brings ruin to all.

The tragedy of the commons manifests in many forms. People may use pesticides on their lawns because the large benefits to its appearance outweigh the very modest pollution it creates, but when everyone does the same thing, the poisons may accumulate with disastrous consequences in the earth itself, which can be viewed as the commons, even though backyards are private property. Backyards are part of a commons whenever toxins spread to other land, or when changes in ownership pass on consequences to other parties. Hardin worried about human overpopulation as another form of commons problem.

Hardin saw "mutually agreed upon coercion" as the only way out of the commons dilemma. This requires centralized states that mandate behavior with respect to situations where individual self-interest conflicts with societal welfare. Just as we pass laws prohibiting robbing banks and punish those who do so, Hardin suggests that central regulation (for example, China's one-child policy) is needed to control human breeding to rescue the world from the misery of overpopulation.

Some have suggested that "privatization" can solve the tragedy of the commons. If each herdsman has his fixed land, then only he will experience the gains and losses. But mobility and a number of other factors undermine this solution. A forester can fell all the trees on the land he or she owns and then use the proceeds to buy other land and then repeat the cycle. A mining company can exhaust a resource and then abandon the site, leaving lethal byproducts behind. Furthermore, consequences of actions extend beyond borders. A pig feedlot on a single farm can lead to groundwater contamination and to a huge release of ammonia that affects people in neighboring farms and communities. Inuit mothers have dangerous amounts of dioxin and other toxins in their breast milk, even though no one within hundreds of miles of them has ever used dioxin.

In short, the tragedy of the commons appears to be relentless and inevitable from the perspective of rational-choice theory. Note that the herdsman who is morally troubled by overgrazing and reduces his herd produces losses exclusive to himself, but shares the gains with everyone. Ultimately it makes no difference what he does or doesn't do, because it is the collective action that matters.

Hardin's view is pretty pessimistic and seems to require an abandonment of many individual freedoms in favor of central control. It is hard to argue with the logic and implications of rational-choice theory, according to which the tragedy of the commons is inevitable. But there is an important alternative view according to which the tragedy of the commons is not inevitable. Its focus is on collective action.

COLLECTIVE ACTION

Does the dilemma of the commons relentlessly lead to resource depletion? There certainly are some dramatic cases, such as Easter Island—known for its huge sculptures left behind by its people—where apparently the residents eventually cut down all the trees and had to abandon the island. However, other work suggests that Easter Island may be the exception to the rule.

Elinor Ostrom, Roy Gardner, and James Walker (1990) have studied resource dilemmas around the world and documented a very large number of cases where the commons has been managed successfully for extended periods of time. These case studies allow some important generalizations concerning sustainability. The general idea is that collective action can produce results that are "better than rational"—in other words, better than would transpire under a "rational-choice" regime.

On a social level the key elements are cooperation and reciprocity based on communication. Imagine that our hypothetical commons creates a "cattlemen's association," where, after discussing the problem of overgrazing, herdsmen reach a voluntary cooperative agreement to the effect that no one will graze more than forty head of cattle on the commons.

Such a solution will work as long as no one "defects" by putting more than his share of cattle on the commons. But one cannot automatically assume reciprocal cooperation. Instead, there must be procedures in place for monitoring other people's behavior. If some person defects, then the others have to be willing and able to sanction or punish this noncooperation. Sanctions can take the form of immediate punishment and also the longer-term loss of "reputation," which could affect other players' future willingness to enter into cooperative agreements with violators. Such agreements require relatively "closed access" to the commons, in order for the processes of communication, monitoring, sanctioning, reciprocity, and reputation to be effective. Elinor Ostrom and Vincent Ostrom (1997) provide a nice review of both laboratory experiments and field observations that support the efficacy of these factors.

Collective action does not necessarily require the sort of centralized control envisioned by Hardin nor the privatization suggested by others. Instead, local groups with common interests may often organize themselves so as to establish norms and create shared monitoring systems that encourage reciprocal cooperation.

The work of Ostrom and her associates provides an important new perspective on resource dilemmas. In fact, social organization in local contexts may be an effective alternative to centralized mandates, especially given that in the latter case, central authorities may have difficulty in monitoring and enforcing compliance.

However, in our view some caveats are in order. Ultimately, the perspective of collective action is grounded in the same idea that inspired Hardin to write of "the tragedy of the commons." Human beings are utility maximizers and unless the framework of incentives and sanctions is correctly set, commons management will be impossible.

Another important point is that neither Hardin's tragedy of the commons nor Ostrom's collective-action approach take into account cultural differences or the semantic side of decisionmaking. But then, how could we envision a monitoring and sanctioning system free of any meaning?

FRAMEWORK THEORIES, CULTURAL MODELS, AND MEANING

Cultural differences can be analyzed in terms of framework theories, theories that cultures develop and that provide individuals with some orientation in meaning making. Religion is a good case in point. Specific religious beliefs about the creation of the world and its ultimate function and cause provide a basis that guides individuals' thoughts and behaviors. In addition, religion provides a causal framework for the events of human lives, such as death or bad luck. Within this wider framework—if it applies—an individual carves out specific meaning for particular contexts and behaviors. An example of a framework theory is the Menominee beliefs that everything in the universe is connected and that one should show respect for animals, even after they have been killed; this belief is understandable within the context of Menominee religious beliefs. Itza' Maya forest management is another case where framework theories and mental models are closely linked to the practices of those who hold the beliefs.

Mental Models

Originally our research group set out to study the cultural models of three cultural groups living off the same environment, the tropical rain forest of the Petén region of northern Guatemala.[2] We hypothesized that people's understanding of nature may affect how they act on it. We use the term "mental models" quite broadly to refer to how people approach and understand nature, and their beliefs about causal processes associated with it. For example, whether one views the forest as a resource to be exploited as one's home may make a difference in how one uses it. You might be willing to sell the timber of a forest you view as a resource but reluctant to sell the timber of trees planted and protected by your grandfather in a forest you view as your home.

We were also interested in people's mental models of the components of the resource itself, in this case the components of the rain forest such as specific trees. Does a farmer think about, say, a papaya tree as an individual thing in isolation, or are his relations with it and with other plants and animals important to his mental model? If differences exist, they may mark cultural differences in meaning attached to entities such as the forest and particular plants and animals.

We assessed mental models and environmental management practices of three groups of farmers (called "milperos") who practice slash-and-burn agriculture in the rain forest of Petén: the Itza' Maya from the municipality of San Jose; Spanish speakers of mixed descent, called Ladinos, from the adjacent community of La Nueva San Jose; and Q'eqchi' Maya from the hamlet of Corozal, about ten miles away. Slash-and-burn agriculture in Petén involves burning clearings in a forested area to clear arable land for agricultural use; it bears some resemblance to "swidden-fallow" planting, since clearings are burned, planted, or left to rest on a rotating basis. Study participants from the three groups did not differ in age, family size, amount of land available for cultivation, nor median family income. In many cases farmers' "milpas," the areas they farm, are adjacent, and we did not detect differences in the quality of land given to participants of the three groups. Itza' are indigenous to this part of Guatemala; the Ladinos and Q'eqchi' migrated to these lowlands more than thirty years ago. All have had extensive experience with slash-and-burn agriculture in Petén's lowland rain forest. Yet, we found dramatic differences among the three groups' mental models and practices. We had reason to believe that Itza' forestry practices were the most sustainable, and those of the Q'eqchi' least sustainable. But this impression was based on anecdotal and informal observation. Our goal was to do a mere systematic analysis.

Mental Models of the Forest

To get a better notion of how these groups think about the forest, we asked members of each group to name the most important plants and animals for the forest. There was substantial agreement across groups, and on the basis of the answers we selected twenty-eight important plants and twenty-nine important animals to see how participants conceptualize ecological relations. Ultimately we wanted to find out how each plant and animal affected every other plant and animal, but first we focused on how plants affect animals and how animals affect plants—812 plant-animal pairs. The interview typically took three to four hours.

There is a body of research that suggests that people around the world generally classify plants and animals in the same ways—they tend to see the same players in nature and put them into similar groupings (Atran 1990; Berlin 1992; Malt 1995). We had done earlier studies with these three populations and found this same pattern of general agreement. The present question is whether people differ in how they think about the activities and interrelationships of these players, whether members of the different cultural groups attribute different roles and meanings to the different plant and animal species in their environment.

They do. In fact, the differences could hardly be larger. First we asked how plants affect animals. The Ladino and Itza' informants reported about four times as many relations as did the Q'eqchi' informants. The relations were almost exclusively helping ones: plants help animals by providing food, shelter, or something else the animals need. Furthermore the Ladino and Itza' informants showed high agreement on which particular plants help which particular animals. The relatively impoverished Q'eqchi' mental model is a subset of the Itza' and Ladino models.

The question of how animals affect plants produced even greater differences. Q'eqchi' informants reached consensus on only 13 of the 812 possible animal-plant relations, whereas the Ladinos and Itza' reported about five times as many relations for ways in which specific animals hurt specific plants. Strikingly, the Ladinos tended to deny that animals help plants. In contrast, the Itza' reported as many helping as hurting relations and four times as many helping relations as the Ladinos. In many cases Ladinos and Itza' appeared to be drawing the opposite conclusions from the same observations. For example, Ladinos tended to report that birds hurt the fruit trees by digesting their seeds. Itza' had a more nuanced interpretation, saying that if the seed coat is soft, eating the seeds destroys them, but that if the seed coat is hard, then digestion plus fertilization by birds by means of their excrement help the seed to germinate.

Overall, one could characterize the ecological models of plant-animal interactions as follows. The Q'eqchi' have a very impoverished model and report few relations for plants helping animals and almost no relations for animals affecting plants. Ladinos appear to have more of a hierarchical model in which plants help animals and animals help people but they do not conceptualize animals as helping plants. Finally, the Itza' have a rich, reciprocal ecological model in which plants help animals and animals help plants.

We also asked informants from each of these groups about how they used various plants and whether people of their own community helped, hurt, or had no effect on the twenty-eight plants (Atran et al. 1999). Surprisingly, the Q'eqchi' tended to report that they neither helped nor hurt most plants. The Ladinos said they help more plants and hurt more plants than the Q'eqchi'. The best predictor of whether Ladinos thought they helped or hurt a plant was its economic importance—Ladinos said they protect plants that have a cash value.

The Itza' show yet a third profile in their ratings of impact on plants. They say that they hurt only a few plants (a few vines and two ubiquitous "weed" trees) and protect most of the other plants.[3] We looked to see what predicts their priority for protection and found two independent factors. One was the total number of uses that the Itza' had for the plant and the other was ecological centrality, an index we developed on the basis of the results from the animal-plant interaction task reported earlier. According to the consensual model of our informants, the more animals a plant helps, the higher its centrality index. In other words Itza' Maya protect plant species that are important to animal species, independent of any utility for humans.

Groundtruthing

Up to this point we have no proof that Itza' Maya actually do what they say they would do, in other words, that these mental models actually guide individual behaviors. Do the meanings as conveyed by ecological models and impact ratings have measurable consequences? The answer is yes. Impact ratings reliably predicted the number of different kinds of trees that we found when we surveyed Itza' farmers' parcels. This indicates that Itza' Maya not only have a rich ecological model, but that they use that understanding in their interactions with the forest. Other analyses of soil samples and number, diversity, and size of trees confirm that Itza' have the most sustainable practices, Ladinos are intermediate, and Q'eqchi' have the least sustainable practices.

The Forest Spirits and Values

Another important component of all three groups' mental model of the forest is the Arux, or forest spirits. Men from all three communities see the Arux as tricksters that may test your valor when you go into the forest. In addition, the Itza' Maya see the Arux as guardians of the forest.

We asked individuals to rank-order the importance of twenty-one plants (a random subset of the twenty-eight species selected from the interaction task) from several distinct perspectives, for example, how members of their own community would value them; how members of the other communities would value them; how God and how the forest spirits would value them. The best predictor of how Itza' say God would rank-order the species is the number of different uses the Itza' report for a given plant. In short, God is looking out for the Itza'. Although the Itza' did not show overall agreement on forest spirit preferences, the group of Itza' men showed a clear consensus. The best predictor of how Itza' men say that the Arux will rank plants is again ecological centrality (as measured from the interaction task). In other words, according to the Itza' men, who spend much time in the forest, the Arux are looking out for the forest. Itza' men believe that if they disrespect the forest and violate Arux preferences, the Arux will punish them. For example, one Itza' male told us that he fell out of a tree and hurt his back because he had cut down a tree that he shouldn't have.[4]

Mental Models and Meanings

For the Itza' Maya the forest has a very specific meaning, not shared with the Ladino and Q'eqchi' migrants to the area. For them the forest and nature has a relational dimension—the Itza' term for the forest, "ki-wotch," means "our home." Beyond that, Itza' Maya attribute very different meanings to plants and animals compared to the other two groups of the study. This view is confirmed and reinforced by the Itza' beliefs in the Arux and their role as guardians of the forest.

The Itza' view of the forest has direct consequences for an assessment of the relevance of rational-choice theory to their situation as well as the tragedy of the commons. For the Itza' Maya the forest represents not a passive resource to be exploited but, rather, an active player that is responsive to their behavior. It is not a commodity but an entity with which they have a relationship. They would no more cut down a ramon tree and use it for firewood than American home owners would chop up the wooden doors of their houses for firewood.

Our results also have implications for the collective-action approach (Ostrom, Gardner, and Walker 1990). Itza' Maya have no monitoring and sanctioning system in place that would protect the commons from breakdown. The Itza' relational interaction with the forest—the meanings they attach to the forest and the forest species—leads them to behave in a sustainable manner. The Q'eqchi' have the best structure in place for monitoring and sanctioning, and indeed they use it for managing the use of the copal tree, which is a source of incense. Surprisingly, however, the Q'eqchi', despite their monitoring and sanctioning activities, are the most destructive farmers of the three groups.

The belief that nature will punish you if you do not respect it is fairly common among Native American tribes, including the Menominee. The Ladino term for the forest is "tierra agarrada de nadie," which roughly translates as "land not taken by anyone." This contrasts dramatically with the Itza' notion of the forest as their home.

At the conference on the future of Petén mentioned in chapter 1, we asked representatives of seventeen nongovernmental organizations, or NGOs, to rank-order the importance of the same twenty-one plant species that were used before. Although there was a fair amount of variability in rankings, highest-ranking plants were trees that generated cash-producing products or timber. Notably, the NGO representatives' rank-ordering correlated negatively (−0.23) with Itza' measures of ecological centrality. Apparently, people who work for NGOs see the forest as an extractive resource and either they have little knowledge of important ecological relationships or those relationships, if known, have no consequence for the plants' valuation.

Summary

Cultural models and the meanings people attach to resources matter when it comes to natural-resource management. This is the starting point for the study in this book, the comparison of Menominee Native American and majority-culture hunters and fishermen. The Guatemalan case study supports the idea that it makes sense to take mental models and understandings of nature seriously when trying to understand the bases of environmental decisionmaking.

MENTAL MODELS OF THE WISCONSIN OUTDOORS

The way people think about nature affects how they act on it. In other words, knowledge, beliefs, values, and practices are all interrelated. According to this view, environmental decisionmaking is not utility-based, driven by calculations of monetary value, but rather is meaning-based, driven by people's understandings of their relationship with the rest of nature. Only in the extreme case where people are alienated from the natural world would one expect a strict utilitarian orientation toward environmental decisionmaking.

We think that the values that are critical to understanding environmental decisionmaking are often noneconomic, moral values. The violation of moral values often triggers strong emotional reactions. In Wisconsin our focus was on the relationship of meanings and values internal to the cultures and cross-group misunderstandings and conflict. The Wisconsin setting offered a methodological advantage over the Guatemala setting. In Guatemala, the Itza' are indigenous and the Ladinos and Q'eqchi' are immigrants, from various lowland areas of Guatemala, respectively. Despite thirty years' experience in Petén the migrant groups may have less expertise concerning the lowland rain forest. The Wisconsin study participants from both groups were born and often have a long family history in the area. We were interested in whether different framework theories would exist among our participants and whether they would lead to different goals and different forms of conceptual organization for biological kinds.

Even if, like Menominee and majority-culture fishermen, two groups have the same general goal of resource conservation, the acts of one may be misunderstood and even morally condemned if they are not compatible with the specific goals and meanings through which these acts are interpreted. In principle it is possible to translate across frameworks and achieve mutual understanding, but it's far from easy to do—perhaps analogous to getting a war veteran and a war protester to accept each other as American patriots.

At the outset of our study we hypothesized that we would not find different mental models among Menominee and majority-culture informants; we thought that at least there would be no difficulty in translating across models. There were a number of reasons for thinking this:

- The two groups have more or less the same level of expertise.

- Menominees have lived with majority-culture folk for hundreds of years and are, of necessity, bicultural.

- Both groups are exposed to much the same media and other sources of information, so their ideas should tend to converge.

- Many aspects of understanding are likely based on principles that are universal and likely would be shared.

Our results from Guatemala led us to expect some differences, but we were not prepared for what we actually observed.

Chapter Three | The Study of Culture: A Framework for Theory and Methodology

Everyone can sing and has songs inside. If you don't think you can sing, go into the forest and start singing. Pretty soon the trees will start to respond—swaying and moving their leaves.

—A Menominee elder

IT IS HARD to do cultural research without having a clear definition of culture in mind. Serious questions come up whenever cultural comparisons are undertaken—for example, how to decide what groups are relevant to study; how to select samples of participants; how to measure whatever it is you want to measure; and how to interpret any differences or similarities found. Researchers' specific notions of culture and cultural processes go far to determine the way they answer these and other questions.

The logic of cross-group comparisons is very, very tricky. In the cognitive sciences most of the researchers have been trained on methods where there is an independent variable, which the experimenter varies, and one or more dependent variables, which the researcher measures. For example, the independent variable might be amount of caffeine given to research participants in some drink and the dependent variable might be their speed and accuracy at solving multiplication problems. Culture isn't like that. You can't randomly assign people to cultures in the same way you could assign them to groups given varying amounts of caffeine. Cultural variables are multifaceted. In short, culture is neither an independent variable nor a unitary thing.

The peculiar properties of cultural comparisons create the dilemma that if you compare two groups, there are two possible results and both

23

of them seem like bad news. If one finds no differences between the groups, the results may not be considered particularly newsworthy and you would have gone to a lot of work to show what other people had been taking for granted. But at least then the generality of the results would have been confirmed and would be on firmer ground.[1]

If, on the other hand, one compares two groups and finds clear differences, problems of interpretation quickly emerge. Which of the many ways in which the two groups vary are crucial? For example, Alejandro López et al. (1997) found that U.S. undergraduates and Itza' Maya of Guatemala showed a different pattern of responding on a reasoning task involving mammals. This is an important finding in that it undermines the idea that the particular reasoning phenomenon is universal. So far, so good. But figuring out what causes these group differences is a considerable challenge, because the two groups differ in myriad ways, including age, education, literacy, livelihood, language, and world view. It is practically impossible to disentangle these various factors, because cultural groups cannot be found that represent comparisons of single variables holding other factors constant. A researcher who compares cultures may be confronted by the dilemma of finding either weakly informative similarities or uninterpretable differences.

Here's another problem. Suppose we could control for age, education, literacy, and other features when we compare Itza' Maya and undergraduates. How do we decide which variables represent "culture" and therefore should not be controlled for, and which variables do not, and should be controlled for. The Itza' Maya practice agroforestry and also hunt and collect plants in the forest. To be Itza' is to be connected with the forest. This raises the question of whether intimate contact with the forest is a factor to be controlled or whether we should think of it as part of Maya culture. The answer is not clear. One could require that only American foresters be used in any Itza'–United States comparisons, but then one would be comparing Itza's who have a typical Itza' occupation with Americans who have a culturally atypical occupation, and possess lots of knowledge that is atypical for Americans in general. Or imagine if we controlled for occupation by contrasting a sample of Americans with white-collar jobs with a handful of the very few Itza' holding corresponding positions in Guatemala. That just won't do.

Suppose that we do control for every variable we can think of and still find differences. In this case, it seems that we may be more or less forced to reify or essentialize culture. That is, the only explanation of the cultural difference involves appealing to some abstract notion of "culture." This leaves us caught between two equally undesirable possibilities: either to end up with a notion of culture that solely has recourse to circular explanations of differences ("the Itza' are different because they are Itza'"') or to conclude that cultural comparisons just represent confounded experiments and that the notion of culture is not needed once proper experimental control is achieved.

Another problem associated with comparative research is the issue of sampling. If we want to know how the Itza' categorize and reason, we had better take a random sample of Itza', else our results may not generalize to the Itza' population as a whole. And we had better make sure that we are really taking a random sample. The sample used by López et al. (1997) consisted of Itza' Maya elders who speak Itza' Maya, a dying language; the "typical" Itza' speaks mainly Spanish. That fact alone makes the sample unusual and unrepresentative, a problem if one tries to make universalizable claims.

OUR METHODOLOGICAL STRATEGY

Our methodological strategy for cultural comparisons incorporated two main approaches.

Triangulation

There is no theoretically neutral way to define or study culture (see Atran, Medin, and Ross 2005). The idea that culture is whatever is left when all potentially confounding variables are controlled is self-defeating. It is useful to control for variables that are clearly irrelevant to culture, but decisions about what is irrelevant are necessarily theory-based and commit one to a particular notion of culture.

The general idea of triangulation is to use observations from a third group to get at least modest leverage for understanding initial group differences. The third group should resemble one group in some potentially important ways and the second group in other ways. If the third group performs like one group and different from the other group, then the variables shared by the third group and the group it mimics become candidates for critical variables.

Our triangulation strategy proved to be effective for understanding the difference in reasoning between Itza' Maya and University of Michigan undergraduates. When we found that American parks maintenance personnel used reasoning strategies just like those of the Itza', we were able to rule out language, literacy, and formal education as the basis for the differences between Itza' people and college students reported in the López et al. (1997) paper. Closer analysis revealed that having a lot of knowledge about the domain is the key variable in patterns of reasoning:

undergraduates, who didn't know much about mammals, used abstract reasoning strategies; both Itza' and park maintenance personnel, who did know a lot, employed causal and ecological knowledge in their reasoning.

In the work associated with this book we only made use of triangulation once. After comparing expert Menominee and majority-culture fishermen, we added two additional groups: less expert Menominee fishermen and less expert majority-culture fishermen. The former less expert group allowed us to see how the influence of Menominee culture may vary with expertise and the latter group allowed us to examine the same question for majority-culture fishermen.[2]

Purposive Sampling

Cultures are not static but relentlessly evolve as different coalitions of people dissolve, merge, and mutate. Nonetheless, it seems sensible to look for sharp contrasts by means of selecting subpopulations that have retained more group-specific knowledge. These considerations lead one to employ sampling techniques most likely to reveal cultural differences. Consider again the López et al. studies with the Itza' Maya. Younger Itza' might have notions of biology that differ from those of Itza' elders, differences that reflect assimilation to "Western culture" or a lack of traditional knowledge. Thus, a random sample may tend to hide rather than reveal cultural differences. Instead of randomly selecting participants, López et al. restricted their sample to Itza'-speaking Maya as the best representatives of Itza' culture. This is not that there was some pure Itza' culture in the past that nowadays is being degraded—cultural change is a constant. Itza' cultural life is a rich blend of ideas and habits stemming from different inputs, including a great deal of Spanish influence. A random sample is only appropriate when one wants to make claims about population parameters such as averages, something that we believe is rarely relevant in cultural comparisons. In our studies in Wisconsin, our primary focus has been on expert fishermen and hunters. Again, this is far from a random sample. It does, however, help us separate cultural effects from expertise effects.

With these general methodological issues as background we are ready to take a more direct look at approaches to conceptualizing culture.

WHAT KIND OF THING IS CULTURE?

There is an important distinction to be made between the question of how cultures should be studied and how they should be defined.

The Intuitive View of Culture

One might intuitively define culture as the shared knowledge, values, beliefs and practices among a group of people living in geographical proximity who share a history, a language, and cultural identification. Although we think that a definition of a culture in terms of history, proximity, language, and identification is useful and (if not too rigidly applied) perhaps even necessary, it does not follow that the cultural content of interest must be shared ideas and beliefs.

We see three problems with this intuitive view of culture and its focus on shared content. First, it prejudges the issue of what constitutes cultural content. If a diversity of ideas, values, and practices are in competition, does that mean that they aren't part of the culture because they aren't consensual? There might well be distinctive values, beliefs, and knowledge within a culture that nonetheless are not consensual. For example, a culture may have a set of beliefs and practices known only to a privileged group of people, such as healers, elders, or a ruling elite.

Second, this view of culture is static in that according to it, cultural change either is not a relevant object of study or is treated as (cultural) loss or, in some cases, as extinction. Third, this approach may implicitly essentialize culture by conceptualizing it as an entity with systematic, law-like properties. "Explanations" of differences may simply point to the differences themselves ("Dogs are different from cats because dogs are dogs and cats are cats").

It is very natural to think that the cultural contents of interest must be shared in order to qualify as "cultural." But we have just seen that this commitment undercuts the dynamic side of cultural processes. We believe that scientific cultural research must be able to overcome intuitive notions of culture in order to focus on causal processes associated with both stability and change within and across cultures.

Culture as a Collection of Changing Norms and Rules

Some influential models of culture formation and evolution in biology and anthropology take a somewhat more liberal view of consensus, taking as examples of consensus group-level traits that assume cultures are integrated systems consisting of widely shared social "norms"—or "rules," "theories," "grammars," "codes," "systems," "models," or "worldviews"—that maintain heritable variation (Rappaport 1999; Laland, Olding-Smee, and Feldman 2000; Wilson 2002). Some political scientists also tend to view cultures as socially "inherited habits" (Fukuyama 1995), that is, as socially transmitted bundles of normative traits (Huntington

1996; Axelrod 1997). Richard Dawkins (1976) has launched the concept of memes, analogous to genes, as packets of ideas, knowledge, or beliefs that are culturally transmitted by imitation (see also Blackmore 1999; see Aunger 2000 for an analysis and critique of the meme notion).

The idea of heritable variation loosens the restrictions on consensus and raises questions about the basis for variation. But here cognitive scientists are likely to be disappointed by the implicit assumption that the gist of cultural learning is the automatic absorption of norms and values from the surrounding culture by processes no more complicated than imitation. We believe that these assumptions do not pay sufficient attention to the sorts of inferential and developmental cognitive processes that allow human beings to build and participate in cultural life.[3]

The Psychological View of Culture

Recent studies in the area of cultural psychology have made important contributions to human understanding by showing that knowledge systems and patterns of categorization and reasoning previously thought to be universal (a conclusion resulting from studies on U.S. undergraduates) actually vary widely across the world (for reviews, see Cohen 2001; Nisbett 2003). Much of the data supporting these claims of variability comes from studies with college students in different cultures or from foreign students attending American universities. If anything, these studies probably underestimate the magnitude of cultural differences.

Although this work represents a very important contribution, we have some reservations about it. Perhaps most important, the idea of "culture" typically endures as a commonsense notion that one does not bother to define or identify in any reliable way. Furthermore, the leap from statistically reliable differences in some sample population to "the culture" suffers from precisely the sort of reasoning we criticized in mainstream psychology's leap of generalization from college students to the world. More generally, it is tempting to think of culture as a thing and it becomes easy to essentialize culture. In contrast, we believe that it is more useful to consider culture as more like a verb than a noun. That is, cultural processes are at least as interesting as *products* or outcomes that are then treated as defining culture.

The Distribution View of Culture

It is our view that cultures should be studied as causally distributed patterns of ideas, their public expressions, and the resultant practices and behaviors in given ecological contexts. This distributive view of culture is a significant departure from the shared norms and rules perspective in that the variable distribution of ideas within a culture becomes an important object of study instead of a nuisance. That is, disagreement across observers is treated as signal or information, not noise (random variability). Just as one would not study the United States' political parties by attending only to what Democrats and Republicans agree on, one should not limit oneself to studying shared values and beliefs when investigating the most important aspects of culture. When popular writers discuss "culture wars" within the USA, they explicitly address the fact that cultural notions are often contested, yet these disagreements are assumed to be part of the American culture.

The Cultural-Consensus Model

The distribution view avoids the stereotypical view of "culture" as a well-bounded system or cluster of practices and beliefs (see Bruman 1999 and commentaries for examples). Instead it relies on a set of techniques for assessing groupwide patterns that statistically demonstrate cultural consensus or lack thereof. In our work we have relied extensively on the cultural-consensus model (CCM) developed by A. K. Romney, S. C. Weller, and W. H. Batchelder (1986), an important tool for analyzing commonalties and differences within and across cultural groups.

It is hard to overestimate the importance of the cultural-consensus model as a tool in our research. A considerable amount of research, including cultural research, relies on statistical tests to see if some difference is statistically reliable. There's nothing wrong with this as far as it goes, but in the case of group differences, it is easy to overinterpret or reify differences and as a consequence downplay cross-group agreement as well as within-group differences.

For example, later in the book we will show that when given a free sorting task, Menominee fish experts are reliably more likely to sort fish ecologically (that is, to group them by the habitats in which they are found), yet less than half of the Menominee experts used this strategy. Thus, the Menominee ecological orientation, which is in striking contrast with majority-culture orientation, does not hold equally for all Menominee.

The cultural-consensus model assumes that widely shared information is reflected by a high level of agreement across individuals. It asks whether or not it makes sense to assume that there is a single knowledge or belief base among a group of people for some particular topic or domain. If so, there is a consensus. But if there are subgroups with different knowledge or beliefs—or even dramatic individual variations—then there is no consensus.[4]

In this way, the cultural-consensus model provides a measure for shared knowledge among a group of people and hence a measure of the extent to which an individual shares what others agree on. The model invites one to think about the distribution of within- and between-group differences and the special conditions under which it makes sense to say that there is consensus within a group.

In the case of an existing consensus, the cultural-consensus model justifies combining individual responses into a "cultural model." The degree of agreement can be used to determine the minimum sample size needed to estimate the cultural consensus within some range of tolerance. The notion is quite straightforward but it flies in the face of a natural intuition, that the data or opinions from a hundred people just aren't as convincing as data from a hundred thousand people—that the larger the sample size, the more confident we should be of the result.

But there's another way of thinking about sample size. With small samples, it takes a huge effect for a difference to be statistically reliable. With very large samples, even very tiny effects often prove to be statistically significant. As long as an effect is statistically reliable (unlikely to have been produced by chance or sampling variability), then usually the magnitude of the effect will be larger for smaller samples. Going back to the Lopez et al. study, if one group used a particular strategy 75 percent of the time and the other group used it 80 percent of the time, it's very unlikely that the difference would be statistically significant when there were fewer than twenty participants in each group. If the difference were 10 percent versus 80 percent, then it would no doubt be highly significant. Similarly, the 80 percent versus 75 percent difference would certainly be reliable if we had a thousand participants per group. This difference would probably strike us as small and unimportant (unless we were evaluating some treatment or procedure that might be used with many thousands of people, such as a treatment regimen for cancer).

What all this means is that if you can find a reliable effect for a small sample, you can be confident that it is probably a big effect. The cultural-consensus model can tell us how small a sample is reasonable if we want to see if there's an overall consensus. The more people within a culture agree with each other, the smaller the sample you need. If you ask ten people what day of the week it is and they all say Thursday, then you can be pretty sure that other people you could have asked would also probably say it's Thursday. They may not be correct (if the subjects were passengers on an airplane they may not realize that they have crossed International Date Line), but they do show a consensus. In some of our work, as few as ten informants are needed to reliably establish the presence of a consensus.

As already indicated, general agreement may be coupled with systematic disagreement, and the cultural-consensus model is an effective tool for uncovering both shared and unshared knowledge.[5] In our studies comparing Menominee and majority-culture fishermen we often find that members of the two groups share a common model yet differ reliably on specific submodels. If there are reliable cultural differences, Menominees should agree more with other Menominee than they agree with majority-culture informants and vice versa. Once in a while two cultural groups can differ reliably on some task but there is no reliable within-culture consensus. In this situation one needs to be cautious about making culture-wide generalizations. For example, we saw in the last chapter that Itza' men see the forest spirits as guardians of the forest. In our interviews, Itza' women did not share this description of the forest spirits. In that case there was no overall Itza' consensus.

Analyzing agreement patterns both within and across different populations promotes the exploration of possible pathways of learning and information exchange within and between cultural groups. For example, it allows us to investigate the impact of specific factors such as gender or kinship relations on patterns of agreement. It also gives us leverage for pinpointing relevant sources of variation within and between cultures.

As a concrete example, suppose we find cultural differences relating to a task such as "successfully dunking a basketball," and we think that the difference is associated with cultural differences in height. This seems plausible, but we will have a stronger argument that height is a relevant source of variation if we also find that within each culture dunking ability is correlated with height.

In the present project we find ourselves very much in this sort of situation. Specifically, we find cultural differences in mental models and we think they are linked to stereotyping. To strengthen our argument, it helps to show that within-culture variations in these mental models are associated with within-culture variations in stereotyping.

Summary

We have presented a view of culture that focuses attention on the distributions of ideas and belief systems, in contrast with notions of culture that rely on shared values and attitudes or treat any statistically reliable culture differences as central, without worrying about whether they are even consensual.

Modern biology provides a good analogy to cultural studies. Biology was founded on the intuitive notion of species as uniform, unchanging kinds. Unless you've been exposed to modern evolutionary theory you may still think of species in this way. The consensus in evolutionary biology is that the notion of species is somewhat arbitrary—for example, reproductive isolation as a criterion doesn't always hold—and that we should view species as historically linked populations changing over time

(Ghiselin 1981). Just as it may be difficult for us to give up our notion of species as timeless, unchanging, and identical in their deep underlying properties and genetic structure, it may also be difficult to abandon the notion of culture as an unchanging body of rules, norms, and practices.

But the use of a commonsense notion of culture as a starting point does not leave research on culture stranded or unable to come to a new, more nuanced understanding of the topic. Initially, the use of a commonsense notion of species focused Darwin's attention, but subsequent discoveries revealed only rough correspondence between the commonsense construct of species and historically contingent patterns of evolution, whereby the concept of species is elastic, referring to more or less geographically isolated and interbreeding populations. Darwin continued to use the commonsense idea of species (see Wallace 1889, 1), while denying it any special ontological status or reality.[6] Likewise, intuitions about what constitutes a "culture" may continue to help orient research, but should not be mistaken for a final or correct framework of analysis or explanation.[7]

Like modern biology, the distributive view of cultural phenomena takes individual variation not as deviation but as a core object of study. From this perspective, issues of cultural acquisition, cultural transmission, cultural formation, and cultural transformation are intricately interwoven and together constitute the object of study.

DATA COLLECTION

If you're trying to immerse yourself in culture in order to understand it, then the idea of collecting data in a formal manner may strike you as artificial. Indeed, some anthropologists and cognitive psychologists criticize other cognitive psychologists on just these grounds—as presenting "toy problems" in unfamiliar contexts that have little to do with reality. The critics of data collection argue that richer, more meaningful contexts are needed to achieve anything but the most superficial understandings.

Those who would learn about a culture by collecting data about it defend themselves by pointing out that if the only thing an ethnographer can report is his or her "impressions," then cultural studies become a form of literature, because there's no way of dealing with the situation where two ethnographers study the same culture and come away with different impressions.

In fact, anecdotal and statistical evidence—qualitative and quantitative measurement—are complementary, and both are needed. In our case this means that we used both structured interviews and quantitative probes in our study. If two descriptions disagree, we can look at the measures and the contexts in which they were made to begin to understand the basis for the disagreement.

Some further cautions. First, taking a distributional view of culture means that the goal of cultural comparisons cannot be solely to figure out what or how people of some culture think. One might be able to determine the consensus on some body of knowledge or opinions or strategies, but whether or not there is a consensus is itself an empirical question. Frequently the most interesting questions will be about the distribution of ideas within and across groups, including changes with development and expertise.

Second, what's true for cultural groups may also be true at the level of individuals. If we ask the same questions of a person in several different ways and in different contexts, there's no guarantee we'll always get the same answer. People's attitudes, beliefs, and strategies are often multifaceted and some contexts bring out facets that other contexts conceal. Wendi Gardner, Shira Gabriel, and Angela Y. Lee (1999) have shown that the patterns of independence and interdependence revealed in tasks that have been used to demonstrate differences between Asian and Western cultures can be dramatically changed by asking people to read a paragraph with a lot of personal pronouns in it: reading lots of "I's" is associated with an individualistic orientation, whereas reading lots of "we's" shifts Asians and Westerners alike toward a collectivist or interdependent orientation.

In our studies, we have found that whether or not we observe cultural differences sometimes depends on the pace of the task. In other studies, concerning how children's knowledge of the natural world develops, we find substantial differences in the answers young Menominee children give in response to questions that are identical but that have been embedded in different contexts. A skeptical anthropologist might take these context effects as evidence that we're not getting at people's "true" beliefs. We believe that these context effects in fact are crucial for understanding how people's knowledge is organized and how it gets recruited in different settings. It is signal, not noise.[8]

Our research strategy, therefore, is to collect multiple measures in a variety of contexts. In so doing, we often enlist participants as aids and seek their advice about what sorts of tasks are meaningful and relevant. More than once an informant has said, "Gee, I thought you were going to ask me about . . . " and then gone on to describe some probe or issue that we hadn't thought about. Often this issue became the central focus of a new round of interviews.

We were also careful about the timing of our questioning—when we asked what we asked. Researchers who have studied primarily undergraduates know that you get down to business quickly: explain the task, run it, give a debriefing, and wait for the next set of undergrads to come to the lab. Ideally, the undergraduates won't find the task so interesting that they talk with other undergraduates about it so you don't have to worry about them passing on any information that could affect how later students might perform on the task.

Such conditions do not obtain with field interviews. Trust and rapport are necessary for work in the field, and this requires more detailed knowledge of groups and their social conventions. For example, in the first visit with a Menominee elder, your goal may just be to introduce yourself, say a little about your general aims, and then sit back and listen. Once you start the formal interviewing process, your fond hope is that people have been talking about your interviews and that your reputation (hopefully a good one) has preceded you. If the interview is with a majority-culture hunter, you must make clear that you are neither a rabid environmentalist nor connected with the animal-rights movement. So it's helpful if you come into the interview with Wisconsin word-of-mouth approval.

Of course, we present the informed-consent forms associated with all research projects, but these forms are themselves often more intimidating than helpful. One person read our standard consent form carefully and asked, "Does this mean I need to hire a lawyer before helping out with your study?"

Some of our most valuable information has come from chatting informally before and after the "official" interviews. Some of our questions on values and attitudes might seem to touch on sensitive areas, but these probes typically come on the seventh, eighth, or ninth interview with that person. By spending considerable time in both the Menominee and majority-culture community, we got to see our informants in a variety of other contexts, including when we were ourselves fishing.

Ethnographers espouse the practice of "participant observation," meaning that one comes as close as possible to becoming a member of the community one is studying. Our experience is that both communities welcomed us and took us in—one of us, Douglas Cox, is himself Menominee and lives on the reservation, but the other two researchers did not become members of either community. It was always clear that our role was as researchers, that we benefited from that, and that we in turn had a moral obligation to give back to each community. We tried to do so in ways ranging from hiring local research assistants and teaching courses at the local college to baking cookies and attending meetings of service organizations.

Chapter Four | Categorization in Cultural Perspective

My brother seems to be getting to be quite a spokesman, even though he doesn't live on the reservation and doesn't know the traditional ways. I gave him a headdress to wear when speaking so people can see he's a real Indian.

—A Menominee elder

SINCE WE'RE GOING to be talking about how two different groups think about nature, it seems like a good idea to place our work in the context of other work on cross-cultural similarities and differences in categorization of biological kinds. If you're just interested in intergroup conflict over environmental resources, you might think we are straying a bit, but as we mentioned earlier, the intention of this book is to show that meanings matter. If meanings matter, the various components of understandings of the biological world, values, and practices are all interrelated and provide part of the story told in this book. In this chapter specifically we will take on the puzzle of categories—the building blocks of thought.

Do people in different cultures organize nature in the same way? It is easy to be of two minds on this question. There's a case for expecting large variation across cultures. First of all, there are clear examples of variation. For the Itza' Maya of Guatemala, bats are birds. Other cultures do not consider the cassowary a bird. The traditional Menominee notion of "alive" includes materials such as water or rocks which are inanimate according to Western science and convention.

Second, there's no obvious reason why different peoples should have the same categories. One could argue that "similarity" is a universal organizing principle—that we put things in the same category because they are similar. If we think that similarity is an objective relation—that things

35

seem similar if and only if they are similar—then we should expect cross-cultural agreement. But, as Nelson Goodman (1972) pointed out, similarity isn't an objective relation. The number of shared aspects or features between two things depends on what is allowed to count as an aspect or feature and how much weight or importance is attached to each feature. Even if we restrict ourselves to perceptual features, assuming we can define what is and what isn't a perceptual feature, we may be little better off—there is now fairly strong evidence from studies of perceptual learning that features themselves can change with experience (see Goldstone 1998). Instead, the perception of similarity may be the result of category learning, not the cause. Even if we delimit the features that we are considering, similarity will depend on how much weight is placed on the various features—a canary and a grapefruit belong to the same category if we only pay attention to color.

Third, there is also good evidence that people's concepts are organized in terms of their theories about the world (Carey 1985; Murphy and Medin 1985). In most cases these theories are framed in terms of causal principles and not in terms of similarity. A pair of siblings may be similar because they are twins but they are not twins *because* they are similar. The general line of argument from the theory view takes the form, if different theories lead to the formation of different categories and if the theories people have vary across cultures, then people in different cultures will have different categories.

But the issue is not one-sided. First, if concepts are so different across cultures, why do we find it so natural to ask "What's the name in your language for X?" where X usually is some object, including a plant or animal? Suppose we point to a tree and ask for the name. When we're given the name, we naturally and usually correctly assume that the word we are given corresponds more or less to the level of detail that we expect. It is not a superordinate label, such as "living kind," that encompasses far more than the ash tree, nor will it be a highly specific or subordinate label, such as "Thompson's seedless green ash," that applies to just one narrow example of the plant or animal. Rather, the word we are given will be an intermediate, informative level of description such as "ash tree" or perhaps "tree."

A second and related counterargument is the way that things are in the world sets boundary conditions on both perceptual learning and the forms that theories can take. It matters a lot whether you categorize a mushroom as poisonous or not if you then take the additional step of eating the ones you call nonpoisonous. Since people in every culture face the common task of making predictions and inferences about the things that they categorize, the properties of those things strongly encourage, and possibly outright guarantee, convergence on more or less the same categories.

The most compelling argument against major cultural differences in categorization is the research done by anthropologists on how different peoples classify nature (see Atran 1990; Berlin 1992; Berlin, Breedlove, and Raven 1973, 1974), which shows remarkable cross-cultural agreement in how people organize their knowledge about plants and animals. People of all cultures classify living kinds into ranked, hierarchical taxonomies (for example, plant, tree, oak, red oak); and one particular level of rank is especially salient and stable across cultures (see Malt 1995). This level corresponds more or less closely to the genus or species level (for example, oak) in scientific taxonomy. Locally, most genera have just one species so it's not practical to distinguish genus and species. Let's take a closer look at this evidence.

CROSS-CULTURAL COMPARISONS OF FOLKBIOLOGY

Ethnobiologists studying systems of classification in small-scale societies (see, for example, Atran 1990, 1999; Berlin 1978, 1992; Berlin, Breedlove, and Raven 1973, 1974; Brown 1984; Bulmer 1974; Hunn 1977; Hays 1983) have argued that taxonomies of living kinds are organized into hierarchical systems in these societies. Not only are categories related to each other by class inclusion (for example, all robins are birds; all birds are vertebrates; all vertebrates are animals; and so forth), but taxonomic categories at a given level in the system also share linguistic, biological, and psychological properties with other kinds categorized at that level. For example, the names for things at the folkgeneric level typically consist of single words, such as robin, crow, or eagle. These regularities in folkbiological classification and nomenclature can be seen in disparate cultures throughout the world. Indeed, these common principles observed in culturally diverse populations are often taken as evidence for universal cognitive constraints on folkbiological thought. Brent Berlin (1992, 8) argues:

> The striking similarities in both structure and content of systems of biological classification in traditional societies from many distinct parts of the world are most plausibly accounted for on the basis of human beings' inescapable and largely unconscious appreciation of the inherent structure of biological reality—human beings everywhere are constrained in essentially the same ways—by nature's basic plan—in their conceptual recognition of the biological diversity of their natural environment.

These claims are supported by research that extends beyond the cataloging of folk taxonomies. For example, James S. Boster, Berlin, and John

O'Neill (1986) examined disagreement between Aguaruna and Huam-
bisa Jivaro natives, of northern Peru, by having members of the groups
identify prepared bird specimens. Although the groups are both from
the same region, their cultures are distinct in the sense that members of
the communities are not in direct contact and speak different but related
languages. These authors demonstrate that the two groups exhibit similar disagreement patterns during identification that can be predicted by
taxonomic relatedness; in other words, both groups are more likely to
confuse species that are more closely related from the point of view of
their scientific classification.

Boster (1988) extended the results of these experiments to include a
task where the participants sorted unfamiliar birds. He chose a subset of
the birds used in the 1986 study and presented them in a sorting task to
U.S. undergraduates. He then compared the data to previous results and
found that specimens the college students saw as perceptually similar
corresponded with closely related birds according to scientific taxonomy,
and also tended to be the ones found to be most similar and thus confu-
sable by Peruvian natives. This finding is impressive in that it shows two
completely distinct cultures performing quite similarly with the same biological kinds.

Formal scientific taxonomy is something of a yardstick, and the distance between any two biological kinds in folk taxonomies tends to
correlate with their distance in scientific taxonomies (Atran 1990). Formal taxonomy can also be a yardstick in the sense of providing an in-
ventory or list of local species and looking to see which species are given
distinct names. For example, one might hypothesize that people are
more likely to name plants and animals that have utility for them (Ellen
1993). The alternative view is that people's natural curiosity and drive
to understand the world undermines any utilitarian bias (Malt 1995;
Hunn 1999). Eugene Hunn (1999) has attempted to specify the principles
determining which kinds are named, and the most significant factor appears to be size—the smaller something is, the less likely a culture is to
name it.

Although it appears that the universalists have won by a TKO in the
third round, the fight isn't over. There is, in fact, a lot of wiggle room.
The strong agreement at the level of genus or species doesn't extend as
well to more abstract categories. Many cultures don't have a superordinate term that covers all animals or all plants, and few if any have a single term for all living things. Even at the level of class (for example,
birds, fish, vines), folk taxonomies may diverge and they certainly conflict with science. Folk everywhere recognize trees as a category, but taxonomic science has rejected it. For example, the genus Hydrangea com-

prises shrub, vine, and tree species. In general, plant families often crosscut folk labels for life forms.

Finally, it is worth emphasizing that folk taxonomy is only a component of a folkbiology, not the whole. It provides the dramatis personae for a drama that is played out among animals, including humans, plants, and other features of the natural world. For example, the native Itza' Maya as well as Ladino and Q'eqchi' Maya migrants of the Petén in Guatemala all share general categories of animals and plants (same life forms). However, the previously presented study makes it clear that members of each group have very different concepts with respect to the folkecology, their view of interactions among members of these categories. Obviously, then, cultural variables can have a large influence on how humans, plants, animals, and other features of the natural world are understood by individuals.

THE USE OF CATEGORIES IN REASONING

One reason to categorize is to be able to make inferences. If you categorize some fish as a walleye, you can infer that it spawns in the spring and likes to eat minnows and shiners, and that if you caught the walleye and cooked it, it would make a tasty meal.

This example makes it clear that these inferences are not to be taken as natural properties of members of a category but include relational properties such as edibility. Therefore, we might expect cultural differences with respect to these inferences. For example, knowing that a fish is a bass will lead Menominee and majority-culture fish experts to very different inferences. Members of both groups know that you can eat bass, yet only the Menominee value the bass as a food source. Majority-culture fish experts make a very different inference, looking at the quality of bass as "good fighters" and as a trophy fish for which catch and release should be employed. Members of the two groups make different inferences and as a result attach different meanings to the same fish. We argue that these differences in understandings lead to intergroup conflict, as they suggest different interpretations of observed behavior.

But categories are used not only to assign concepts to specific instances but also to reason about novel events or properties. If you were to find some new fishing lure that smallmouth bass seem to love, you might make some plausible guesses about other kinds of fish that might like this lure. For example, it's probably a safer bet that a largemouth bass would also go for the same lure than would a musky.

Our research group has used reasoning tasks for two purposes. One is to show that the sorting tasks we have employed result in meaningful groupings. If we can predict patterns of reasoning from the way people sort examples into groups, then we know that these groups are not arbitrary and weren't created simply to entertain us. The other purpose for these tasks is to get a better understanding of how people use categories to reason.

One good way to understand how categories are used in reasoning is to work with a testable theory of category-based induction. One such theory is the similarity-coverage model developed by Dan Osherson et al. (1990), which we have found useful for our own research. The similarity-coverage model relies on the notion of similarity and similarity relations as a guide to induction.

The similarity-coverage model predicts that the strength of an argument from a premise to a conclusion will vary with the similarity of the premise category to the conclusion category. This is the same as the logic underlying our conjecture that a largemouth bass is more likely than a musky to like a lure that we know smallmouth bass like. Largemouth bass are more similar to smallmouth bass than are muskies. The similarity-coverage model also predicts that typical members of a category will have greater inductive strength than atypical members for generating conclusions about the entire category. For example, an inference going from bears to all mammals should be stronger than an inference going from mice to all mammals because bears are more representative of the mammal category than are mice. This prediction follows because in the terms of the SCM, "bear" provides better "coverage" of the category than "mice," because bears have greater average similarity to other category members than do mice.

For our purposes two of the empirical phenomena that the similarity-coverage model predicts are notable: typicality and diversity. We just explained typicality in terms of average similarity to other category members. Diversity also relies on the notion of coverage. Consider the following argument: "Cows and horses get one disease. Cows and squirrels get another disease. Which disease is more likely to affect all mammals?" The similarity-coverage model predicts that people will prefer the argument having the more diverse premises, in this case, the disease that cows and squirrels get rather than the one that afflicts cows and horses. According to the similarity-coverage model, the argument with the more diverse premises is stronger because it provides better coverage. Cows and horses each likely have greater average similarity to members of the mammal category but this coverage is redundant—the mammals to which cows are very similar are the same ones to which horses are very similar, whereas the mammals to which squirrels are similar are different from the ones to which cows are similar. The similarity-coverage model relies on a measure of maximal average similarity and thus is sensitive to the presence of redundancy. Hence, the model predicts that diverse arguments will have greater inductive strength.

In all these types of reasoning phenomena, the properties (for example, having ulnar arteries) are selected to be "blank" in the sense that people will not have any meaningful content associated with the property, and will have to rely on their knowledge about the entities involved in order to make predictions. This is important, as the point is to understand people's reasoning strategies with respect to the categories, not the property.

Our research group has made extensive use of reasoning tasks in order to understand people's use of categories. One striking finding is that experts use very different reasoning strategies than nonexperts do. Undergraduate students use the categories employing strategies predicted by the Osherson et al. model. This means they reason about animals and plants using category membership and resulting similarity calculations to generate inferences. Data from experts look strikingly different. Independent of the domain (birds, trees, mammals, or fish) U.S. experts perform more like Itza' Maya and Menominee than like undergraduate students in that they usually employ their specific knowledge (beyond category membership) when reasoning about folkbiological species (Bailenson et al. 2002; Burnett et al. 2004; López et al. 1997; Medin et al. 1997; Proffitt, Coley, and Medin 2000).

These findings suggest that American undergraduates have a deficit in knowledge about the folkbiological world, which forces them to use category membership as the main reasoning strategy, mainly because they lack any more specific knowledge. This undermines the common strategy in the cognitive sciences of treating data derived from studies of U.S. undergraduates as the golden standard for human thought and consequently treating differences from these results as deviations, if not deficiencies. In the light of the expert data, this assumption seems no longer valid.

A ROLE FOR GOALS IN CATEGORIZATION?

A study by Boster and Jeffrey Johnson (1989) provides a nice illustration of cross-group consensus in categorization. They asked commercial fishermen and undergraduates to sort ocean fish into categories. They found that undergraduate sortings of fish pictures actually correlated more highly with scientific taxonomy than the sorts of the commercial fishermen. Boster and Johnson argue that commercial fishermen are influenced by goals and additional goal-related knowledge about fish. Undergraduates, in contrast, only know what the fish look like from the pictures they've been given, and the morphological information revealed in the pictures is just the sort of information that scientists use in their taxonomic schemes.

You might think that this sort of study is not fair because pictures give everything away. Since undergraduates don't know anything about the fish, they have no choice but to rely on the pictures. This would be basically another example of what we just talked about. Compared to novices, experts use additional knowledge when thinking about folkbiological species. However, it isn't that simple. In another study using pictures, Jeremy Bailenson et al. (2002) asked undergraduates, birdwatchers, and Itza' Maya elders to sort either birds native to the United States or birds of Guatemala into categories. They found that Itza' Maya sorts of U.S. birds actually correlated better with scientific taxonomy than the sorts of undergraduates! The difference was even larger for birds of Guatemala, where the Itza' had a home field advantage. It likely is the case that their experience with birds helps Itza' appreciate which morphological components in pictures of birds are most relevant (see also Johnson and Mervis 2000). Of course, this does not explain why Boster and Johnson (1989) did not find a corresponding advantage for experts in achieving relative congruence with scientific classification systems in their sorts.

One speculation is that a single goal can pull a person away from a general-purpose taxonomy, but multiple goals tend to preserve a single, general organization. Itza' have multiple goals with respect to birds, seeking some as game, using others, the fruit eaters, to monitor forest regeneration, and appreciating others as the subjects of stories.

It would be interesting to see how Boster and Johnson's commercial fishermen would have performed on a category-based induction task; for a good guess, see Pat Shafto and John D. Coley (2003). A goal-based categorization scheme wouldn't necessarily affect reasoning. In studies we did with tree experts (Medin et al. 1997) we found different patterns of sorting trees among different types of experts. Park-maintenance personnel sorted on the basis of a variety of properties of trees, and their sorts correlated well with scientific taxonomic distances. Landscapers sorted into goal-relevant categories such as "good street trees" or "nice specimen trees," and their sorts correlated only very weakly with scientific taxonomic distances.

We then gave landscapers and parks personnel reasoning probes in which we used the same local trees that were employed in the sorting task. The reasoning of parks personnel could be predicted very nicely from their sorting data—the more similar two trees were, as indexed on the basis of the previous sorting task, the more likely they were to infer that a property true of one tree would also be true of the other one. The results of landscapers' sorting, however, did not predict their reasoning at all well. We did a little detective work and found that the best predictor of landscaper reasoning was sorting done by parks personnel. This finding suggests that even though the landscapers preferred to sort in terms of their goals, they also had another organization for thinking about trees that came into play on the reasoning task. Later on we'll see that fish experts have multiple ways of thinking about fish, but that there are cultural differences in which forms are most natural.

The moral of the story is that it's a good idea to collect multiple measures in order to get a more complete picture of categorization and conceptual organization. We'll be getting ahead of ourselves to say this but it turns out that the pattern of results can even hinge on procedural factors such as whether the pace of the task is fast or slow.

SUMMARY AND IMPLICATIONS

This chapter has served to illustrate some of the kinds of studies that are done to see how people organize their knowledge about biological kinds. Although people show fairly good cross-cultural agreement on categorization of biological kinds, this agreement is coupled with sufficient residual disagreement that it is useful to probe for the basis of sorting.

Another excellent way to assess how people organize biological knowledge is to look at the use of categories in reasoning. These types of studies consistently find large differences between undergraduates, who seem to have impoverished biological knowledge and populations that have closer commerce with nature. The differences center on the use of abstract, similarity-based reasoning strategies versus sorting based on more concrete causal and ecological knowledge. In our previous work we have found that cultural differences in categorization pale in comparison to cultural differences in the salience of ecological knowledge. Hence, a key component of our studies in Wisconsin is assessing ecological understandings.

This chapter has also spotlighted varying potentials for cultural differences. For example, people may use similar categories, but the concepts that are attached to these categories might differ widely. In a preceding chapter we alluded to the possibility that these conceptual differences are caused by differences in epistemological frameworks which are employed by people to understand the world. These frameworks may inform the goals individuals employ, which in turn, we propose, leads to different conceptual schemes and associated cultural differences. In our case study we believe that the cultural differences in framework theories and conceptual organization lead to intergroup conflicts, despite the groups' shared values and goals.

Chapter Five | Contemporary Setting and Conflicts

"Start with the rising sun and work toward the setting sun, but take only the mature trees, the sick trees, and the trees that have fallen. When you reach the end of the reservation, turn and cut from the setting sun to the rising sun, and the trees will last forever."
—Menominee leader, usually identified as Chief Oshkosh
(quoted in Spindler and Spindler 1971, 201)

THERE IS CONSIDERABLE tension over Native American hunting and fishing rights in Wisconsin. Letters to sporting magazines commonly urge the boycotting of casinos run by Indian tribes until the tribes give up their right to set their own hunting and fishing regulations. Many majority-culture fishermen believe that Indian fishing practices are a threat to the sportfish populations of Wisconsin. This is seen as having important economic consequences, for in Wisconsin, hunting and fishing for sport are multibillion-dollar enterprises.

To get the flavor of some of the more extreme anti-Indian views, one has only to visit the websites of organizations such as Protect Americans' Rights and Resources (P.A.R.R.), an organization that actively advocates the revocation of Native Americans' rights to fish, game, and water.

Although the conflict is statewide, and often becomes nationwide, we chose to focus on one locale, sacrificing breadth in favor of depth.

HOW WE PICKED OUR RESEARCH SITE

On hindsight it often seems that an event can be both completely accidental and carefully planned. One day, Douglas Medin was surfing the internet and chanced on a site linked to Menominee Tribal Enterprises, a

44

forestry business that, among other things, operates a sawmill on the Menominee reservation in northeastern Wisconsin. The Menominee are renowned for their one-hundred-fifty-year record of sustainable forestry. The tribe also has its own college, the College of the Menominee Nation, which offers training in natural resources and sustainable development.[1]

Two factors made this accidental discovery significant. One was that two of the authors of this volume were part of a team of researchers who had been studying the relationship between how people think about nature and how they act on it. Specifically we had been doing research with three groups who live in the rain forest of lowland Guatemala and practice agroforestry. The groups differ dramatically in the sustainability of their practices and we had been trying to find out why. The Menominee appeared to represent another positive instance of sustainable resource management. We also wanted to perform studies where we could equate for expertise—in Guatemala the group that had the most sustainable practices was far more expert than the other two.

Second, one member of the research team, Medin, was already planning to do research in Wisconsin related to people's understanding of biology. We had been frustrated by the lack of knowledge of plants and animals among Northwestern University undergraduates. Although many of them know a lot about microbiology, most of them couldn't tell a maple from an oak. Of course, we could find tree experts by going to places like the Morton Arboretum, the Chicago Botanical Garden, and the Evanston Parks Department. However, we wanted a sample of people who would have considerable knowledge about plants and animals where this knowledge was not based on professional training but rather on activities in their everyday lives. We thought that a small, rural community in Wisconsin might be a good place to find such people. Finally, we aimed to be in an area where there were lakes and rivers because we wanted to interview fishermen. These factors converged in and around the Menominee reservation, which lies about forty miles west of Green Bay, Wisconsin, on both banks of the Wolf River.

When you get to Green Bay it makes a big difference whether you head east or west. East takes you to Door County, something of a tourist's delight. In addition to the wonderful Lake Michigan shoreline and resorts with all the amenities, there are plenty of excellent restaurants, plenty of opportunities for shopping, plenty of art galleries, and plenty of other tourists.

If you head west instead, you'll come to Shawano County, more of a sportsman's delight. The patches of forest intermingled with cornfields support a high deer population. There are also lakes, rivers, and streams of all sizes, containing a diverse population of fish species. There are

many more bait shops, boat shops, and gun shops than there are art galleries. In many ways the area has a 1950s flavor. In Shawano County the
extended family, both non-Indian and Indian, is alive and well—some
people leave, but the average adult has parents, brothers, sisters, aunts,
and uncles living there, too. One of our Menominee friends recently told
us that he was going to get married and that they had decided to have a
small family wedding—meaning that about seventy relatives from in
and around Menominee County would be attending.

THE MENOMINEE RESERVATION

People whose careers lead them to move every few years may not appreciate how important a sense of place can be. By "sense of place" we
mean the close proximity of family who have also lived in the place a
long time, of the surrounding environment, and a conciousness of relevant histories and memories associated with some context (Basso 1996).
In the case of the Menominee, the forest is a core feature of home and
identity.

The Menominee Forest

Menominee County is just north of Shawano County. On Landsat satel-
lite images one can readily locate the Menominee reservation because of
the salience of the forest, even on the northern section, where the reservation forest borders Nicolet National Forest. The Menominee forest is
richer in larger trees, has a richer mix of species, and is denser than the
Nicolet Forest. It also has a higher per-acre production of timber and
maintains a higher number of board-feet of commercial species (Davis
2000). This is not because the Menominee forest is untouched and pris-
tine. To the contrary, the Menominee forest has been managed for timber
production for more than a century, so this impressive forest is the consequence of a careful and quite successful forest management system.
The Menomonee forestry chief, Marshall Pecore (1992, 16), has described
the productivity of the forest:

> When the Menominee Reservation was established in 1854, there were an
> estimated 1.5 billion board feet of sawtimber growing stock. From 1865 to
> the present more than nearly 2 billion board feet of sawtimber had been
> harvested. The most recent inventory indicates that sawtimber stocking is
> still at least 1.5 billion board feet, even after 138 years of harvesting this
> same acreage.

The forest not only provides timber for the Menominee but also is a place for hunting deer, bear, and other game, as well as for gathering nontimber products such as berries and ginseng and other medicinal plants. As in the past, game is an important food source. Menominee Indians are avid hunters, and hunt deer, turkey, ducks, and geese with both bow and rifle. A number of Menominee also hunt bears, which are used for their meat, fur, and for medicinal purposes. The bear population appears to be healthy on the reservation. There are no moose and the wolf population is quite small in the Menominee forest.

The forest is also represents the place where ancestors are buried and contains culturally important landmarks that serve to remind Menominees of their cultural heritage. Some Menominee hunters have mentioned a sense of connection to the past as they realize that they are walking where their ancestors walked.

Hunting is regulated by the tribe and individuals who want to hunt have to apply for a deer tag for each deer they want to kill. Limits are based on targets set to maintain the size of the herd, just as off the reservation.

The reservation's other major natural resource is water. Over three hundred miles of trout streams, more than forty lakes, and several rivers make the reservation a destination for whitewater rafting and fishing.[2] Fishing has been and continues to be a major activity for the Menominee. Menominee fish during all seasons, in ponds, rivers, streams, and lakes, using a variety of methods. Trout are very important, as are the different species of panfish (small fish that are good for eating). As with hunting, the tribe sets fishing regulations that are comparable with the state's off-reservation regulations. Recent surveys have revealed that the fish population on the reservation shows above-average health and abundance (Schmidt 1995). Fish are stocked in only a minority of the reservation's lakes.[3]

Native American beliefs and relations to the environment are often described in terms that may not be very transparent to majority-culture people. For example, David Beck 2002, 23) writes of the pre-contact Menominee:

> The most startling difference between the Menominee and the European invaders who appeared in Menominee country must certainly have been the very essence of their world-views. The Menominee culture was steeped in the values of respect, kinship, and reciprocity. The Menominee and the world surrounding them interacted in ways that were beneficial to both. The Menominee viewed the world as integrated and holistic. The European cultures, however, viewed the world hierarchically and highly val-

ued both the domination-submission paradigm and property rights. While individual responses varied, these values generally permeated the cultures at all levels, from religious to political to domestic to commercial.

These descriptions may conceal as much as they reveal. How does one go about observing a holistic worldview—or any worldviews? It also isn't so clear what "holistic" means, and dominance-submission may sound like a strange descriptor to majority-culture ears. Further, as noted, almost everyone endorses respect for nature. Nonetheless the visible results of the Menominees' invisible worldview are quite impressive: their maintenance of the forest and resistance to constant economic incentives to abandon their practices, as compared to large-scale deforestation in the nearby off-reservation areas. Whenever we make cultural comparisons, we find differences that many would interpret as indications that the Menominees take a more holistic stance with respect to nature than the majority culture. And Menominee people themselves often say the same thing. Later we provide data rather than description and generally it supports Beck's claims.

As suggested earlier, perhaps the critical element in natural-resource use is not values per se but rather what happens when one set of values comes into conflict with another (Kempton et al. 1995). The Menominee have demonstrated time after time that they are unwilling to trade their forest, lakes, and rivers for money or better-paying jobs. Many Menominee believe that the Menominee would not be the Menominee without the forest in the same way that a farmer cannot be a farmer without his land. For example, the Menominee Tribal Enterprise Management Plan for 1996 to 2005 (Huff and Pecore 1995, 110) states:

> The Menominee do not see themselves as separate from the forest, or the forest and its creatures independent from them. The Menominee culture exists in harmony with Mother Earth, understanding the circle of life. The forest, properly treated, will sustain the Tribe with economic, cultural, and spiritual values today and for future generations.

Obviously, these values are ideals and do not describe the behavior of every single individual Menominee. Some Menominee individuals litter the forest and behave in ways not in line with a "respect for nature" ethic. Nonetheless, as a people they have an environmental record that they can be proud of.

Demographics

In 2000, median family income on the reservation was about $26,000, compared to $38,000 in Shawano County; the average annual income on the reservation is about two-thirds the average income in counties adjacent to the reservation. These figures are somewhat misleading, however, because the average household size on the Menominee reservation is considerably larger, 3.7 individuals, than in Shawano County, where it is 2.5. About 36 percent of the people on the reservation live below the poverty line, compared with about 8 percent in Shawano County.[4] The age distributions are also substantially different on and off the reservation. Slightly more than half of the Menominee are under eighteen, compared to 25 percent for Shawano County.

Today about four thousand Menominee live on the reservation and a slightly larger number live off the reservation, mainly in Milwaukee and Chicago, but also in smaller nearby Wisconsin towns such as Green Bay, Appleton, and Shawano. The large off-reservation population is in part a cumulative effect of efforts by the federal government in general and the Bureau of Indian Affairs in particular to assimilate Indians into the majority culture.[5] The reservation is made up of three old communities, Keshena, Neopit, and Zoar, as well as the recently established "Middle Village," founded in 1995. Further housing areas can be found at Legend Lake, South Branch, and West Branch.

Government

The 1970s saw the formal recognition of hundreds of Native American tribes, including the Menominee. Under the terms of the Menominee Restoration Act of 1973, Menominee lands were protected and the Menominee achieved a great degree of autonomy.[6] Shortly after restoration of U.S. governmental recognition of the tribe, the Menominee developed their own constitution, and in 1977 a tribal government was established (Ricciuti 1997). Today this government consists of nine tribal legislators, one of whom serves as the chairperson. Members are elected for staggered three-year terms. The tribe has its own court system and police department. One major source of employment and revenue is Menominee Tribal Enterprises, which controls the forestry business; another is the Menominee casino operation. Contrary to the stereotype that tribes are getting rich from casinos, gambling revenues are barely enough to keep up with the costs of running an autonomous government.

Summary

In many ways Menominees today appear to follow a majority-culture rural life style. Many look for employment outside the reservation and some even send their children off-reservation to Wisconsin public schools in Shawano County. There are similarities to majority-culture individuals with respect to activities that are very popular in this area and also attract many tourists such as fishing, hunting, and snowmobiling. But such superficial similarities conceal large underlying differences reflecting history, values, and distinct perspectives on nature.

SHAWANO COUNTY

Since the Menominee see the forest as their home, it is important to look at the origin of the town of Shawano and Shawano County. Shawano County is adjacent to and south of Menominee County (which is co-extensive with the Menominee reservation). The history of Shawano County prior to 1843 would rightfully be Menominee history. Around that year the settlement of Shawano was established in order to extract the precious lumber of the area. Once the area was largely deforested, German settlers arrived and converted the land to agricultural use. Landscapes that bespeak both these waves of migration can be seen today when one travels through the area and encounters deforested agricultural land that gives away to forest once one crosses from Shawano County onto the reservation.

According to the 2000 census the population of Shawano County was 40,944. Both agriculture and light industry are important; the county purchased an industrial park in 1958 and it has prospered. Perhaps the major economic change over the last half century is the emergence of outdoor recreation as a major industry. Hunting, fishing, snowmobiling, boating, and jet skiing not only keep the county's residents active but also attract a large number of visitors. Shawano Lake is a particular attraction.

The recreational resources are one factor leading to a sense of stability. Another source of stability is that many people have extended family living in Shawano County and are reluctant to leave. In this respect Shawano County resembles the Menominee reservation, where family proximity and surrounding natural beauty make people reluctant to relocate just for higher-paying jobs. People of Shawano and Menominee counties tend to think of their work in terms of vocations, avocations, and jobs and not so much in terms of careers. Getting ahead and advancing oneself are means to an end (for example, enjoyment of family, outdoor activities) and not ends in themselves.

INTERCOMMUNITY RELATIONS

Community relations are multifaceted. Quite a few Menominees live in the town of Shawano and some Menominees living on the reservation send their children to the Shawano public schools. There is also some back and forth when it comes to employment in schools and business operations. Menominee Tribal Enterprises awards logging contracts on a competitive basis that includes a point system that rewards contractors who are Menominees or hire Menominee loggers.[7]

More than a few majority-culture adults from the surrounding community attend the College of the Menominee Nation, which employs an ethnically diverse faculty. The Menominee casino has provided an economic stimulus to both Menominee and Shawano counties. So there is a fair amount of interchange between the peoples of the two counties that is mutually beneficial.

In some other respects things are not so rosy. There is also a fair amount of real and perceived prejudice and stereotyping. Menominees complain about being followed about when they shop in certain stores, which they consider a form of ethnic profiling. Some Menominees tell of hearing more overt expressions of prejudice from majority-culture people who don't realize that they are talking to an Indian. Sometimes there are confrontations involving hunting and fishing near the border of the Menominee reservation.

Thus, the picture is mixed when it comes to majority-culture–Menominee relations. On the one hand, on issues such as supporting U.S. troops in Iraq or fighting a proposed mining operation that threatens the Wolf River, the communities become one (McNutt and Grossman 2003). On the other, there is always the potential for sharp divisiveness on issues where the interests of the communities are not perceived as shared.

Natural-Resource Issues

As mentioned earlier, there is resentment on the part of majority-culture sportsmen of tribes' setting their own hunting and fishing regulations, especially when those regulations are more liberal than those of the state of Wisconsin. Typically, majority-culture sportsmen see the tribal regulations as leading to resource depletion. Some white hunters and fishermen are under the impression that Indian tribes have no regulations at all.

There are four major specific natural-resources issues that generate strong feelings among majority-culture sportsmen.

One is that whites are not allowed to hunt and fish on the Menomineee reservation, but Menominee can hunt and fish off the reservation if they purchase licenses and follow state laws. Many whites view the asymmetry as unjust.

This frustration is exacerbated by the second issue, which is that court decisions have ruled that the Ojibwe, also called Chippewa, tribe of Wisconsin, whose members live in several bands in the northern half of the state, have off-reservation hunting and fishing rights. These rights allow the Ojibwe privileged access to fish and game and also give them the right to use the traditional methods by which they take them. The Ojibwe have off-reservation rights to spear game fish in the spring when they are spawning, whereas the season for white fishermen does not open until later, when spawning is over, and state regulations prohibit spearfishing.[8] The limits for non-Ojibwe fishermen for certain fish, such as walleyes, are adjusted downward after the tribe declares the waters where it is going to spear; these limits may be adjusted upward later on if tribal members take less than their quota. In the early 1990s demonstrations at boat-launch sites by whites against these practices received a great deal of publicity and the protests occasionally spilled over into violence.

The Ojibwe treaty rights do not directly affect Shawano County, and most of the white fishermen who are residents of the county go outside the county to fish either to Lake Michigan or to less-developed areas of Canada. Nonetheless, they are aware of the issue; many majority-culture folk do not draw a distinction among tribes and carry over their resentment to the Menominee.

A third source of conflict that relates to this lack of differentiation is that the Menominee tribe allows spearfishing on the reservation during the spawning time. Many majority-culture fishermen consider this "unsporting." Furthermore, it seems intuitively obvious that spearing females full of spawn would threaten the fish population.

The fourth source of conflict is that tribes set their own hunting regulations, which may allow hunting for deer at night from roadsides by "shining," blinding a deer with a spotlight or headlights. Not only is this illegal for nontribal members, but it is also seen as not sporting.

Overall, then, many majority-culture hunters and fishermen see Indians as having unfair rights and engaging in unsporting practices. They see both of these characteristics as transparently and intrinsically wrong, and also as a threat to fish and game populations—hence the comments about not seeing deer on the reservation.

The resentments are not all on one side. Menominees have difficulty understanding why whites honor the U.S. Constitution but often regard more recent treaties as outdated. They also see many of these views of treaties for what they are—threats to tribal sovereignty. With respect to "unsporting" practices, many Menominees grew up during times when white hunters would drive through the reservation and offer to buy deer—especially bucks, and the bigger its antlers, the better—that Menominee hunters had shot, instead of hunting or bringing down their own. Being poor, some Menominee hunters would sell their deer, but it hardly seems likely that this would leave them with much respect for the white "hunters." Stories about majority-culture hunters shooting game for fun or being focused solely on trophy game also fail to inspire confidence in Menominees that whites have respect for nature.

STORIES, THREADS, AND OTHER OBSERVATIONS

Observations and narratives by members of the two populations convey a feeling of worldviews.

On the reservation the medium of exchange is acts and memories for acts, of both individuals and families. People have long memories for acts and your reputation is important. That's why people returning to the reservation sometimes don't know how to act and don't know where they fit in.

A Menominee woman educator

When I was young my mother would give me medicine from the forest. She would sing to it. She'd point to the little flecks in it and tell me that they were little people. She told me that these little people had clubs and that they would beat up on the disease. The little men would go clockwise and the women counter-clockwise throughout the body. . . . I think the herb was mandrake root, which looks like a person when it's pulled up.

A Menominee elder

When I came home from World War II I met a girl that I really wanted to date. But her parents wouldn't let me go out with her because I was a pagan.

A Menominee elder

The table is important. It is where children are born and where we would lay out a person at death. When we sat for meals it was also a time for our mother and father to teach us. Although I am not a Christian, there is a picture of the Last Supper in my kitchen along with numerous other Native American spiritual symbols.

An elder appreciates the dinner table

I've been a logger, been in the military, worked in a casino, and was a sheriff for a number of years. I figure now it's time for me to get a little book learning.

An older Menominee who attends the
College of the Menominee Nation

I went to the medical clinic and a white nurse said to me almost accusingly, "Your people are susceptible to TB." I responded, Your people brought it."

A Menominee elder

Getting you to do the dishes is like getting a dead horse to walk.

Menominee expression

One day I [Medin] met with the chairperson of one of the Menominee tribal committees. Partly to indicate that we didn't plan to do what the Menominee call "parachute research"—fly in, do the measures, fly out—Medin mentioned that my wife and I had bought a house on the Wolf River about a mile south of the reservation. The Chairperson's response was direct: "If you look around the reservation, you won't find many houses on the rivers. If people build their houses away from the river, then everyone can enjoy the view. If houses are all crammed together on the riverfront, the view becomes spoiled."

Two Menominee men who were brothers, both of them well over eighty, were reminiscing about their youth, and each independently told us about his earliest fishing experiences. They didn't have rods and reels or even fishhooks. They would carve wooden lures by hand, make a hole in the ice, fold a blanket over the ice hole they made to reduce the light, and then move the lure, hoping to get a northern to follow it so that they could spear it.

The Federation of Fly Fishers announced the Wolf River as the most endangered fishery in the nation at its annual conference. It was listed because the Wolf River fish habitat faces immediate danger due to Nicollet Minerals Company's proposed Crandon mine. NMC is seeking state and federal permits to extract 55 million tons of zinc, copper, lead, silver, and gold from a sulfide ore body in Crandon.

If NMC were to receive mining permits, the mine would be built at the headwaters of the Wolf River. Thirty-two million tons of tailings, crushed rock and water treatment sludge would either be permanently backfilled into the mine or be permanently placed in an above ground tailings landfill covering 282 acres. Sulfide and heavy metals contained in this waste have the potential to contaminate ground and surface waters. Since the mine waste would be stored at the headwaters forever, the possibility of long term damage to this precious ecosystem is real.

Menominee Nation News, September 9, 1999

O Great Spirit whose breath gives life to all the world, hear me! I am small and weak I need your strength and wisdom. Let me walk in beauty and make my eyes ever behold the red and purple sunset. Make my hands respect the things you have made and my ears sharp to hear your voice. Make me wise so that I may understand the things you have taught my people. Let me learn the lessons you have hidden in every leaf and rock. I seek strength not to be greater than my brother but to fight my greatest enemy, myself. Make me always ready to come to you with clean hands and straight eyes so when life fades as the fading sunset, my spirit comes to you without shame.

An Indian prayer

One day Linda Powers (Medin's wife), a clinical psychologist, looked through the Yellow Pages for the Shawano area. She noticed that only three psychologists were listed; then she noticed that there were fifteen taxidermists in the directory. She got the idea of doing a psychologist-to-taxidermist ratio, which she called the P:T, a measure of the relative attention given to therapy and clinical services compared to hunting and fishing. The P:T ratio for Shawano was 3:15, or 1:5. In Evanston, Illinois, where Northwestern University is located, the P:T ratio is 251:2!

Douglas Medin, "Yellow Pages ethnography"

For converging evidence on her measure Linda Powers looked up "pizza" and "cheese." Since the Evanston area is more populous and has lots of college students it is not surprising that Evanston beat Shawano 73 to 12 for pizza parlors. But Shawano wins on cheese shops 18 to 3.

A: I filled my gas tank two weeks ago and it's still full.
B: You drive a lot—how did that happen?
A: I take the cap off when it rains.

Heard in a local bar

One day I went to the local hardware store to buy a water pump to get water from the Wolf River to water our lawn. The clerk carefully explained the setup I'd need and showed me the proper PVC piping. After cutting me a piece of piping he told me that I'd need to glue it onto its fitting, paused for a second, and then said "You know there's no point in your buying a whole container of glue just for this. I've got some glue here so I'll just glue it for you." He proceeded to do so. Then he said "You're going to need some fine screen to use as a filter on the intake side. You only need a little piece . . . . You know, I think I've got some extra out back—I'll go get it." By the time I had recovered from his generosity he had not only found the screen piece but had installed it on the piping. Just doing his job.

One Sunday afternoon in the early fall, my wife and I [Medin] decided to visit the Green Bay Botanical Gardens. When we entered the main building we were greeted by a matronly woman who appeared to be somewhat distracted. After we made our contribution, her attention shifted back to a small television set she had next to her desk. My first thought was that she was reviewing a videotape tour of the gardens or perhaps some nature film. My wife had moved around so she could see it and as we walked away she said to me, "The Packers are ahead."

J.B., one of our study informants, mentioned that in 1942 he had taken a course in wildlife ecology at the University of Wisconsin from Aldo Leopold, the author of *Sand County Almanac* (published in 1948), whom some consider the father of modern ecology. Only a freshman at the time, J.B. needed Leopold's permission to take the course, so he went to talk to him. Leopold was so impressed with J.B.'s knowledge of the outdoors that he let him into the course. After his freshman year J.B. volunteered for military service and was never able to return to the University of Wisconsin.

> I've lived in Shawano for fifteen years, most of my adult life. People are really friendly here but I still feel like an outsider. It seems that many people have known each other all of their lives.
>
> A majority-culture teacher

> Thirty years ago Shawano was a sleepy town of 7,598 people. Now with various business initiatives and organizational efforts, we are a bustling town of 7,598 people.
>
> A local realtor

In this part of Wisconsin the weather changes dramatically at different times of the year, and almost everything seems to be attuned to these changes. The growing season is short enough that one can watch the week by week changes in wildflowers, from the skunk cabbage that pushes up though the early spring ice and snow to the asters and goldenrod of fall.

Hunters shift their sights from rabbits and coyotes in the winter to turkeys in the spring to scouting for signs of deer in the summer and deer, ducks, geese, partridge, grouse, and bear in the fall. Fishermen, too, adjust their targets and techniques with the seasons: rod and reel for walleyes and crappies in the early spring, flyrods for trout from late spring to early fall, heavy casting equipment for muskies in the late summer and fall, and tip-ups for northerns and panfish in the winter. The only thing that doesn't seem to change with the season is the extensive coverage of the Green Bay Packers; any day of the year the sports segment of the local news will feature at least one comment on the Packers.

Menominee tradition organizes human lives around the seasons. A person's life starts in the north, when he draws his or her first breath. Then the focus of life turns to the east and south as a person tries out ways of being and accumulates wisdom. At first you are tense and hold the reins with both hands; then you let go with one hand, then with both, crossing your arms comfortably. Your people are in the west, waiting for you.

Chapter Six | Ethnographic and Historical Background

"On my vision quest I found myself thinking about trees. They are strong because they stand all the time, some grow together in groups, they are different ages, and even dead ones are standing. My guiding elder said that the trees were sending me their thoughts. Trees have spirits and must be respected."

—A Menominee educator

IN THIS CHAPTER we provide historical background on the Menominee and the majority-culture communities.

THE MENOMINEE

The Menominee have been in Wisconsin for a long, long time—evidence from the tribe's oral tradition and archaeological records both provide clear evidence that Menominee residence in the area dates back at least several thousand years (Beck 2002). The name of the tribe in the Menominee language is Kayaes Matchitiwuk, which means "original people." Today, however, they are known and also describe themselves as Menominee, a word that derives from the Algonquin word "manomin," for wild rice (Zizania aquatica), or "manomini," "the wild rice people" (Spindler and Spindler 1991). Traditionallly the Menominee have depended on wild rice as a major staple of their diet.

According to Menominee legend, their history began when the Great Bear emerged from the mouth of the Menominee River and soon was followed by other spirit beings, including the eagle, beaver, sturgeon, elk, crane, and wolf. These spirits became the Menominee. These animals correspond to the Menominee clans; the clan system continues to this

58

day and marks the Menominee sense that people are not separate from the rest of nature. ("Animals are our cousins; we're all related," they say.) The major clans initially were Bear and Eagle.

The Menominee are a woodland tribe. Prior to contact with white people, the Menominee seemed to have followed a semi-sedentary seasonal-village pattern that was organized around hunting, fishing, gathering, and horticulture. They occupied a considerable area of what is now Wisconsin, 9 million acres by one estimate, and were concentrated in part in villages along the Menominee River. The glacial drift left this area with networks of streams, small lakes, and swampy areas linked to rivers flowing either east, to the western shore of Green Bay, or west, to the Mississippi (Keesing 1939/1987). In the 1600s the area was covered with mixed hardwood-coniferous forest, and birch, basswood, oak, cedar, butternut, and hickory were particularly important.

Although hunting was important to their survival, at no season did the tribe move far from rivers or lakes. Spearing sturgeon, the largest freshwater fish of the area, carried special meaning, for sturgeon were important to both physical survival and to social and ceremonial life (Beck 2002). In the spring, thousands of sturgeon migrate from Lake Winnebago upstream on the Wolf River to look for spawning sites.

On the banks of the river Menominee fishermen waited for the sturgeon's arrival in order to spear "the first food of the year." According to mythology, sturgeon provided the first food to the bear, the first ancestor of the Menominee. Subsequently, sturgeon became the first offering to the powers that provided this food (Hoffman 1896/1970).

After the harsh winter, the arrival of the sturgeon in the spring must have been an anxiously awaited event, providing not only a change in diet but also a large quantity of food and a harbinger of warmer weather. In addition, sturgeon skin was used for different kinds of medicines, certain bones were used to make utensils, and the backbone was processed into glue (Beck 2002). To this day, the role of the sturgeon in Menominee culture goes beyond material value, and one can still hear Menominee conversations in which individuals talk about the sturgeon as "grandpa" or "uncle."

In the late pre-contact era, around 1600, two Menominee bands fought over a dam built by the band that lived downstream from the other, along the river. This created an obstacle to the sturgeon in migrating upstream and hence posed a serious disruption of the supply of sturgeon to the upstream band. A fight broke out, leading eventually to the departure of the downstream band. According to the U.S. army officer who recorded the story in 1853, this was the only civil dissension of importance in pre-contact history (Beck 2002). Today, the sturgeon's annual migration to their spawning fields at Keshena Falls on the Wolf River, located within the Menominee reservation, are once again interrupted by a dam, this one built in 1904 by white settlers in order to create a paper mill, near the neighboring community of Shawano. This downstream band is unlikely to depart, so one can only hope for a negotiated settlement.

At the time of contact in the early 1600s—1637 is one "official" date that is given—the Menominee inhabited several villages in an area that extended roughly from Escanaba, Michigan, in the north to Oconto, Wisconsin.

The survival of the Menominee as a people is something of a miracle, given the various assaults on the tribe's existence over the last few hundred years.

The Fur Trade Era

Soon after the arrival of French explorers in the area sometime around 1637, they rapidly established the fur trade (for example, buying pelts from the Indians and shipping them to Europe), mostly to supply Europeans with furs for hats and other items of clothing. The Upper Great Lakes area was ideal territory for such an endeavor, as it featured large tracts of forests intersected by rivers, allowing easy transportation, and inhabited both by a multitude of fur-bearing animals and by an indigenous population that was very skilled in both hunting and trading. The trade for furs introduced sweeping changes to the local economy, as more and more tribes encroached on the Menominee land in search of pelts, leading to an increasing number of intertribal conflicts. The French fur trade era was perhaps the most benign threat that the Menominee faced after contact with Europeans. The French had no designs on Menominee lands, preferring to profit from trade than to settle new lands. The traders had more or less congenial relations with Indians, and intermarriage between French traders and Menominee women was not unusual. The fur trade did change the social structure of the Menominee. As the beaver pelts closest to Menominee settlements began to run out Menominee men had to travel longer distances in search of furs. As a consequence, for significant portions of the year the village structure was replaced by smaller hunting bands. It is difficult to estimate the impact of this shift on Menominee culture, but it no doubt disrupted the clan system to some extent and may have contributed to uncertainty concerning the precise structure of the Menominee clan system pre-contact (Hoffman 1896/1970).

At the end of the seventeenth century both reports of the corrupting effects of the fur trade as well as a dramatic drop in fur prices in Europe led the French crown to suspend the fur trade in the western Great Lakes. The defeat of France in the French and Indian War (1754 to 1763) marked the end of French influence in the Great Lakes region.

Disease

Contact with Europeans meant contact with diseases for which native peoples had no natural immunities. The effects were devastating throughout the New World, and the Menominee were not spared. A 1736 survey put the number of Menominee warriors at 160 (Keesing 1939/1987). It is hard to get precise figures, but it is probably safe to assume that at least half the Menominee population fell victim to disease; in some areas there are records of 90 percent of the population falling prey to nonnative diseases.

Religion

The Menominee were fairly receptive to early French Catholic missionaries, in part because Menominees did not conceive of religious beliefs as mutually exclusive. Christianity was an addition to, not a replacement of, traditional spiritual beliefs. In fact, the French gave the Menominee much more religious freedom than Spanish or English settlers gave to Native Americans.

Religious pressures on the Menominee to give up their traditional beliefs and practices continued into the nineteenth century. In the mid-nineteenth century, when the Menominee people settled in villages on the Menominee reservation, those who were Christians tended to settle in and near what is today Keshena and South Branch and the pagans, those who followed more traditional Indian religion, settled farther away, north and west of Keshena. The present village of Zoar, established in 1881, continues to be a center for traditional spiritual practices. Although most Menominees today are Catholics, many of them integrate this faith with beliefs and practices associated with their traditional religion.

The Treaty Era: 1812 to 1856

The French and, later, the British came to Menominee country for trade. After the War of 1812, British influence all but disappeared, to be replaced by Americans who wanted more than trade—they wanted the land itself. Settlers poured into the Midwest in general and Wisconsin in particular. The treaty era had begun.

The initial interest in this area focused on the timber that grew on it, not on agriculture. But for the timber to be harvested the land had to be owned. Following deforestation, new waves of settlers converted the land into agricultural land, mostly dairy farms.

The idea that land is something that one could own was somewhat alien to Indian sensibilities. Tribes and, within tribes, families did have rights to use the land and to exclude others from using it, but land was not a commodity. Consequently, Indian conceptions, at least for initial treaties, were that they were receiving gifts in exchange for usufruct, or use privileges, not giving up land ownership.

Treaties meant displacement to less hospitable areas, often several thousand miles away from home. When the implications of treaties became clear to Indian tribes, they began to resist them, yet it soon was evident that the U.S. government was going to take the land, treaty or no treaty. For example, in 1832 the U.S. Supreme Court upheld the sovereignty of the Cherokee Nation, but the federal government under President Jackson simply ignored the ruling and proceeded to remove the Cherokee, and even challenged the Supreme Court to enforce its ruling.

Although the treaties usually included payment for the land, the amounts were paltry and at best symbolic, providing a veneer of legality to what were essentially uncompensated takings. In one treaty, in 1831, the Menominee received $285,000 for 3 million acres, or about eight cents per acre.

When Americans made their first appearance at Green Bay in 1815, the Menominee did their best to adapt to the new situation, as they had done previously, when the British replaced the French in 1761. They signed their first treaty with the United States in March 1817, in St. Louis. There was a second treaty in 1831, and a third in 1836. In the last one the Menominee surrendered another 4.2 million acres.

White settlers continued to pour into Wisconsin, and as statehood approached in 1848, Chief Oshkosh and the Menominee were pressured into ceding their remaining Wisconsin land in exchange for a 600,000-acre reservation on the Crow Wing River in Minnesota. Back then the governor of Wisconsin Territory wrote, "The extinguishments of the Indian title to the Menominee County is a subject of the first importance to the growth and prosperity of Northern Wisconsin" (cited in Beck 2002, 167).

Chief Oshkosh sent scouts to the Crow Wing area, and they reported back that the land was desolate and inhospitable. This served to strengthen the Menominee resolve to resist displacement from their remaining land. Although the Menominee signed the treaty in 1848, they nevertheless refused to move to Minnesota. Instead they pleaded for a reservation in Wisconsin—their homeland. This was finally granted after many negotiations and interventions from outsiders, missionaries (including Father Florimond Bonduel, for whom the nearby town of Bonduel is named), and settlers.

The final major treaty, the Wolf River treaty, signed in May 1854, established a reservation for the Menominee in northern Wisconsin. In this treaty twelve townships were assigned to the Menominee reservation. This treaty was amended in 1856, when the Menominee ceded two townships for the purpose of creating a separate reservation for the Stockbridge Indians, who had been displaced from the Northeast. The new established Menominee reservation contained 235,000 acres of their original homeland, less than 3 percent of the lands they had originally occupied.

Timber Interests

Before, during, and after the treaty era, businessmen and settlers, aided by governmental officials, were eager to exploit Wisconsin's timber resources, including those on tribal lands. The tribe had to fight off numerous schemes that would have let whites harvest the Menominee forest, and poaching, especially of valuable white pine, was a constant problem. James Newman (1967) estimates that about 1 million board feet of timber were stolen from Menominee lands between 1871 and 1890. The so-called "Pine Ring," a group representing white logging interests, was involved in a number of efforts to gain control of and clear-cut the Menominee forest.

The Dawes General Allotment Act of 1887

More generally known as the Dawes act, the Dawes General Allotment Act, sponsored by Senator Henry L. Dawes of Massachusetts, authorized the U.S. president to end tribal ownership of land by allotting 160-acre plots to heads of families and 80 to other family members. Any lands left over would be auctioned off or given to homesteading white settlers. In states such as Oklahoma, the "left-over" lands were extensive and white settlers benefited from what can only be called a theft of land.

The consequences of the Dawes Act were disastrous. The idea was to "civilize" or assimilate Indians by forcing them to adopt the white model of ownership and individual industry. But where allotment took place, most of the land assigned to individual Indians quickly ended up in the hands of whites.

Although the Menominee tribal council approved the Dawes Act—in effect, they were forced to—they and other Menominee leaders successfully stalled off its implementation until the disastrous consequences of allotment were so transparent that talk of allotment died out. The Menominee had dodged another bullet.

Wardship and the Bureau of Indian Affairs

Although the tribe had some autonomy, many of its activities were under federal supervision. The Bureau of Indian Affairs, created in 1849 as a special section of the new Department of the Interior (and sometimes called the Indian Department), held tribal lands in trust, and tribes were wards of the government. Early Menominee efforts to develop sustainable logging as a source of employment and income were hardly aided by U.S. authorities. In 1871 the Secretary of the Interior agreed that Menominees could cut and sell logs to mills off the reservation and in 1872 a tribal logging camp was organized (Grignon et al. 1998). But in 1878, in response to pressure from the Pine Ring, the Indian Department issued orders to stop Menominee logging. In 1882 a congressional act gave permission to the tribe to cut dead and down timber, but six years later the U.S. attorney general ruled that Menominees had the right of occupancy only and that the timber on the reservation was the property of the United States. This was again reversed in 1890, when cutting of timber was allowed under the supervision of white superintendents in the employ of the Department of the Interior. One index of just how inept this regulation and oversight was is that in 1951, the Menominee were awarded close to $8 million dollars for damages caused by the Department of the Interior's logging superintendents between 1912 and 1926.

As this book goes to press (spring 2006), the Bureau of Indian Affairs is being sued by numerous tribes for literally billions of dollars for misuse and misappropriation of tribal trust funds. A major problem hampering the investigation is the B.I.A.'s inability to locate relevant records in its offices.

Boarding Schools

In the 1920s and 1930s there was an attempt to assimilate Indians to white culture by "taking the Indian out of them." Many Indian children were forced to attend boarding schools at considerable distances from their homes. Children from different tribes and language groups were thrown together and students were punished for speaking their native language. One product of this experience for many Native Americans was distrust of and disidentification with the mainstream educational system. Many parents avoided speaking the Menominee language in front of their children so that their children wouldn't be punished when they went to school. Menominee became a dying language. Over the past few decades, however, the tribe has made extensive efforts to keep the language alive. Currently there are about eighty to one hundred relatively fluent Menominee speakers.

The Termination Act of 1954

The most recent threat to the Menominee as a people was the Menominee Indian Termination Act of 1954, which ended federal recognition of Indian rights and privileges guaranteed by treaties. It was in effect an effort to legislate the Menominee tribe out of existence. No new names were to be added to the Menominee tribal roll after 1954. The idea was that all Menominees would become American citizens instead of wards of the federal government, the tribe would receive no more financial support from the federal government, the land would be divided up, and the reservation would become nothing more than another Wisconsin county. When the plan went into effect in 1961, it meant that the Menominee were subject to a crushing financial burden. Not only was federal support cut off but also the Menominee government had no tax base to generate revenue to substitute for federal aid. The tribal clinic and hospital soon closed. The tribal court system broke down, and the sawmill, the primary business on the reservation, had to focus on efficiency rather than maximizing Menominee employment. Menominee County became a pocket of poverty almost overnight as the tribe struggled to provide essential services.

In desperation the Menominees, in 1968, were led to make a major concession with respect to their precious land: from several smaller lakes on the reservation, they created a man-made lake, Legend Lake, and sold shoreline lots to non-Indians.

But once again the Menominee people proved to be resilient. The Legend Lake decision had been made by the board of directors of Menominee Enterprises, on which several non-Indians served. When news of the decision reached the tribal grass roots, the development triggered a storm of protest over the loss of land and the energy released by it fueled a broad, sustained effort to restore federal recognition of the tribe. One key development in this restoration movement was a 1968 U.S. Court of Claims ruling that the Menominees did not relinquish their hunting and fishing rights when the tribe was terminated, which set the stage for a Supreme Court ruling that Termination had not abrogated treaty rights and obligations.

After more than a decade of resolute struggle, the tribe succeeded. The Menominee Restoration Act was signed by President Nixon in 1973. Under its terms the Menominee lands would be protected under the treaty trust relationship with the U.S. government (though the Legend Lake development stands, and non-Indians continue to own and occupy much of the shoreline). Through it, the Menominee achieved their greatest degree of autonomy since before the treaty era (for more on the restoration movement see Beck 2002; Davis 2000; Peroff 1982).

Casinos and Continuing Threats to Sovereignty

The relatively recent development of gaming compacts and tribally operated casinos has given an economic boost to many tribes, including the Menominee. It has allowed them, among other things, to create and support the College of the Menominee Nation.

But there is also a strong downside to casinos. One is the misperception that Indians have all been made wealthy from casinos profits. In the case of the Menominees, the highest per capita annual payment to enrolled tribe members over the past five years from casino profits has been one hundred dollars, and for the past two years when the tribe has had some budgetary problems, the per capita payment has been zero. (Compare this figure with the payment that every Alaskan citizen receives each year from oil and gas revenue; in 2002 this figure was $1,540.)

A more significant downside grows out the fact that tribes are only semi-autonomous. The need for state approval of gaming compacts has led to pressure from members of the state legislature and from a former governor, Tommy Thompson, on Wisconsin's tribes to give up certain treaty rights in exchange for the renewal of gaming compacts. One Wisconsin state legislator has stated, "The tribes should determine what is more important to them—fish or chips" ("Petition Seeks to Separate Spearfishing, Gaming," *Beloit Daily News*, 23 October 23, 1997).[1]

In the case of the Ojibwe, the aim has been to force them to relinquish their hunting and fishing rights in the ceded territories. Of most relevance to the Menominee tribe is the attempt to remove any legal standing Menominees may have for fighting off-reservation threats to the Wolf River, such as the proposed Crandon mine some forty miles north of the reservation.

This list of threats to the Menominee people over the past few hundred years is by no means complete; one could add to it involuntary sterilizations and plans to site a nuclear waste dump on the reservation. The U.S. government has consistently been extremely paternalistic to Indians, in the worst sense of the word. As Charles Hobbs (1969, 1268) notes in his review of court cases on Indian hunting and fishing rights: "It may come as a surprise to realize that most persons who identify themselves as American Indians are `restricted.' Also known as `noncompetent' or 'unemancipated.' The 'restricted' Indian is legally assumed to be incapable of managing his property wisely, and as a consequence of this presumption he may not sell his land without approval of the federal government."

Anyone who knows Menominee history cannot fail to come away impressed with Menominee resiliency.

MAJORITY CULTURE

In part because majority-culture history in Wisconsin is shorter, there is less to be said about it in general and Shawano County in particular than about the Menominees. For the first few hundred years post-contact, there was only a modest white presence in the form of explorers, traders, and soldiers. Then, in the nineteenth century, came an explosion of white settlers and an associated removal of Indians from their lands via treaties.

According to Shawano County historical records, the first white man to explore this area, Samuel Farnsworth, paddled his canoe up the Wolf River in 1843 to identify an area for logging operations. He and Charles Wescott set up a sawmill where the channel from Shawano Lake joins the Wolf River. Shawano County was established in 1853, at which time there were 254 registered inhabitants. The county's first school was established in 1860, and by 1898 there were 108 public schools staffed by 124 teachers. Shawano was incorporated as a village in 1871.

Business and industry in the early days were not dramatically different from today's: primarily logging, sawmills, cheese factories, and agriculture. The relative prominence of agriculture increased as the forests began to disappear. In the late nineteenth century a paper- and fiber-manufacturing company was established, and the paper mill continues to be a source of employment to this day.

The early immigrants tended to come from New England and Canada, many from Germany and Norway; 4,524 of the 27,475 residents counted in Shawano County in 1900 were born in Germany. Two factors that spurred the county's growth were the establishment of a road from Green Bay to Copper Harbor, Michigan, that passed though Shawano and north through the Menominee reservation, and the railroad, which provided an important transportation link.

Religion was and is important to the residents of Shawano County. Early on, Catholics worshipped with the Jesuit priests who had come to Keshena with the Menominees. The first Protestant church, a Methodist church, was established in 1860, and other churches soon followed. The *Shawano Evening Newspaper*, evolved from earlier publications, was founded in 1881. The first public library was built in 1916.

Chapter Seven | The Folkbiology
| of Freshwater Fish

"I fish because I love to: because I love the environs where trout are found, which are invariably beautiful. . . . Because of all the television commercials, cocktail parties, and assorted social posturing I escape. . . . Because trout do not lie or cheat and cannot be bought or bribed or impressed by power. . . . And finally, not because I regard fishing as being so terribly important, but because I suspect that so many of the other concerns of men are equally important . . . and not nearly so much fun."
—John Voelker, *Anatomy of a Fisherman* (1964)

THIS BOOK IS about intergroup conflict over natural resources, mainly fish and game. Even though experts from the two groups included in this study, Menominee Indians and majority-culture sportsmen, more or less agree on their basic values with respect to conservation, they are often in conflict. Our hypothesis is that different ways of looking at nature and the species that make up nature constitute different frameworks used to evaluate activities and practices. These meanings and associated judgments lead to stereotyping, misunderstanding, and intergroup conflict. To make our argument we shall elaborate each group's understanding of nature; in this chapter we look at understandings of freshwater fish.

One of the best ways to find out who the experts are is to ask around. Once you find a few experts you can ask them to identify other experts. This is known as the "snowball method" of sampling and it works pretty well. How do we know it works? We get an index of knowledge by asking informants about their familiarity with local species of fish, not only about the popular game fish but also non-game-fish species such as gar (Lepisosfeus sp.), dogfish (amia calva), darter (Etheostoma sp.), dace (Phoxinus sp.), and stickleback (Culaea inconstans). Our experts were familiar with all but a handful of the forty-four to forty-six kinds of fish we asked them about. We also asked experts to nominate more typical fisherman—people who fished a lot but would probably know less about fish. With one or two exceptions, these less expert fishermen were, in fact, less familiar with local species of fish, which confirmed our judgment of who were truly expert.

In order to select the group of fish species that would work for testing local knowledge, we needed to find out what fish were inhabiting the local water bodies. We started out by asking fishermen to list the fish found in the area. This also acquainted us with the local names for fish. We then supplemented this by referring to Wisconsin Department of Natural Resources fish surveys of the area and asking a few majority-culture and Menominee experts if the various fish were found locally. Questions about names helped not only to select kinds of fish but also the level of specificity at which to name them. For example, we had to decide whether to distinguish between black crappie and white crappie or to just use the folkgeneric term crappie. As a general rule (see Hunn 1999), finer distinctions are made for larger fish. For example, experts distinguish between white and black crappie, and largemouth and small-mouth bass, but not between specific kinds of darters and dace. Smaller fish that are used for bait and differ in habitat and goal-relevant characteristics—examples of these are river shiner and golden shiner; fathead minnow and bluntnose minnow—are also conceptualized at the folk-specific level. Our selection procedures allowed us to use relevant local names and to narrow our set of local fish down to forty-six.[1]

THE LOCAL FISH SPECIES

The full listing of the fish species knowledge of which would be tested to assess expert knowledge is given in table 7.1. The most relevant species are discussed here.

Walleyes and Perch   We have already mentioned walleyes (Stizostedion vitreum) in describing the controversy over Native American spearfishing rights. Walleyes and their smaller cousins, yellow perch (Perca flavescens), are among the most prized fish for eating. Friday-night fish frys pretty much feature walleyes and perch.

Northern Pike   The northern pike (or simply, "northern" Esox lucius) is one of the larger predator fish. Northern pikes have an elongated body shape like that of a barracuda and they also have voracious appetites. They can grow to be quite large and it is not rare for them to exceed

Table 7.1   Fish Species used in the Different Studies

Common Name	Scientific Name	Study 1	Study 2	Study 3	Study 4
American eel (lawyer)	Anguilla rostrata	X		X	
Black (hog) sucker	Hypentelium nigricans	X	X	X	X
Black bullhead	Ameiurus melas	X		X	
Black crappie	Pomoxis nigromaculatus	X	X	X	X
Blacktail (hornyhead) chub	Nocomis biguttatus	X		X	
Bluegill	Lepomis macrochirus	X	X	X	
Bluntnose minnow	Pimephales notatus	X		X	
Brook trout	Salvelinus fontinalis	X	X	X	X
Brown trout	Salmo trutta	X	X	X	
Carp	Cyprinus carpio	X	X	X	X
Channel catfish	Ictalurus punctatus	X		X	
Dace	Phoxinus spp. or Rhinochthys spp.	X		X	
Darter	Etheostoma spp.	X		X	
Dogfish (bowfin)	Amia calva	X	X	X	X
Emerald shiner	Notropis atherinoides	X		X	
Fathead minnow	Pimephales promelas	X	X	X	
Flathead (Mississippi) catfish	Pylodictis olivaris	X			
Gar (billfish)	Lepisosteus spp.	X	X	X	
Golden shiner	Notemigonus crysoleucas	X	X	X	
Green sunfish	Lepomis cyanellus	X		X	
Lamprey eel	Ichthyomyzon spp.	X			
Largemouth bass	Micropterus notius	X	X	X	X
Mudminnow	Umbra limi	X		X	
Musky	Esox masquinongy	X		X	
Northern pike	Esox lucius	X	X	X	X
Pumpkinseed	Lepomis gibbosus	X		X	
Rainbow trout	Oncorhynchus mykiss	X		X	
Redhorse	Moxostoma spp.	X	X	X	X
Redtail chub	Nocomis effusus	X	X	X	

Table 7.1   Continued

Common Name	Scientific Name	Study 1	Study 2	Study 3	Study 4
River (blackback) shiner	Notropis blennius	X	X	X	
Rock bass	Ambloplites rupestris	X	X	X	X
Sauger	Stizostedion canadense	X			
Sheephead (drum)	Aplodinotus grunniens	X		X	
Smallmouth bass	Micropterus dolomieu	X	X	X	X
Smelt	Osmerus mordax	X			
Spottail shiner	Notropis hudsonius	X		X	
Stickleback	Culaea inconstans	X		X	
Sturgeon	Acipenser fulvescens	X	X	X	
Walleye	Stizostedion vitreum	X	X	X	X
White (brown) sucker	Catostomus insignis	X		X	
White bass	Morone chrysops	X		X	
White crappie	Pomoxis annularis	X		X	
Yellow bullhead	Ameiurus natalis	X	X	X	X
Yellow perch	Perca flavescens	X	X	X	X

Source: Medin et al. (2006).

twenty pounds; the state record is close to fifty pounds. Many majority-culture fishermen practice catch-and-release with northern pikes. Others pickle smaller northerns, called "hammer handles," and fillet larger northerns.

Musky   Muskies (Esox masquinongy) are the largest freshwater fish that anglers in this part of Wisconsin are allowed to catch. They are like the big brothers of northerns in shape and habit but they are much less common. Muskies are known as "the fish of ten thousand casts," and a successful outing might involve simply seeing a musky rise toward one's lure. Actually the Wisconsin Department of Natural Resources (WDNR) estimated a few years ago that anglers needed about three thousand casts to land a musky). The state record for size is sixty-nine pounds, eleven ounces for a fish caught in 1949.

Majority-culture fishermen almost always release muskies they catch (though a trophy-sized musky may be kept to be mounted).[2] Killing a musky is grounds for dismissal from the Shawano Musky Club. There are also musky fishing contests featuring prizes of $25,000 or more. The Menominee treat muskies pretty much the same way they treat northerns—they eat them. There are fewer muskies on the reservation than off, perhaps because the tribe does not stock them. The WDNR does stock lakes with muskies and the Shawano Musky Club buys eighteen-to-twenty-inch fingerlings and stocks Shawano Lake with them.

Panfish   The term "panfish" is used for a group of smaller, fairly abundant fish that are good for eating such as bluegills (Lepomis macrochirus), green sunfish (Lepomis cyanellus), and crappies (Pomoxis), and many people also call perch (genus perca) panfish. Some people suggest that they are called panfish because of their round frying-pan-like shape, but the large majority of fishermen include perch in this category, which suggests a more functional interpretation: that they are good for frying up and eating. Although they may run up to a pound or two at most, success in hooking panfish is driven less by numbers than by size—it's no fun to clean twenty-five small panfish, when a good meal for a small family can be had with ten larger panfish. Locals start their children out fishing by letting them fish for panfish because there's usually plenty of action.

Smallmouth and Largemouth Bass   Some fishermen would be annoyed to see these two cousins lumped together, and protest that smallmouth (Micropterus dolomieu) are "much better fighters." Largemouths (Micropterus notius) are basically a lake fish and smallmouths are much more common in rivers. Majority-culture fishermen pretty much confine themselves to catch-and-release with both species, because of the fishes' sporting qualities; There are also bass fishing contests. This shift away from eating bass reflects an increasing emphasis on fishing for sport instead of food. Menominees eat both largemouth and smallmouth bass.

Brook Trout and Brown Trout   Trout generally like clear, cool, fast-moving waters. There are some rainbow trout in the area but brook and brown trout are by far the most common. Brown trout (Salmo trutta) is an introduced species and they run considerably larger than brook trout (Salvelinus fontinalis). Brookies spawn in the spring and browns in the fall. Tastes differ, but most people prefer to eat the brook trout. Although both majority-culture and Menominee fishermen target trout, Menominees place greater emphasis on them. Conversely, majority-culture fishermen place relatively more emphasis on walleyes, northerns, and muskies. The Menominee reservation has many trout streams. Shawano County has fewer trout streams, and majority-culture fishermen often drive up to Langlade County north of the reservation to flyfish for trout.

Minnows and River Shiners   In addition to flies and other artificial lures, many fishermen use live bait (though not for fishing contests). Mudminnows (Umbra limi) and river shiners (Notropis blennius), either seined or purchased at a bait shop, are commonly used to catch walleyes, northerns, largemouth bass, smallmouth bass, and crappies.

Suckers and Redhorses   Small black or hog suckers (Hypentelium nigricans) are also used as bait fish for walleyes and northerns, and large dead suckers are sometimes used as bait for muskies. Many people consider suckers and redhorses (Moxostoma species) as undesirable—"garbage" fish—but Menominee elders say they taste fine when they are smoked. Members of older generations in both communities may grind them up to make fish patties. Menominee youths may either spear or catch suckers with their hands in the spring when the suckers come into the shallow water to spawn.

Sturgeon   The sturgeon (Acipenser fulvescens) is the largest Wisconsin freshwater fish. Sturgeon are protected by law, except for a two-to-three-day winter spearing season on Lake Winnebago, when Native Americans are allowed to spear them. They are a big local attraction in the spring when they swim upstream to spawn in the shallows of the Wolf River (they do not reproduce until they reach about twenty-five years of age), and the sight of thousands of huge sturgeon in the shallows, so close that children reach out to touch their backs, is stunning. Some majority-culture fishermen like pretending to be fishing for suckers in the river in hopes of getting a sturgeon on their line. Game wardens will force them to cut their lines as soon as they see what is going on, but the fishermen like the idea of even a brief wrestling match with sturgeon.

According to legend, in the spring, the high water and rains beat against the mass of rock at Keshena Falls, making a drumming sound. This is the music of a mystic drum belonging to the manitou, or spirit, who controls the falls area and it calls the sturgeon upstream. A series of dams built on the Wolf River in the late nineteenth and the twentieth centuries prevents sturgeon from reaching the Menominee reservation, and the fish must spawn downstream of the ideal spot by the falls. The tribe is trying to negotiate to have fish ladders installed, which would allow sturgeon to return to the reservation, but many majority-culture fishermen are opposed to this plan because they think that the Menominees just want to get sturgeon "so they can kill them." The tribe also is stocking Legend Lake with sturgeon. Each spring the Menominee have a sturgeon pow-wow which features a fish dance showing the movements of the sturgeon as they swim upstream and prepare their spawning beds.

PROCEDURE

In an earlier chapter we noted the strong cross-cultural agreement in the categorization of biological kinds. This has been attributed to the correlational structure of the environment (see Rosch 1977), according to which correlated features or properties create natural "chunks," or basic-level categories, that any well-adapted categorization system must acknowledge or exploit.

Agreement on categories does not necessarily imply identical bases for categorization. The same categories can result from very different sources of information, and similar outcomes in categorization processes are no guarantee of similar underlying features. For example, woodticks have categories that correspond very closely with the human concept mammal, but ticks rely on sense organs to detect animal scents, carbon dioxide, and body heat to detect the presence of warm-blooded mammals, rather than on visual features to classify an organism as a mammal. One consequence of the assumption of correlated features is that two people or two groups may have roughly the same categorization scheme but have very different underpinnings for it. For example, Alejandro López and colleagues (1997) noted that undergraduates in the United States and the Itza' Maya of Guatemala both sorted mammals into categories that corresponded fairly well with science. However, the justifications they gave for their sorts, and other evidence, suggested that the American students relied heavily on size as the basis of sorting, whereas the Itza' Maya used a broad range of morphological and ecological criteria and only used size to describe differences within categories.

Earlier we also mentioned the James S. Boster and Jeffrey Johnson (1989) finding that free sorting of ocean fish by commercial fishermen who were looking at pictures actually agreed less with scientific taxonomy than the free sorts of novices. Expert comments suggest that the experts were using goal-related knowledge to structure their categories (see Barsalou 1985). Recall also that Douglas L. Medin et al. (1997) also used a free sorting task with different kinds of tree experts (landscapers, parks-maintenance personnel, and taxonomists) and found that landscapers tended to sort trees into goal-related categories but that the sorts of maintenance personnel and taxonomists corresponded more with scientific taxonomy.

One hypothesis that summarizes the current literature is that the correspondence of expert sorts to general-purpose scientific taxonomy is driven by the relationship between that taxonomy and how experts' goals structure the domain. If the goals crosscut the taxonomy, as landscapers' do, then the correlation with science will be reduced. If the goals are concordant with the taxonomy, then expertise should increase the correlation between expert sorts and science. For example, given that the goal of birdwatching is to identify birds, one might expect higher agreement between the sorts of expert birders and science than between the sorts of novices and science—and this is indeed the case (Bailenson et al. 2002). A corollary of this hypothesis is that the sorts of different groups that have the same goals and characteristic activities should converge as they become more expert.

People may use more to identify category members than merely a set of features. Different groups may use the same features to categorize things like fish and forest plants, but may have very different conceptualizations or understandings of these categories. They may differ in their conceptions of how that knowledge is to be organized in memory. We wanted to know whether Menominee and majority-culture experts differed in any of these ways in their understanding of local fish. If goals have a large influence on sorting, then we might be able to learn a lot about goals by the pattern of sorting and associated justifications or explanations.

Comparison of Populations

The two populations in our studies are closely matched for both expertise and characteristic activities. There were three types of tasks that we used to look at several facets of folkbiological knowledge, within a framework of four separate studies. The three tasks are:

1. Free sorting

2. Reporting of fish-fish interactions

3. Ecological sortings of fish (according to shared habitats)

The sorting task is designed to answer the question as to whether shared expertise leads to a convergence how local fish are categorized. The alternative possibility is that cultural differences in framework theories for understanding nature have an influence on conceptual organization. Finally, all of the tasks bear on the question of whether cultural variables play any role beyond that reflected by characteristic practices and activities.

The literature we have reviewed so far gives us little reason to expect differences between Menominee and majority-culture fishing experts. Both groups share the general goal of catching adult fish, both groups target essentially the same set of fish, and both use the same set of methods; they use live bait and artificial lures, do fly-fishing and ice-fishing, and so on. These common goals and practices, coupled with their very extensive fishing experience of on average several decades should lead to a convergence of the two groups with respect to how they think about fish. Previous literature provides every reason to expect that we will not observe any substantial group differences.

Against this background of similarities there are some differences in orientation toward fish and fishing that are important to bear in mind. Our informal observations suggest that fishing for food is a higher priority goal for the Menominee than it is for the majority-culture experts. Furthermore, the Menominee informants typically consider a broader range of species appropriate for eating. As we noted before, Menominee usually eat largemouth and smallmouth bass, whereas majority-culture fishermen often practice catch-and-release for these bass, describing them mainly as sportfish. Thus, majority-culture informants focus relatively more on fishing for sport than for food.[3]

There are also some modest differences in the particular fish that are targeted. Majority-culture fishermen associate prestige with catching and releasing muskies—the bigger, the better, so they are more likely than Menominee fishermen to target muskies. Majority-culture fishermen also target two other game fish, walleyes and northern pike. Larger northerns and walleyes are typically released, but majority-culture fishermen may eat smaller northerns and walleyes, the latter being considered one of the best-tasting freshwater fish by both informant groups. Menominee fishermen also eat northerns and walleyes and both groups eat panfish such as bluegills, sunfish, crappies, and perch. Menominee are somewhat more likely to target trout than are majority-culture informants. Trout are very good to eat, according to the informants, and, as we noted before, trout streams are abundant on the reservation.

These modest differences show up on an open-ended task where we asked thirteen Menominee and fifteen majority-culture fish experts to generate names of local fish off the top of their heads. Majority-culture fishermen were reliably more likely than Menominees to mention northern pike, musky, and walleye in their first five names and Menominees were reliably more likely to mention either trout or specific kinds of trout such as brown, brook, or rainbow in their first five names.[4]

Differences in the species of fish targeted could lead to differences in knowledge. For example, we might expect majority-culture experts to know relatively more about the large species of game fish (northern, musky, walleye) and Menominee experts to know relatively more about trout. Note, however, that differential experience with particular species would be unlikely to lead to overall differences in conceptual organization.

It seems clear that what one might call a "practice account" leads one to expect only tiny differences between experts in the two groups. According to this view, any effects of goals and attitudes would be mediated by the particular activities and practices associated with fishing.

But then there's the other side of the coin. Framework theories may serve to guide the interpretation of experience (Keil 1995; Keil et al. 1999) and make accessible and highlight certain features over others. We suggested earlier that cultural beliefs may act as a framework theory, either in the form of so-called "skeletal principles" (ideas such as: nature seeks a balance, or every fish has a role to play) or in the form of more concrete stories and examples that might serve to guide reasoning by analogy, for example, knowledge about cowbirds tricking other birds into caring for their young may lead one to be alert for the possibility that some species of fish might spawn on the bed of another species of fish with the same goal in mind. Thus, cultural factors may produce different "habits of the mind" that have consequences for how nature is conceptualized. This raises the possibility that shared activities and decades of experience may be insufficient to produce a common way of thinking about fish. This view would lead us to predict clear levels of agreement due to shared experience, but with important underlying differences in the ways cultural life shapes the interpretation of experience and attention to various aspects of nature.

On the basis of previous studies by our research team (Atran et al. 1999, 2002; Ross 2002; Shafto and Coley 2003), a strong candidate for an area where differences between the groups could be revealed is in the conception of ecological relations. The two groups' different knowledge bases might lead them to differ in their likelihood of noting ecological relations or in their assessment of the role that ecological relations play in organizing their knowledge of fish. In the latter case the two groups might have the same knowledge base, but what is a major organizing principle for one group may be a minor principle for the other.

STUDY 1: SPONTANEOUS SORTING

The first study examined spontaneous, hierarchical sorting of fish species by majority-culture and Menominee fish experts. We wanted to see if there were cultural differences in the ways informants group fish into categories because we thought it might provide an indirect measure of cultural differences in goals and orientations toward nature.

The participants were sixteen majority-culture and sixteen Menominee fish experts. We could have used more participants but we were confident that sixteen participants per group would be enough to establish a group consensus and we were interested only in differences that were fairly large and thus would show up in a small group. The two groups were similar with respect to age (the mean age was forty-six), fishing experience (both groups' members averaged about forty years—our experts started fishing at an early age), and education. It's also the case that most fishermen in each group fish year-round, often on a daily basis. All fishermen had English as their native language and all interviews were conducted in English. None of our informants had any formal training in ichthyology and all informants had experience fishing streams, rivers, ponds, and lakes in all seasons.

Stimulus Materials

The common and scientific names of the forty-four species of fish used are listed in table 7.1. We initially included two more fish species, jumping jack and mully, but they were excluded when we determined that almost none of the Menominee and only a few of the majority-culture experts were familiar with these common names. For the few fish that had more than one common name, both names were listed on the stimulus card (for example, the species Anguilla rostrata was called both American eel and lawyer). For the forty-four fish used in the task there were no differences in common names used by group members. The fish were selected to be broadly representative of the fish genera and families found in this part of Wisconsin. Experts confirmed that all these fish are found in this general area, although a few are less common locally. Specifically, smelt (Osmerus mordax) are mainly found in Lake Michigan and the rivers feeding into it, white bass (Morone chrysops) are more common slightly south of the research area, and flathead catfish (Pylodictis olivaris), sheephead (also called drum, Aplodinotus grunniens), and sauger (Stizostedion canadense) are not locally common. Carp (cyprinus carpio) are not found on the lakes or rivers on the reservation but they are common in nearby lakes and rivers and everyone is quite familiar with them.

Familiarity Task

We interviewed the experts individually in their homes, at our research house, or at their place of work. Often it was easier to catch participants during their lunch hour at work than on the weekend, when family and fishing were the priority. Our procedure was to present each fish name on a small card and ask the informant to indicate his general familiarity with the fish by saying a sentence or two about it. This familiarity task was relatively unconstrained both with respect both to how long informants talked and to content. The expert might mention the physical appearance of the fish, where it is found, its habits, how to fish for it, or simply tell a story about it. The responses ranged from the requested sentence or two up to long stories. Fish names that the fisherman was unfamiliar with were set aside and not used in the sorting task.

Sorting Task

Immediately after the familiarity task, fishermen were asked to sort the fish names into meaningful categories. In previous work (López et al. 1997) we found that the instruction to sort on the basis of similarity is typically met with the question "Similar in what respects?" and yields large cross-informant inconsistency (except in undergraduate populations), whereas the instruction to "put the fish that go together by nature into as many groups as you want" yields coherent patterns of sorting in all of the populations we have studied. Informants were told that there were no right or wrong answers and that we wanted to know how they thought about fish. After the sorting was completed, the informant was asked to explain the basis for each of the categories created. Asking for explanations or justifications is important because identical groupings can be conceptualized in very different ways.

The sorting task was unconstrained in the sense that there are many possible ways to place kinds of fish into groups. Our idea was to see the ways of organizing the categories that informants find most natural and straightforward.

Results

The richness of information provided by the sortings and justifications enables us to present a variety of measures of category organization. To compare experts' results, we converted each informant's sorting into a measure of distance of each fish from every other fish. If two fish were placed in the same category, their distance is zero; if they were sorted into different categories their distance was one. Unfamiliar fish were scored as missing data for all pairs (distances) involving the unfamiliar fish.

These fish-fish distance measures can be used to see how well experts agree with each other in their sorts. Two experts agree if fish that are far apart for one expert are also far apart for the other expert and fish that are close for one are close for the other. In other words the sorting distances for pairs of fish should show a positive correlation. We use correlation as our measure of agreement.

Familiarity with the Species   On average experts indicated considerable familiarity with the forty-four fish, and there were no reliable between-group differences.[5] All the experts were least likely to be familiar with three small fish not used in fishing: stickleback, dace, and darter. Overall, the pattern of unfamiliarity is consistent with Eugene Hunn's (1999) observation that characteristic size is correlated with psychological salience.

Consensus Analysis   Recall that we use the cultural consensus model to evaluate within and across group patterns of consensus. If the groups do not differ then we should find a single overall consensus.

Each informant's fish-distance matrix was correlated with that of every other expert. Evidence for overall consensus will be found to the extent that each expert's sort tends to be similar to every other expert's. Evidence for a cultural difference will be found if Menominee experts agree with each other more than they do with majority-culture experts, and the same for majority-culture experts. The technical term for this type of analysis is a principal-components analysis on the inter-subject correlation matrix. We then see how well it fits the cultural-consensus model developed by A. Kimball Romney, Susan Weller, and William Batchelder (1986).

The results showed a clear overall consensus.[6] If we stopped the analysis here, it would seem to suggest a common model across the groups. In order to test for group differences in sorting patterns we predict how much any two people will agree with each other if there is just a single overall consensus. Then we compare predicted agreement with actual agreement. If Menominees agree with other Menominees more than they agree with majority-culture fishermen, or vice versa, then there likely is a cultural difference.[7] In fact, only the Menominee informants displayed reliably greater within- than between-group residual agreement. Therefore, it appears that the Menominee and majority-culture informants share a common cultural model of fish but that the Menominee, in addition, share a somewhat distinct conceptual organization of fish. The sorting justifications provide converging evidence on these differences.

Sorting Justifications

For the initial analysis it was determined for each justification, or reason that the fish was categorized as it was, whether it involved taxonomic or morphological properties (for example, bass family), ecological properties (for example, river fish, bottom feeders), or goal-related properties (for example, game fish, garbage fish). These categories were not mutually exclusive—the justification "pond-dwelling bait fish" would be scored as both ecological and goal-related.

The majority-culture expert justifications were primarily taxonomic or morphological (62 percent), followed by goal-related (32 percent). Ecological justifications were rare (6 percent). Menominee experts were much more likely to provide ecological justifications (40 percent), less likely to give taxonomic justifications (33 percent), and about as likely as the majority-culture informants to give a goal-related justification (27 percent).

A finer level of analysis reveals more detail concerning these cultural differences. Here and elsewhere, if we mention a difference, it is statistically reliable (we won't discuss statistics that have been reported elsewhere). Eleven of the Menominee informants mentioned rivers, streams, lakes, or ponds for at least one justification, compared with only two majority-culture informants. Eleven majority-culture and seven Menominee informants, out of sixteen, mentioned bait fish, and seven and five, respectively, mentioned food or eating value. Twelve majority-culture informants described a group as undesirable, or as "garbage fish," whereas just five Menominees did so. Eight majority-culture informants as against just two Menominees described a group as being game fish or sport fish, so majority-culture experts are somewhat more likely to give evaluative ("garbage," "sport") justifications for fish sorts.

Multidimensional Scaling (MDS)

Multidimensional scaling is an effective method for depicting similarity relationships among a set of stimuli. Similarity is represented by spatial proximities. The more similar two things are, the closer they are in space.

The aim of the scaling procedure is to try to find a set of spatial proximities that best corresponds to the various item similarities. For example, with twenty fish types there are one hundred ninety similarity pairs when each fish is paired with every other fish. Depending on the pattern of similarities across items, one may be able to represent similarities using just a few dimensions; since we want to be able to visualize these similarities it helps if we can get by with two or three dimensions. The patterning of similarities along a dimension or dimensions may suggest an interpretation of what that dimension represents. For example, if the items being scaled are positioned in terms of increasing size, then it raises the possibility that judgments were being based in size similarities. The inference isn't ironclad but it is suggestive. Let's see what we found.

The consensual sorting distances, averaged across all informants of a group, were used as a measure of similarity and were analyzed using multidimensional scaling. The results are shown separately for the two groups in figures 7.1 and 7.2. The closer two fish are conceptually, the closer they are spatially in the figures. As we noted, one advantage of multidimensional scaling is that one may be able to identify dimensions along which the stimuli (in this case, fish) cluster. For the majority-culture a two-dimensional solution accounted for 96 percent of the variance.[8] The best scaling solution for Menominees involved a three-dimensional solution covering 94 percent of the variance. As shown in figure 7.1, the majority-culture solution appears to consist of three or four clusters, corresponding to bait fish, garbage fish, trout, and desirable sport fish (with trout perhaps forming a separate cluster), as one moves from left to right. Within a cluster, folkgenerics (for example, bass, catfish, sucker, chub) are closer to each other than to other members.

Although we failed to see any obvious interpretation of the two dimensions in figure 7.1, we did uncover some reliable correlates of them. Using the sorting justifications to categorize a fish as desirable (+1), undesirable (−1), or neutral (0), there is a +.67 correlation between the first dimension and desirability. This fits with the observation that a fair number of majority-culture experts sorted fish into desirable versus undesirable categories. The second dimension correlates reliably (−.54) with characteristic adult size, as determined by consulting fish guidebooks. This may mean that the second dimension corresponds to size, but note that there are a number of important features of fish that are correlated with size. For example, desirable game fish tend to be large and bait fish tend to be small, so the four clusters we noted in figure 7.1 may be captured fairly well in terms of size and desirability.

The picture is more complex for the Menominee fishermen, as shown in figure 7.2. First, there is no grouping corresponding to garbage fish. Second, the trout are closer to suckers and to bait fish than they are to more desirable fish. This probably reflects ecological sorting in that trout, shiners, and suckers are often found in the same waters. Shortly, we describe evidence consistent with this hypothesis. In general, there is more dispersion in the MDS solution for the Menominee fish experts.

Again we were able to uncover factors that correlate with position on each of the three dimensions. Using the sorting justifications, we categorized each fish by habitat as mainly associated with lakes and ponds (+1), mainly with rivers and streams (−1), or about equally with lakes and rivers (0). For a fish to be scored as occurring mainly in one habitat, more than 75 percent of the informants had to assign the fish to that location. In the area of Shawano and Menominee counties, trout, dace, darter,

Figure 7.1 Majority Culture Multidimensional Scaling; Euclidean Distance Model

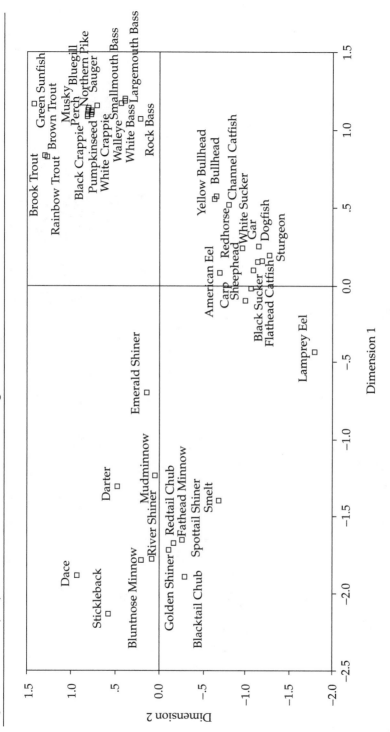

Source: Medin et al. (2006).

Figure 7.2 Menominee Multidimensional Scaling; Euclidean Distance Model

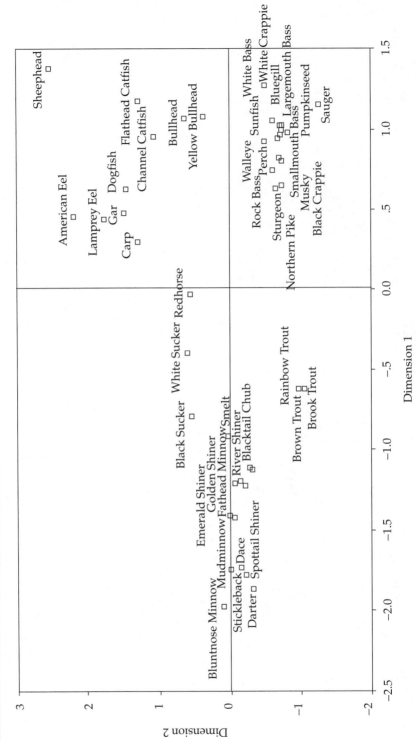

stickleback, black sucker, redhorse, chubs, white bass, and sturgeon are mainly associated with rivers; sunfish, crappies, perch, dogfish, bluegill, and largemouth bass are mainly associated with lakes; and bullhead, gar, musky, northern, carp, walleye, fathead minnows, and smallmouth bass are associated with both. This resulting habitat factor correlated +0.72 with values on the first dimension. Desirability, again determined by the sorting justifications (different for Menominee than for majority-culture informants) correlated +.82 with value on the second dimension, and size correlated +.60 with value on the third dimension.[9]

Overall, the MDS solutions yielded values that correlate with size and desirability for each of the groups. In addition, however, the Menominee informant solution had a third salient dimension that correlated highly with habitat. As noted earlier, desirability was mentioned by many informants, though Menominee experts were less likely to do so, and Menominee fish experts were very likely to mention habitat. In short, the correlates of the dimensions seem to correspond fairly well with the sorting justifications. A notable exception is the correlation with size, which is never mentioned as a justification. This observation suggests that the correlation involving size is an artifact of the correlation of size with other categorization schemes such as bait fish versus sport fish or taxonomic relatedness.

In follow-up work we have given less expert Menominee and majority-culture fishermen this same sorting task (Medin et al. 2002). Nonexpert majority-culture fishermen were significantly less likely (41 percent) than experts to give taxonomic justifications and more likely (43 percent) to give goal-related justifications. Interestingly, the same difference in ecological orientation remains: Menominee nonexperts showed the same tendency as Menominee experts to give ecological justifications.

SUMMARY OF RESULTS OF STUDY 1

Study 1 revealed clear cultural differences in how equally expert fishermen from two groups performed on a basic sorting task. The majority-culture experts were more likely to mention taxonomic or morphological justifications for their sorts than the Menominee informants, who were much more likely to organize categories in terms of ecological relations than the majority-culture informants. In the multidimensional scaling only the Menominee had a dimension corresponding to habitat. The justification data also suggest that the majority-culture experts were somewhat more likely to have categories organized around evaluative dimensions such as prestigious sport fish, or garbage fish, than the Menominee.

Both groups, however, showed a dimension correlated with desirability in their MDS solutions. Overall, then, the Menominee consensual model has an ecological component not seen in the majority-culture sorting. These differences indicate that framework theories and general orientations toward nature affect the two groups' conceptual organization of local fish species.

Chapter Eight | Ecological Orientation

"In the winter I follow the otters' trail to see where the minnows are, because I know that's where the predator fish will come."
—A Menominee fisherman

TO BE SUCCESSFUL in fishing, you have to know where certain species are found and usually that means knowing what they are eating; what they are eating often consists of other fish. Are the two groups of experts equally knowledgeable concerning where fish are found and which fish are found together? Here we describe studies probing further into ecological orientation. A key question is whether majority-culture fishermen, despite their expertise, have less knowledge of ecological relations than their Menominee counterparts.

STUDY 2: ECOLOGICAL SORTING BY HABITAT

In study 2 we used forty of the original set of forty-four local species of fish. We dropped four species—lamprey, smelt, flathead catfish, sauger—that tend not to be found locally. Each species had a name card. We asked fourteen Menominee and fourteen majority-culture experts to "put those fish together that live together, that share a common habitat." Because some fish have a wider range of habitats than others, we also told the fishermen that a given species could appear in more than one group. If an informant noted that some fish lived in two different habitats, such as rivers and lakes, we gave him a copy of the name card so that this species could be included in more than one pile. There was no limit on the number of groups a given species could be placed into and name cards were added as needed. The informants were asked to ignore seasonal differences in habitats (spawning season and so forth), and to give their general assessment of the dominant habitats over the whole year. Once all the fish had been sorted into groups, we asked each informant to give a short description of the type of habitat, for example, "clear, fast running water." If a person was not familiar with a given species, the name card was dropped for that informant.

Again, the cultural-consensus model was used to explore the existence of an overall model as well as culture-specific models of fish habitat sharing.[1] If the two groups of experts have the same knowledge base, we would expect to observe an overall consensus and no reliable cultural differences.

Results

In our analyses we first looked for consensus among all the informants taken together, and then examined patterns of residual agreement. The principal-components analysis showed a strong consensus among all the experts.[2] First-factor scores were positive for everyone, and the average first-factor score was .85. This means that a great deal of the experts' knowledge is shared across the two cultural groups. No group difference was found in an analysis of residual agreement. In other words, both groups share essentially the same model and knowledge base for fish habitat. Figure 8.1 presents the MDS for average sorts of both groups. Trout and other river fish are clearly separated from fish found in lakes, and at a finer level of detail, fish found in clear running water such as trout, chubs are separated from fish found in slower-moving water, such as mudminnows.

Summary

As we expected, study 2 produced no reliable group differences in the sorting of the fish species by habitat. This finding is important for two reasons. First, it provides converging evidence that our experts do not differ in ecological knowledge per se. Second, the data support the idea that the differences noted in study 1 are linked to the differential salience of ecological information in the two groups.

STUDY 3: SPECIES INTERACTIONS

In study 3 we explicitly targeted expert ecological knowledge in the form of understandings of fish-fish interactions. On many grounds one would not expect to observe group differences in perceived fish-fish interactions. These experts engage in more or less the same activities in terms of when they fish and how they do so—their use of hook and line, artificial

Figure 8.1   Fish Habitat Relations, Multidimensional Scaling (Both Groups)

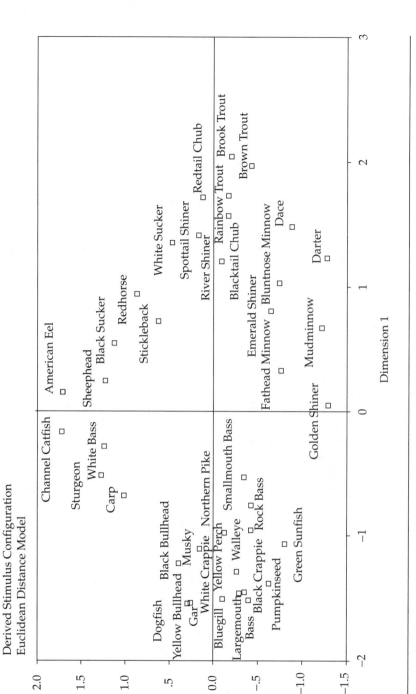

Derived Stimulus Configuration
Euclidean Distance Model

Source: Medin et al. (2006).

lures, and so forth. Second, goals and activities associated with fishing are intimately intertwined with fish-fish interactions. To be successful in fishing, one needs to know where fish are found and what they are eating. Food chains are an important component of fish-fish interactions. Third, our experts have been fishing on average for several decades, and one might expect a convergence of knowledge, especially when that knowledge is relevant to certain activities.

But these reasons for expecting a convergence do not exclude other factors that work against convergence. If we were to observe cultural differences, what form might they take? It is possible that notions of balance and reciprocity may affect Menominee notions of fish-fish interactions. One normative injunction of Menominee culture is to take from nature only what is needed. Menominee fishing regulations outlaw the "wanton destruction" of any fish. Some Menominee pray before taking fish or game to apologize to and thank the animal for giving its life. Menominee may also offer tobacco to the spirits as a sign of respect and as a token of reciprocity. To maintain this balance, they might report more reciprocal relations where each species affects the other species. They might also be more likely to attend to and think about the various stages in the fish cycle of life rather than focusing on adult fish. Finally, if their knowledge of fish is organized along ecological lines—and we did find in study 1 that Menominee fishermen were more likely to sort fish ecologically—then Menominee fishermen should have highly accessible information concerning fish-fish interactions.

Majority-culture sportsmen also express appreciation of nature; however, they also tend to view fish in terms of specific goals, such as the challenge of catching a large fish. As a result, majority-culture fish experts may be less inclined to spontaneously report relations that are not pertinent to their goals. These differences may be expressed in terms of the number of relations, and the kinds of relations that the members of each group perceive. For example, if a person has the goal of catching the biggest fish, then he might be more likely to reason in terms of adult fish if asked about fish-fish interactions.

Because it would not be practical to probe each of the nearly one thousand pairs formed by forty-four local species of fish, we narrowed the set to twenty-one species. We selected familiar species varying in range of habitat, desirability, and status in food chains. There was a name card for each species. In the few cases when an informant was not familiar with a given species, the name card was dropped. The informants were fifteen Menominee and fifteen majority-culture fishing experts.

To generate the fish pairs, we began by randomly picking one fish as a base-card and comparing it with every other species, presented in random order. Then a second card was randomly picked and so on through the twenty-one species. This procedure yielded 210 pairs and 420 potential fish-fish relationships for each participant to comment upon. For each fish-fish pair, the participant was asked if the base species affects the target species and vice versa, thus: "Does the northern affect the river shiner?" and "Does the river shiner affect the northern?" If an expert mentioned an effect he was then asked whether the species affect each other in any other way; this question was repeated until no more relations were mentioned. It is important to note that the task was presented at a fairly rapid pace and it took about an hour to an hour and a half to get through all the possible pairs.

Scoring

Relations mentioned were initially coded into one of nineteen categories, for example, species A eats species B; species A eats the spawn of species B; and so forth. Later on, we combined categories in various ways to examine responses at different levels of specificity. Agreement between two fishermen was calculated as the number of the 420 cells of all the fish pairs and the two sets of questions posed on which the fishermen's answers agreed. Agreement between each pair of fishermen was categorized at one of four levels:

1. Both experts agreed that some relation between the fish was present, though the specific relation could be seen to be different.

2. Both agreed as to whether the relationship was helping or hurting, regardless of what the specific relation was.

3. Both agreed that there was a food-chain relation.

4. Both agreed on a reciprocal relation, one where fish 1 affects fish 2 and fish 2 affects fish 1 in some separate way, regardless of the character of the specific relations.

Overall, Menominee fishermen report reliably more relations than their majority-culture counterparts, reporting relations in 62 percent of the possible pairs versus 46 percent for the majority-culture informants. The pattern of agreement and disagreement across groups is interesting. For all relations cited by at least 70 percent of the members of one group, we found that 85 percent are reported by both groups; forty-five relations, or 14 percent of all possible relations, are reported by Menominee

but not majority-culture participants; and just four relations, or 1 percent, are reported by majority-culture but not Menominee experts.

With the exception of the four last-named fish-fish relations, the majority-culture ecological model appears to be a subset of the Menominee
model, a finding that parallels our results from study 1. Looking at the
four relations, it is interesting that these relations were between species
that basically are not encountered in the same habitat as the rest of the
local species.[3] The four relations that majority-culture experts report that
Menominee experts do not are overgeneralizations. For example, in this
part of Wisconsin, large mouth bass are mainly found in lakes and river
shiners in rivers. On this pair majority-culture fisherman tended to say
that large mouth bass eat the river shiner. In contrast, Menominee fishermen tended to say there would be no effect since they are not found in
the same waters.

Food-Chain Relations

There are no group differences in the number of food-chain relations
mentioned that were "one-way" and were not part of a reciprocal relationship. The presence of a high cultural consensus across the two groups
undermines the possibility that each group reports the same number of
relations but attributes them to different species.

Reciprocal Relations

A reciprocal relation between two species was coded whenever there
was at least one helping relation reported in each direction, so that each
member of the fish pair benefits the other fish. There was much less
agreement on these types of relations, and only Menominee experts
showed above-chance agreement, 69 percent, in naming these reciprocal
relations (by chance, half should be positive). On average, Menominee
informants mention nearly twice as many reciprocal relations, sixty, as
majority-culture fish experts, who mention thirty-five. These reciprocal
relationships tended to be reciprocal predation or feeding habits, including eating spawn or fry.

Summary and Analysis of Study 2

One significant difference between the two groups of experts was that
majority-culture experts were more likely to report only relations between adult fish, for example, that northerns eat walleyes, and not mention that a large walleye may eat a small northern. Similarly, majority-

Table 8.1   Most Prominent Reciprocal Relations Elicited in Study 3 (Percentage of Members of Each Group Agreeing on a Reciprocal Relation Between a Pair of Species)

Majority	Menominee	Species A	Species B
0.13	0.67	Walleye	Smallmouth bass
.07	.60	Northern pike	Walleye
.07	.53	Yellow perch	Black crappie
.07	.50	Carp	Black (hog) sucker
.21	.50	Northern pike	Dogfish (bowfin)
.00	.47	Brown trout	Black (hog) sucker
.00	.47	Walleye	Black (hog) sucker
.33	.47	Brown trout	Brook trout
.20	.47	Walleye	Largemouth bass
.20	.47	Black crappie	Rock bass
.13	.47	Smallmouth bass	Rock bass
.20	.47	Largemouth bass	Smallmouth bass

Source: Medin et al. (2006).

culture experts were likely to mention that brown trout and walleyes eat black suckers but not report that black suckers eat the spawn of brown trout and walleyes. (See table 8.1 for the most prominent pairs of reciprocal relations and a summary of the group differences.)

This difference in reciprocal relations suggests that majority-culture fish experts tended to answer in terms of adult fish, rather than taking into account the whole life cycle of each species. As another test of this idea we looked at relationships involving eating spawn. The median number of reports of one fish eating the spawn of another was one for majority-culture informants and twelve for the Menominee.

The results indicate that experts of both cultural groups share a substantial amount of knowledge concerning interactions among freshwater fish.[4] This should not come as a surprise; much expert knowledge stems from actual observation while looking for fish, fishing, and even from cleaning the catch, for stomach contents usually tell what a fish has been eating recently. Despite this common knowledge we also find reliable group differences. Menominee experts see many more positive fish-fish interactions, such as one fish helping another as well as more reciprocal relations, such as two species affecting each other, than their majority-culture counterparts.

What is the origin of the differences between these results for majority-culture and Menominee fishermen? Our speculation is that cultural attitudes and beliefs reinforce what one might call "habits of mind," or characteristic ways of thinking about some domain. In the present case we think that the two groups have much the same knowledge but that they organize it differently. Responses of majority-culture informants concerning ecological relations may be filtered through a goal-related framework. Goals may lead to reports of ecological relations that apply to adult fish rather than those associated with the entire life cycle. Many of the relations reported by Menominee experts but not majority-culture experts involve spawn, fry, or immature fish.

It is often difficult to distinguish between any knowledge that we have in memory and "highly accessible knowledge." Despite the cultural differences noted, the majority-culture experts had very extensive ecological knowledge, as demonstrated in study 2, knowledge that was not recruited for the sorting task of study 1 and, at least some of the time, not in response to the direct probes of study 3. Overall, we believe that the major source of cultural differences is in the accessibility of knowledge as a consequence of different cultural models of fish as a resource. Fortunately, these speculations could be tested in study 4.

STUDY 4: SPECIES INTERACTION—FEWER PROBES AT A SLOWER PACE

One way to examine the role of knowledge as opposed to knowledge organization is to change the speed at which probes are administered and compare the results. In study 3 we probed for over four hundred relations in about an hour, which means that experts were answering questions at the rate of about six to ten per minute, or a speed of six to ten seconds per item. About a year after study 3, in study 4, we probed thirty-four pairs of fish-fish interactions (a subset of the study 3 probes) at a leisurely pace of about thirty seconds per item, in the course of related interviews we conducted.

We had three general predictions. One was that we would no longer observe the group differences noted in study 3. We also predicted that majority-culture fish experts would show considerable improvement, and would now start mentioning more relations than just those involving adult fish, such as, say, reciprocal relations and relations involving immature fish such as a fish eating spawn of another. The third prediction was that Menominee experts would show modest improvement as a result of the slower pace, because their ecological knowledge is relatively more accessible. Here's our logic in a nutshell: if the two groups have the same knowledge base of ecological relations and if they are given plenty of time to answer, we should no longer observe group differences in performance for study 4. This outcome, in turn, would suggest that the differences in study 3 reflect group differences in how readily or easily ecological knowledge comes to mind. If Menominees organize their knowledge ecologically, they should find it easier to answer questions concerning ecological relations.

The thirty-four probes were given to fourteen Menominee and fourteen majority-culture fish experts. The instructions were exactly like those for study 3, except that we explicitly told informants that there would be many fewer probes than before. The probes were given as part of a longer interview on attitudes regarding different fishing practices.

Results

For the results of study 4 to be meaningful, we needed to verify that the overall group difference in reported relations in study 3 was also reliable for the subset of thirty-four probes used in study 4. For this subset, majority-culture informants had reported an average of 17.3 relations and Menominee informants had reported an average of 28.3 relations in study 3—a considerable and statistically reliable difference. For these same pairs in study 4, majority-culture and Menominee informants reported an average of 29.3 and 32.6 relations, respectively. The more relaxed pace led to significantly more relations being reported by majority-culture fish experts but just a few more by Menominee fish experts. This difference is nowhere near reliable.

Moving to specific relations, the data were broken down into relations involving eating spawn, basic food-chain relations, and reciprocal or mutual relations. The majority-culture experts reported reliably more relations involving eating spawn in study 4 than they did in study 3. The majority-culture informants showed a large increase in reported mutual relations between study 3 and study 4; the median went from one such relation to five, and the mean from 4.0 to 8.1. As predicted, Menominee informants showed essentially no change. Thus, the group differences found in study 3 virtually disappeared in study 4.

Study 4: Conclusions

Slowing down the task made a huge difference. The more leisurely pace of study 4 as a basis for answering probes produced two related shifts: the group difference in total reported relations essentially disappeared, and this change was concentrated in reciprocal relations and relations involving eating spawn. This pattern is consistent with a reduced focus on adult fish on the part of the majority-culture fishermen.

The data fit with the idea that the difference between majority-culture and Menominee informants is in the accessibility of knowledge rather than in the knowledge base per se. The two groups of experts appear to have more or less the same knowledge about fish, but they differ in how that knowledge is organized. The Menominee ecological orientation, revealed in task 1, is very compatible with the fish-fish interaction task, and their answers varied little as a function of whether the task went at a slow or fast pace. The taxonomic and goal-related organization characterizing majority-culture experts makes it harder to retrieve information about fish-fish interactions other than the most straightforward ones, such as that of game fish eating bait fish.[5]

SUMMARY OF FOUR STUDIES

We began our studies by asking whether expertise leads to a convergence on how fishermen conceptualize and organize their knowledge about fish. In addition, we wanted to see whether cultural variables play any role beyond that reflected by characteristic practices and activities. Earlier studies suggest that shared expertise may be more important than large cultural differences in influencing categorization and category-based reasoning. For example, North American experts perform more like Itza' Maya silviculturalists than like North American novices (Atran 1998; Bailenson et al. 2002; Coley et al. 1999). There were good reasons not to expect any cultural differences.

Given that background, the differences we did observe are striking. First of all, study 1 found that in a free sorting task, Menominee experts differed from majority-culture experts by being much more likely to sort ecologically. Justifications for sorts provide further evidence of this and other cultural differences. Majority-culture informants were more likely to use evaluative descriptions than Menominee informants, designating some species as garbage fish and other as desirable and prestigious fish.

Study 2 showed that the cultural difference in sorting by habitat was not produced by differences in knowledge about habitat. These cultural differences emerged once more on the fish-fish interaction task associated with study 3. Menominee experts reported more positive relations such as fish helping other fish and more reciprocal relations than did majority-culture experts. Majority-culture responses were influenced by characteristic goals; they answered the questions from the perspective of adult fish, which are the ones fishermen want to catch.

The second and fourth studies support the idea that the cultural differences represent differences in knowledge organization, which in turn are associated with differences in the accessibility of ecological information. The slower pace of study 4 led to the disappearance of group differences in the number of reported fish-fish interactions. The group differences appear to be differences in the salience of different kinds of information rather than differences in knowledge per se.

Our data show that meanings matter a great deal, even for basic processes such as category organization. Menominee fishermen appear to approach freshwater fish from the perspective of multiple goals and expectations or cultural frameworks that express notions of balance and reciprocity and of each fish having a role, that lead them to develop a more ecological, nature-centered concept of the biology of fish. In contrast, majority-culture experts appear to be more likely to approach fish from the perspective of a smaller set of goals and with a cultural model that focuses more on intrinsic than relational properties. These are two very different models of fish and of nature in general.

If we are correct in assuming that ecological conceptions are linked to environmental behaviors and ethics, then these data should have significant consequences. In addition, differences in ecological orientation and related conceptions of nature may be associated with real and perceived differences in environmental ethics and behaviors. That will be our focus in much of the rest of this book.

Chapter Nine | Values, Attitudes, and Practices

"That's why the fish are there. If you put the fish you catch in your holding tank, you can't expect them to be around when you come back to that spot to fish again."

—Majority-culture fisherman who practices catch-and-release almost exclusively

BY MEANS OF studies 1 to 4 we have established that Menominee fishermen tend to use an ecological framework to conceptualize fish. Menominees also commonly express the attitude that every fish has a role to play and are less likely than majority-culture fishermen to think of fish in terms of positive (game fish) or negative ("garbage fish") utility.

Now, we shall examine values and attitudes toward various fishing practices more directly. Both groups report wanting to save fish as a resource, but the goal of conservation is supported by different strategies in the two groups. Menominees have a strong "do not waste" ethic which comes down to not taking more than you need, whereas majority-culture experts tend to focus on catch-and-release as a conservation strategy, at least for the fish that they tend to target as sportfish, namely, musky, smallmouth bass, largemouth bass, and larger walleyes.

Superficially it looks as though both groups are equally goal-oriented, with majority-culture experts fishing for fun and Menominee experts fishing for food. Although there is some validity to this, there is a deeper, more subtle difference. Majority-culture experts tend to see themselves as caring for nature in what one could call a subject-object or agent-patient relation. Menominees tend to see themselves as part of nature, as participants in the ecosystem. In this view humans have equal status with other biological kinds—no more, no less. The "do not waste" ethic invites Menominees to assume their natural role in the ecosystem. If everything follows its role, the ecosystem will be healthy. In related work, Norbert Ross has found that Lacandon Maya have a similar notion of a "natural" act. For example, it is considered acceptable to chop down a tree to get to a beehive and its honey, but wrong to chop down a tree to sell its wood.

DIFFERING WORLDVIEWS

These assertions are based on our interviews with expert fishermen and hunters, but there is reason to think that it constitutes a broader cultural difference and not only one that manifests in the fishing and hunting community. As part of an ongoing project aimed at improving science education, we interviewed rural majority-culture and both rural and urban Native American (mostly Menominee) parents and grandparents (Bang et al. 2005). One of our questions was "What are the five most important things for your children or grandchildren to learn about the biological world?" We coded the responses into categories representing different perspectives on the natural world.

We found differences between urban and rural cultures and and between the majority culture and Native American culture. Rural parents were more likely to mention survival skills ("I want my child to be able to recognize poison ivy") than urban parents. Parents in general also took a moral stance. For example, majority-culture parents commonly said that they wanted their children to realize that they have a responsibility to *take care of* nature. Native American parents tended to talk about "Mother Earth" and wanting their children to understand that they are *a part of* nature. They were also more likely to mention continuity between the past and the future, mentioning both ancestors and coming generations. Overall, eighteen of twenty-two Native American parents mentioned at least one of the three related values of spiritual-relational, part versus whole, and intergenerational compared with two out of twelve majority-culture parents.[1] Note also that the term "Mother Earth" used by Native Americans implies that the earth takes care of us rather than vice versa. It also embodies a relational view of nature, rather than seeing it as something external. Our hypothesis is that this cultural difference lies at the heart of the other differences that we report.

Although both groups presumably share the goal of preserving fish as a resource, we wondered how the differences in orientation might be reflected in values and attitudes toward different fishing practices. Differences in these values and attitudes as well as related differences in behaviors (catch-and-release versus fishing for food, but do not waste) might lead to differences in how each group perceives and evaluates the behavior of the other group (discussed further in chapter 10).

MEASURING VALUES, ATTITUDES, AND PRACTICES

In order to get some quantifiable data on these different worldviews, we developed a series of three rating tasks, which took about thirty minutes to an hour to complete.

The purpose of the first task was to see if majority-culture fishermen place greater value than Menominee fishermen on the "big five" sport-fish: walleye, northern, musky, largemouth bass, and smallmouth bass. We asked seventeen majority-culture and fifteen Menominee fishing experts to rank-order species according to the importance each fish has to them and gave them fifteen to choose from: sturgeon, black sucker, yellow bullhead, bluegill, brook trout, brown trout, gar, bluntnose minnow, musky, largemouth bass, smallmouth bass, northern pike, river shiner, walleye, and perch. Each species had a name card and participants were asked to arrange these cards in order of descending importance.

Our second task was geared toward generating data on goals connected with fishing. We asked our experts to rank a set of six goals for fishing in the order of their importance to themselves that we had extracted from previous interviews and the literature:

- Fishing as a way of being close to nature
- Fishing as a challenge to outsmart the fish
- Fishing as a food source
- Fishing to get a trophy-sized fish
- Fishing for relaxation
- Fishing as an activity to pass on to future generations

If an expert indicated that he couldn't rank-order the goals, he was asked to rate them on a seven-point scale with 1 representing no importance and 7 representing a very important goal. We later converted these ratings into rank orderings. Participants were allowed to have ties.

For the third and final task, measuring attitudes toward various fishing practices, experts were asked to rate seventeen different fishing practices on a seven-point scale, where 1 represents strong personal disapproval; 4, a neutral attitude; and 7, strong approval. The seventeen tasks were as follows:

1. Doing catch-and-release only

2. Spearfishing suckers or carp

3. Spearfishing walleyes or northern

4. Having a trophy fish mounted by a taxidermist

5. Fishing for bluegill or sunfish for food

6. Fishing for northern or musky for food

7. Fishing for largemouth or smallmouth bass for food

8. Using setpoles to catch trout

9. Selling a fish

10. Keeping undersized fish

11. Participating in fishing contests

12. Fishing on spawning beds

13. Pretending to fish for suckers hoping to get a sturgeon on the line

14. Culling out smaller fish to get the largest possible limit

15. Using fish finders

16. Taking more than one's limit in order to feed one's family

17. Giving away all of the fish one has caught

These practices (the list was developed on the basis of previous interviews) included both commonly accepted activities, such as fishing for bluegills and sunfish for food, and practices that are roundly condemned and in fact are illegal on and off the reservation, such as selling fish or using setpoles (an unattended pole set in the riverbank) to catch trout. It probably speaks to our good rapport with our informants that several individuals in each community mentioned that they themselves had engaged or sometimes engage in some of these activities—for example, using setpoles or pretending to fish for suckers while hoping to get a sturgeon on the line. (The objection to using setpoles is that people tend to put out many lines and leave them unattended, trout swallow the bait and the hook and ultimately die, and in the end undersized fish are killed and not released.)

We expected divided opinions on some of the practices. For example, we expected Menominee experts to ascribe greater importance to catching largemouth and smallmouth bass for food than majority-culture experts. We also thought that Menominees might approve of keeping undersized fish more, in cases where the fish is badly hooked and to release it would be to waste it. Finally, informal discussions with Menominee and majority-culture fishermen had led us to expect within-group differences of opinion on practices such as spearing walleyes or getting a trophy-sized fish mounted. Spearfishing walleyes is illegal for majority-culture fishermen and illegal for Menominee fishermen in waters outside the reservation. Often the participants explained the basis or justifications for their ratings or simply told a story about various values or practices.

Results

Rank Ordering of Species   Table 9.1 gives the rankings of the fifteen fish species' importance (lower numbers correspond to higher importance). The two groups agreed with each other to a surprising extent. For example, the six fish ranked lowest are not only the same for both groups but also are even placed in exactly the same order. The overall correlation of rankings was +.81.

Despite the overall agreement there were predictable group differences.[2] Menominees assign a higher value to the two trout species, and majority-culture fishermen high a higher value to musky and walleye. The biggest differences are in the rankings of brook trout and brown trout: the average Menominee rankings were 2.1 and 2.6, respectively; the average majority-culture rankings were 6.2 and 7.2, respectively; the differences for both fish are highly significant.[3] There was also a difference for musky and walleye: the average Menominee rankings were 8.7 and 4.5; for the majority culture they were 5.3 and 3.0.[4] Given the role played by the sturgeon in Menominee culture it is surprising that Menominees did not rank sturgeon higher than majority-culture fishermen.

Goal Rankings   The average rankings for the six goals are given in the first and fourth columns of table 9.2. Since each goal had been endorsed by several experts in earlier interviews, we had no strong reason to expect consensus either within or across groups or even a clear ranking of goals, and in fact we did not find consensus across groups or for either

Table 9.1   Average Species Rankings by Menominee
and Majority-Culture Fish Experts (Lower Numbers
Indicate Higher Value)

Species	Menominee	Majority Culture
Sturgeon	9.1	8.6
Black sucker	12.0	12.1
Yellow bullhead	11.1	10.0
Bluegill	5.4	4.8
Brook trout	2.2	6.8
Brown trout	2.6	7.9
Gar	14.5	13.7
Bluntnose minnow	13.0	12.0
Musky	8.7	5.4
Largemouth bass	4.4	6.4
Smallmouth bass	7.3	6.5
Northern pike	6.5	5.5
River shiner	11.9	11.0
Walleye	4.6	2.9
Perch	5.9	5.9

Source: Medin et al. (forthcoming).

of the two groups individually. This important finding indicates the diversity of goals among members of both groups.

Despite the lack of consensus, we were nonetheless able to detect group differences when it came to specific goals. As we anticipated, Menominee experts give significantly higher importance to "fishing for

Table 9.2   Rankings of Goals of Fishing Broken Down by Group
(Lower Numbers Indicate Higher Priority)

Goal	Majority Culture	Menominee
Being close to nature	2.4	3.0
For the challenge of finding fish	3.4	4.4
As a source of food	4.6	2.7
To catch a "trophy fish"	4.6	5.0
As a way to relax	2.6	2.4
As an activity to pass on to future generations	2.9	3.2

Source: Medin et al. (forthcoming).

Table 9.3   Ratings of Fishing Practices by Each Group
(1 = Strong Disapproval; 7 = Strong Approval)

	Majority Culture	Menominee
1. Doing catch-and-release only	4.5	4.7
2. Spearfishing suckers or carp	5.9	5.1
3. Spearfishing walleyes or northern	1.0	4.0
4. Having a trophy fish mounted by a taxidermist	4.4	4.9
5. Fishing for bluegill or sunfish for food	6.0	6.9
6. Fishing for northern or musky for food	2.9	6.1
7. Fishing for largemouth or smallmouth bass for food	3.4	6.5
8. Using setpoles to catch trout	2.5	3.3
9. Selling a fish	2.0	1.3
10. Keeping undersized fish	1.6	2.3
11. Participating in fishing contests	4.9	4.3
12. Fishing on spawning beds	3.0	2.8
13. Pretending to fish for suckers hoping to get a sturgeon on the line	3.6	2.1
14. Culling out smaller fish to get the largest possible limit	2.9	1.9
15. Using fish finders	5.9	3.6
16. Taking more than one's limit in order to feed one's family	2.9	5.2
17. Giving away all of the fish one has caught	3.9	4.8

Source: Medin et al. (forthcoming).

food,"[5] while majority-culture experts tend to place higher value on "fishing as a challenge to outsmart the fish."[6] These data are in line with the observation that majority-culture fishermen tend to see fishing as a contest or sport.

Ratings of Fishing Practices   We expected to observe a number of differences in ratings of practices related to both specific goals and historical practices. For example, for centuries the Menominee have speared fish in the spring when they are spawning as an efficient means of food gathering. Consequently, it would have been surprising if there were no group differences in rating practices like spearfishing for walleyes.

The full set of ratings is given in table 9.3. We found modest, marginally significant overall consensus and statistically reliable group differences.[7] Menominee experts gave higher ratings than the majority-culture experts in three areas: Menominee experts strongly approved of catching bass, northerns, and muskies for food, compared to just neutral ratings for the majority-culture experts; modest approval for taking more than the limit to feed their family, compared to modest disapproval on the part of the majority-culture fishermen; and neutral ratings to spearfishing walleyes, compared to strong disapproval from the majority-culture experts. The Menominee fishermen were sharply divided on spearfishing walleyes and the average reflects an equal mixture of strongly positive and strongly negative ratings. Menominees opposed to it say that females are being speared and their spawn wasted. Menominees in favor of spearing say that they only spear the males.[8]

Majority-culture fishermen gave srong approval to using fish finders, compared to the Menominees' neutral rating;[9] and gave a neutral rating to pretending to fish for suckers hoping to get a sturgeon, compared to the Menominees' strong disapproval. It is illegal to fish for sturgeon with hook and line; but some fishermen engage in this practice in the spring when sturgeon swim upriver to spawn. Again, several majority-culture fishermen reported having engaged in this practice occasionally.

Conclusions: Modest Differences and Large Similarities

These results form a coherent pattern that lends credence to the existence of cultural differences that were noted in previous chapters. The Menominee experts place a higher priority on fishing for food and majority-culture fishermen are more inclined to view fishing as a challenge. These differences in goals are reflected in differences in attitudes toward specific practices such as spearfishing or targeting bass, northerns, and muskies for food. One surprising result was that majority-culture fishermen endorsed using fish finders, which on first glance doesn't appear to be sporting. A common comment was that it is one thing to find fish and quite another to catch them. Also, some experts said that they only used fish finders to map out the underwater terrain, for example, noting changes in depth to identify dropoffs where certain fish might be found.

It is important to note the broad commonalities across groups. For example, the rank ordering of species was highly correlated across groups. The Menominee rank trout higher, perhaps reflecting their food orientation, but also reflecting the presence of many rivers and streams on the reservation and the fact that one doesn't need a boat to fish for trout. Most important are the similarities in attitudes toward various fishing practices. Both groups condemn selling fish, keeping undersize fish, fishing on spawning beds, using setpoles to catch trout, and culling out smaller fish to get the largest possible limit.[10]

The key question to be answered in the next phase of our research was the extent to which these groups were aware of their substantial shared values as well as their modest differences.

OBSERVATIONS AND ANECDOTES

We conclude this chapter with some less formal observations that convey some of the majority-culture and Menominee differences in perspectives.

Walleye spearing goals declared by the state's six Chippewa tribes have resulted in reduced bag limits on 283 northern Wisconsin lakes for the 2001 season. Based on those declarations, 134 lakes will have a bag limit of three walleyes per day, 140 lakes will have a bag limit of two walleyes per day and three lakes will have a daily bag limit of one walleye per day. Overall, this year's tribal walleye declarations are at about the same level as recent years. The state is beginning its 17th year under court-affirmed tribal hunting and fishing rights.

Wisconsin Outdoor News, April 13, 2001

The limit for walleyes in the rest of Wisconsin is five per day.

I'm opposed to bass tournaments. People don't know how to release fish properly and a fair number of fish die. An even bigger problem is that the release is often remote from the nest, and besides, other fish will quickly destroy the nest anyway.

An older majority-culture fisherman

The state of Wisconsin has a sturgeon spearfishing season on Lake Winnebago in the winter. The target for sturgeon is 5 percent of the population because they take so long to mature, as compared to the 30 to 35 percent that is considered safe for the walleye population. Spearfishing is carefully monitored by the Wisconsin Department of Natural Resources and the season may be reduced from three days to two if harvest quotas are met. In the year 2001 a total of 1,585 sturgeon were speared, including 586 adult females. One of the fish was eighty-one inches long and weighed 146 pounds.

I have fished for 50 years. We grew up with fishing being a relaxing way to spend time away from work. It was a noncompetitive no-contact sport. Now I wonder why oversized boys feel so compelled to prove they can catch the most fish? I think it's an ego thing. I guess if I had a $30,000

Ranger, a 200hp outboard, three locators, etc., I'd have to tell my wife something.

Jim Cox, *Wisconsin Outdoor News*, September 15, 2000

There were several responses over the next several issues to Cox's comments. One defender of contests argued that though there may be some deaths associated with released fish, at least the survival rate was greater than for fish not released. The same letter writer noted that a photo of Cox with an eleven-pound fish had appeared in *Wisconsin Outdoor News*; had Cox released that fish? Cox responded that the fish was a dogfish, which many fishermen consider to be an undesirable "garbage" fish. Cox also noted that dogfish are voracious predators, so by killing the dogfish he was saving the lives of hundreds of bluegills. Another reader offered a final comment, that dogfish play an important role in controlling the bluegill population so that populations do not get out of hand, resulting in stunted growth.

One Menominee fisherman had a brook trout mounted on his wall. He called our attention to it and was proud of the fact that none of its fins were damaged, explaining that this meant that it had not come from a fish hatchery—fish in hatcheries are usually so crowded that they have some fin damage. Possibly this fish symbolized a past, better, time of natural, uncontaminated conditions, before Wisconsin Department of National Resources management or other forms of human intervention.

This fisherman believes that Menominee values are under pressure from majority-culture influences. Children see movies showing implausible scenes like a bear cuddling a raccoon like a baby, scenes that treat animals as if they were humans.

Chapter Ten | Intra- and Intergroup Perception of Goals and Values

"One time I caught an eight-pound smallmouth bass. A guy I know asked me if I was going to get it mounted. I said to him, 'If your wife died would you put her head up on the wall?'"

—A Menominee fisherman

THE STUDIES DESCRIBED in chapter 9 established the existence of substantial agreement between our two groups, and some second-order differences.

Majority-culture fishermen were slightly more approving of practicing catch-and-release exclusively and reliably more approving both of using fish finders to locate fish and of "pretending to fish for suckers in the spring in hopes of getting a sturgeon on the line."

Menominee fishermen were more approving of fishing for smallmouth or largemouth bass for food, spearfishing walleyes, and someone with a large family taking more than his limit to feed his family. One important result was that the Menominee men were sharply divided on the question about spearfishing walleyes—about half of them strongly approved of it and half strongly disapproved. These differences seem to reflect the relative priorities of the two groups in fishing for food and fishing for sport.

Our next step was to evaluate whether our experts were aware of the group differences in orientation and how accurately they perceived both their own group and the other group—in other words, intra- and intergroup perceptions. Our approach was to ask experts to make predictions for their own and the other group, and then, in a feedback part of our study, show experts how their predictions about their own and the other group matched with the actual data. The goal of feedback was to clarify the assumptions, and mental models, and associated values of each group regarding the other group.

There is fairly good evidence that people tend to perceive the views of both their in-group and of out-groups as more extreme than they actually are. A study of own-group perception (Prentice and Miller 1993) found that college students systematically overestimated the amount and perceived desirability of alcohol consumption among other students (their own group) and that, for male students, this misperception led to an increase in drinking. Thus, misperception of a group norm can cause a self-fulfilling prophecy that feeds back to make the perceived group norm even more extreme. This has obvious implications for negotiation and conflict resolution (see Ross and Stillinger 1991; Thompson and Gonzalez 1997).

Our focus, however, was the perception of other groups. There is lots of evidence that people tend to negatively stereotype outgroups (see Eagly and Chaiken 1993). Given the tendency to assume more exaggerated stances in both one's own and other groups, one might expect members of both groups to see majority-culture fishermen as more sport-oriented than they truly are and Menominees as more food-oriented than they are. We also strongly expected that majority-culture fishermen would think that Menominee experts endorse spearfishing walleyes more than they actually do.[1] In fact, we thought that this was going to be our big finding, but we were wrong.

INTRA- AND INTERGROUP PERCEPTION STUDY

The aim of this study was to explore the relationship between the actual similarities and differences noted in chapter 9 and the perceived within- and between-group similarities and differences. In this task we asked the same questions as before, but instead of exploring each informant's own goals and values we asked each one to report how he thought equally expert members of his group and the other group would answer the probes concerning values, goals, and attitudes.

The informants were fourteen majority-culture and fourteen Menominee fish experts, virtually all of whom had participated in the prior study. The time that elapsed between the earlier study and this one was a minimum of several weeks and in some cases several months, so it is unlikely that informants remembered their judgments from before. The average age, education, and years spent fishing was similar in the two groups. We used the same species-ranking, goal-ranking, and practices-

Table 10.1   Predicted Fish-Value Rankings Own- and Other-Group

Raters	Menominee		Majority Culture	
Rated	Menominee	Majority Culture	Menominee	Majority Culture
Sturgeon	9.6	8.7	5.4	10.9
Black sucker	11.9	11.7	11.5	11.9
Bullhead	10.9	10.3	10.6	10.0
Bluegill	4.7	6.7	6.1	4.0
Brook trout	1.6	5.5	2.4	5.1
Brown trout	2.3	5.6	3.1	7.1
Gar	14.4	13.9	13.9	14.1
Bluntnose minnow	13.4	13.4	12.2	13.2
Largemouth bass	4.2	2.8	6.8	4.3
Smallmouth bass	7.5	7.3	7.5	7.2
Northern	6.0	5.5	6.2	5.4
River shiner	12.4	12.9	12.6	12.5
Walleye	4.3	1.4	4.8	2.1
Perch	7.5	7.8	6.2	6.2
Musky	8.6	4.6	7.9	5.9

Source: Medin et al. (forthcoming).

rating tasks as before. The only difference was that each participant was asked to answer each of the probes twice. The first time they were to answer the questions the way they thought a typical and equally expert fisherman from their community would answer them. We explained that in many cases the answers would probably be the same as they themselves would give, but that sometimes people recognize that their preferences and values might not agree with a typical expert's answers. Then informants were asked to repeat the task, this time giving answers reflecting the views of an equally expert fisherman from the other community. After these tasks were completed we showed participants the actual mean ratings for each group from the study described in the last chapter.

Intra- and Intergroup Perceptions of Relative Importance of Fish

First let's look at the results from the condition where we asked informants to rank-order the importance of fifteen species of fish for members of their own group and members of the other group. The predictions were remarkably accurate.

The main data appear in table 10.1. Each number represents the aver-

Table 10.2   Own- and Other-Group Predicted Goal Rankings[d]

	Majority Culture			Menominee		
	Self[a]	Group[b]	Other Group[c]	Self[a]	Group[b]	Other Group[c]
Being close to nature	2.4	3.2	4.6	3.0	3.0	3.2
For the challenge of finding fish	3.4	3.7	3.3	4.4	4.6	3.7
As a source of food	4.6	3.9	3.7	2.7	1.7	2.5
To catch a "trophy fish"	4.6	3.9	1.9	5.0	5.4	4.5
As a way to relax	2.6	2.4	2.6	2.4	3.1	3.5
As an activity to pass on to future generations	2.9	2.9	4.2	3.2	3.3	3.5

Source: Medin et al. (forthcoming).
[a]The average of the individual ratings broken down by group.
[b]Predictions for one's own group.
[c]Predictions by the other group in study 2.
[d]Lower numbers indicate higher importance.

age ranking, so smaller numbers correspond to more highly valued fish. Both Menominee and majority-culture informants correctly thought that trout were more important for Menominee than for majority-culture fishermen. Informants in both groups also predicted that majority-culture fishermen would rank walleye and musky very highly—more highly than the Menominees—and that also was the case. So our predictions were accurate.

Overall, each group very accurately anticipated the rankings that members of the other group would give. The two groups generally agreed on their rankings (the cross-group correlation was +.87), but accuracy in predicting the other group's rankings extended well beyond general agreement. Menominee estimates of majority values correlated +.95 with actual majority values and majority-culture estimates of Menominee values correlated +.93 with Menominee values.

Intra- and Intergroup Rankings of Fishermen's Goals

The predicted rankings for the two groups are summarized in table 10.2.[2] Each group was fairly accurate at anticipating the goals of members of their own group. Menominee experts thought that majority-culture experts would be much more focused on catching a trophy-size fish than they actually are. Menomonee fishermen also underestimated the importance to majority-culture experts of fishing as an activity to pass down to future generations and of being close to nature. The largest discrepancy between intra- and intergroup predictions was the majority-culture experts' underestimation of the importance to Menominee experts of fishing as a way to relax. Overall, the misperceptions were fairly modest in scope.

Values and Attitudes Concerning Practices: Intergroup Predictions

We expected that majority-culture experts would fail to predict that Menominee experts are divided on the question of spearfishing walleyes and that Menominee experts might think that majority-culture fishermen are more sports- and trophy-oriented than they actually are. But we were not prepared for just how strongly some perceptions would depart from actual differences between the groups' practices and perceptions of their counterparts—specifically, majority-culture experts' relatively extreme stereotyping of Menominee attitudes (see table 10.3).

Majority-culture models of Menominee are strikingly different from Menominee individual responses and Menominee predictions for their own group consensus. If a practice was condemned by both groups, majority-culture informants predicted that Menominees would support it. Majority-culture experts predicted that Menominee experts would approve of selling fish, keeping undersized fish, fishing on spawning beds, culling smaller fish to get the biggest-sized limit, using setpoles to catch trout—and even that Menominee would approve of fishing for suckers hoping to get a sturgeon on the line (the results discussed in chapter 9 show just the opposite). Overall, these data indicate that majority-culture fishermen hold strong, incorrect expectations concerning Menominee values.

Where do these misperceptions come from? We believe that the source for these misperceptions comes from differences in specific goals and knowledge organization, reinforced by patterns of media coverage. Differences in specific goals can lead to rejection of another group's values and practices.

Individual Differences in Majority-Culture Stereotyping

Individual differences in tendency to stereotype are a key part of our argument that mental models drive values and attitudes. Generally speaking, the greater the sport-fishing orientation for a majority-culture fisherman, the greater should be their tendency to stereotype. Conversely, the

Table 10.3   Reported and Predicted Ratings of Fishing Practices[d]

	Majority Culture			Menominee		
	Self[a]	Group[b]	Other Group[c]	Self[a]	Group[b]	Other Group[c]
Doing catch-and-release only	4.5	3.1	4.3	4.7	3.3	3.1
Spearfishing suckers or carp	5.9	5.9	3.4	5.1	5.0	6.2
Spearfishing walleyes or northerns	1.0	1.1	1.2	4.0	5.4	5.9
Having a trophy fish mounted	4.4	4.8	6.7	4.9	3.9	4.6
Fishing for bluegill or sunfish for food	6.0	6.4	6.2	6.9	7.0	6.5
Fishing for northerns or muskies for food	2.9	3.2	5.6	6.1	6.8	5.7
Fishing for largemouth or smallmouth bass for food	3.4	3.8	5.5	6.5	6.8	5.7
Using setpoles to catch trout	2.5	2.6	1.1	3.3	3.3	6.1
Selling fish	2.0	1.7	1.7	1.3	1.5	4.4
Keeping undersized fish	1.6	2.6	2.2	2.3	2.4	4.8
Participating in fishing contests	4.9	4.9	6.7	4.3	5.0	4.4
Fishing spawning beds	3.0	4.2	4.0	2.8	4.3	5.9
Pretending to fish for suckers to get a sturgeon	3.6	3.8	3.0	2.1	2.9	5.7
Culling for biggest limit	2.9	3.2	3.4	1.9	3.5	4.9
Using fish finders	5.9	5.9	6.5	3.6	4.8	6.1
Exceeding limit to feed family	2.9	4.1	2.8	5.2	5.3	6.0
Giving all fish away	3.9	3.3	3.2	4.8	5.1	4.8

Source: Medin et al. (forthcoming).
[a]The average individual rating in the earlier study.
[b]Own-group predictions for rating of fishing practices.
[c]Other-group predictions for rating of fishing practices.
[d]Higher numbers indicate greater approval; 4 = neutral.

more a majority-culture fisherman endorses values similar to those of Menominees (ecological orientation, fishing for food, not focusing on a single goal), the less stereotyping they should show.

Note that attributing some negative quality to an outgroup does not constitute stereotyping if that same negative quality is attributed to one's own group. For example, someone who exclusively practices catch and release should be bothered when he sees Menominee fishermen keeping the fish that they catch, especially if the fish are "big five" sport fish.[3]

Therefore, the tendency to stereotype among majority-culture fishermen was calculated as the difference between their predictions for Menominees' and their predicted own group's approval of specific fishing practice: using setpoles for trout; selling fish; fishing for suckers hoping to get a sturgeon on the line; keeping undersized fish; fishing on spawning beds; and culling out smaller fish to get the biggest possible limit.

First we examined the correlates of stereotyping using predictors drawn from the sorting justifications for the sorting task (see study 1 in chapter 7). We expected that a knowledge organization similar to the Menominees' might allow a better appreciation of values and attitudes Menominee hold, and thus that majority-culture individuals who shared a basic knowledge organization with Menominee experts might show less stereotyping concerning Menominee values and behaviors. We found that using an ecological justification was negatively correlated (−.45) with stereotyping and that the greater the number of goals reported as justifications, the less the stereotyping (correlation is −.66). The latter correlation is reliable by a directional test. Conversely, stereotyping was positively correlated (+.26) with using a "garbage fish" category and with mentioning sports fish (+.43). Although these correlations are in the predicted direction, neither is reliable.

In a second exploratory analysis we examined relationships between the fish-ranking task and stereotyping. In one analysis we looked at the correlation between how high majority-culture experts, both as individuals and as a group, ranked their "big five" sport fish and their tendency to stereotype their Menominee counterparts' rankings and practices. Assuming that stereotypes are an indicator of a "fishing-for-sport" orientation, we expected a positive correlation with stereotyping. This correlation approaches reliability for the individual rankings (+.62) and achieves reliability for the predictions for majority-culture fishermen in general (+.50). (Although the former correlation is higher, it is based on a sample of ten majority experts compared with a sample of fourteen for the group predictions.)

We also have some evidence that knowledge of Menominee values reduces or eliminates stereotyping by majority-culture experts. Overall, both Menominee and majority-culture fishermen correctly anticipated that Menominee experts rank brook and brown trout higher than majority experts. Using the six fishing practices listed previously to get an overall measure of stereotyping, we also find a reliable negative correlation (−.49) between knowing that Menominees preferentially value trout and stereotyping. The better the majority-culture experts knew Menominee rankings, the less stereotyping they displayed.[4]

One further set of correlations was at first puzzling. A significant number of the majority-culture fish experts thought that the Menominee experts would rank the sturgeon more highly than they actually do. Some majority-culture fishermen may be aware of Menominee efforts to get ladders installed on these dams so that sturgeon could return to the reservation for spawning. Some may know that sturgeon are considered sacred. So it seems reasonable to assume that majority-culture experts would think that Menominee experts would value sturgeon highly. Indeed, we ourselves were initially surprised that our Menominee experts didn't rank sturgeon more highly. The responses of the Menominee experts tend to be pragmatic. A typical comment was "We don't have them on the reservation anymore." One elder didn't rank sturgeon high because he thinks the meat is too rich.

We looked at the relationship between thinking that Menominees would rank sturgeon highly and the combined measure of stereotyping. The correlation between stereotyping and thinking that Menominee experts would rank sturgeon higher than they did was a statistically significant +.65! This seems to reflect knowing a little bit about Menominee values but then interpreting these values from within a majority-culture framework. For example, the majority-culture fishermen who thought Menominee experts would value sturgeon also thought that they would approve of getting sturgeon on the line for entertainment (correlation was a statistically reliable +.70). A further indicator that the informants who thought Menominees would rank sturgeon highly did not have intimate knowledge of Menominee values is that these same individuals tended not to know that Menominee place high value on trout: for brook trout the correlation was −.57, for brown trout it was −.53, and for the trout combined, −.62. These results underline the point that values and goals are not transparent and can give rise to intergroup misperception. The observations also suggest that knowing a bit about Menominee values in the abstract was not enough to undermine stereotyping, but knowing Menominee fishermen's specific values was.

There is evidence that stereotyping is associated with conflicting goals. Both groups catch panfish for food, but the majority-culture community is divided about catching largemouth bass, smallmouth bass, musky, and, in some cases, northerns for food. In a final analysis we looked at the correlation between overall majority-culture stereotyping of Menominees and beliefs about the differences between Menominee and majority-cultures in the level of approval of catching these various fish for food. For each majority expert we looked at the perceived difference in using these fish for food and total stereotyping. As we anticipated, stereotyping was not reliably correlated with beliefs about the panfish bluegills and sunfish (correlation was +.25), but was positively correlated with beliefs about Menominees being more likely to catch bass for food (correlation is +.52) and northern or musky for food (correlation was +.68). Both of these effects are reliable. In short, the perceived difference in how fish should be used was correlated with overall stereotyping. It may be that some of the majority-culture experts' stereotyping of Menominee fishing practices stems from their observing Menominees catch and keep fish that majority-culture fishermen typically catch and release.

THE GAP BETWEEN PERCEPTION AND REALITY

Menominee experts modestly exaggerated the sportsmen's model of fishing, but majority-culture judgments of Menominee values differed wildly from Menominees' stated values. It is not too surprising that majority-culture experts thought that Menominee would be more approving of spearfishing walleyes than they actually are, but they also thought, contrary to fact, that Menominee fishermen would strongly approve of virtually every practice that in fact both groups condemn.

One explanation for these judgments that can readily be rejected is that the Menominees' stated values do not correspond to actual behaviors. Recent surveys of fish populations in lakes and rivers on the Menominee reservation show that fish populations are healthy and abundant (Schmidt 1995), indicating that the Menominee tribe has done a good job of managing fish as a reservation resource.

We suggest that these misperceptions are mediated by differences in framework theories, knowledge organization, and goals, reinforced by patterns of media coverage (for related analysis of effects of media coverage see Gilens 1996; Gilliam and Iyenger 2000). We found not only a large stereotyping effect but also strong positive correlates of stereotyping within the majority-culture group with measures indicating agreement with a fishing for sport orientation and strong negative correlation with ecological sorting and sorting in terms of multiple goals.

We also have fairly strong evidence that knowledge of Menominee values is correlated with stereotyping in a complex but coherent way. The correct belief that Menominees preferentially value trout was reliably and negatively correlated with stereotyping. The incorrect belief that Menominee fishermen preferentially value sturgeon was positively correlated with stereotyping. Finally, the correct belief that Menominees preferentially value northerns, muskies, and bass for food was positively correlated with stereotyping.

Although it may be somewhat risky to generalize these results beyond expert fishermen, there is no particular reason to think that less expert majority-culture fishermen would show less stereotyping. Differences in specific goals can lead to rejection of another group's values and practices. For example, Menominee fishermen endorse eating largemouth and smallmouth bass, a practice that many majority-culture fishermen reject because "they are such good fighters that one should only do catch-and-release." Fishing for sport is institutionally sanctioned and encouraged by the majority culture. For example, the ethic of catch-and-release (Hummel 1994) is reinforced by Wisconsin Department of Natural Resources policy. In parts of Wisconsin the WDNR fishing regulations include a "catch-and-release only" season for largemouth and smallmouth bass in the spring, when bass are spawning (Wisconsin Department of Natural Resources, 2002).

THE ROLE OF THE MEDIA

Media coverage of the controversy surrounding Native American—specifically, Ojibwe—spearfishing exacerbates the effects of these differing orientations, especially when these rights cover off-reservation waters. When we revealed the actual Menominee ratings to majority-culture fishermen, a common response to the mismatch between their predictions and Menominee ratings was, "You know, I think I was answering the way that the Chippewa might answer."[5]

The Ojibwe (also called Chippewa)—as the only tribe with off-reservation fishing rights in the territories they ceded in the nineteenth century, which cover much of northern Wisconsin—have received the most publicity. In these waters, the daily limit on walleyes is lower than in the rest of Wisconsin, and it is a natural inference that spearfishing of walleyes in the spring when they are spawning depletes the resource. A decade ago Ojibwe spearfishing of walleyes and the associated demonstrations and protests in the spring by organizations such as Protect Americans' Rights and Resources and Stop Treaty Abuse attracted almost nightly media attention, which created more heat than light. Moderate voices were rarely quoted and the television coverage focused on the fact of controversy, not on relevant factual information.[6]

In fact, Wisconsin Department of Natural Resources (2000, 2002) records covering the period from 1985 to 2001 indicate that sports fishermen harvested at least ten walleyes for every one taken by Ojibwe spearers.[7] The Ojibwe also maintain fish hatcheries; they strip the spawn from any females they spear and restock the waters where they spear. Thus, in 1998 the Ojibwe stocked ceded territory waters with over 26 million walleye fry and more than 700,000 walleye fingerlings (Wisconsin Department of Natural Resources 2002). This positive information may not prevent many sports fishermen from balking at the image of spearers taking large female walleyes, and WDNR Wisconsin Department of Natural Resources monitoring seems to support their skepticism.[8] Sexing of harvested fish during the period from 1985 to 1999 shows a breakdown of 83 percent males, 10 percent females, and 7 percent of unknown sex. The average length of walleyes taken has been fifteen and a half inches. So the typical image of Ojibwe spearing that best fits is of a fifteen-inch male walleye, not a twenty-five-inch female.

As we suggested earlier, the Wisconsin Department of Natural Resources may indirectly and perhaps inadvertently contribute to the perception that Ojibwe spearers are depleting the walleye population by its policies concerning limits. A 1998 study commission recommended that the statewide limit be set at three walleyes, but a review board overturned this policy. If the Wisconsin Department of Natural Resources is implementing this policy where it can, namely where lakes have been declared for spearing, then the result may be that Ojibwe fishermen take the blame for the lower limits.

Another source of misperceptions consists of anecdotes and stories, sometimes rooted in reality, often not. Lurid stories about Native Americans' tossing walleyes in dumpsters are highly memorable and tempting to repeat, regardless of the authenticity of the source or the veracity of the information. In at least one case, a television station dispatched a TV crew to document this waste, only to discover that what appeared on quick inspection to be discarded walleyes were actually fish heads left intact during filleting.

CONCLUSIONS

Our results on within-group differences in stereotyping show that group means can be misleading. A significant minority of the majority-culture fishermen accurately predicted Menominees' reported values. These tended to be men who had firsthand experience with Menominee fishermen and were familiar with details of the Menominees' preferences, such as that Menominees preferentially value trout. One such fisherman summed up his own philosophy: "I don't care if someone is Native American, African American, Asian or white, the vast majority will have good values and a few won't."

Overall, the most striking finding is the contrast between perception and reality: despite the strong overall consensus across the two groups in knowledge, goals, and values, majority-culture fishermen see Menominees' preferences as vastly different from their own. In retrospect, we should have realized that the differences in worldview (framework theories), conceptual organization, and goals might lead majority-culture experts to view Menominee practices through their own, majority-culture, framework.

These results show that differences in how groups conceptualize nature are critical to understanding intergroup conflict over resources. The next chapter brings in some historical data bearing on cultural support for the differences we have noted in real and perceived values associated with fishing.

Chapter Eleven | Fishing: Cultural Changes

"We have limits on the number of trout and other fish you can take each day. Some of the people accept and follow them. Others say that it's the white man's way and that one should take what one needs and not waste. They say, `In the old days if you needed four trout for a nice meal you caught four. Now with the limit at ten, people may take ten even when they only need four.'"

—A Menominee Conservation Commission member

DOUGLAS MEDIN OF our research team grew up in Iowa and Minnesota in a typical midwestern hunting and fishing family. Here is his first-person perspective on that time: At least in northern Minnesota in the 1950s and '60s, it seemed like everyone was fishing for food. Sure, there were lots of tales about "the big one that got away" (or even more about the big one that didn't) and some people had trophy-sized fish mounted, but these events were incidental to, or a byproduct of, our primary orientation. Mind you, fishing was a lot of fun, especially when you had loon families to watch or a grandmother to tell you stories during the quiet periods. Every part of it was fun. In the morning we'd seine for minnows to use for bait fish. As a teenager I remember pulling the seine with my grandmother or my great aunt, often with middle-aged male relatives watching us from the dock. They paid for their share of the bait fish we gave them with a lot of kidding about why they were so afraid to get wet.

Fishing itself was intrinsically enjoyable. There were white pine and birches along Woman Lake's shoreline, and sometimes we would enjoy the sight of a porcupine climbing in the trees. Fishing was an absorbing activity. It was a pleasure to be able to cast one's lure or bait into a particular location (after many hours of practice from the dock). I liked watch-

120

ing dragonflies land on my bobber. And it was a delight to be able to tell what kind of fish had hit the bait by the way the bobber responded: if it skimmed across the water it was a crappie; if it popped but without any intensity it was a perch; a northern would make it just disappear with a quiet intensity.

Typically, we would go out about four o'clock, provisioned with peanut-butter sandwiches and cookies. We'd fish near drop-offs on the lake bottom, not far from shore. We didn't have a depth locator, so my job was to lower the anchor until I could feel it touch bottom, then pull it up and down until we found the drop-off. For the first hour or so we'd catch a few northerns and perhaps a largemouth bass and the occasional crappie. Then toward sundown the walleyes would start to move into the shallows to feed, and things often got pretty busy. We were happy for what we caught and didn't aim for just the large fish that some consider trophies.

We'd try to time it so that we could leave just before the mosquitoes came out on the lake in search of our blood. The smelly lotion-form 6–12 brand repellent was not much of a deterrent, so we'd rush home just before dark. To complete the fishing activity, we would clean the fish in our six-foot-square fish house, equipped with pliers for holding fish, a scaler for panfish, a set of knives, and a grindstone used to keep those knives sharp. Even cleaning fish was interesting. You could open the stomach of a northern to see what it had been eating. Just learning how to clean different kinds of fish made me feel less of a novice. My grandmother showed me how to cut out the infamous Y-bones on a northern or what my great-aunt called the "stinkbone" on a crappie. I learned that you can age fish by the growth rings on their scales. I'm sure that when I regaled my parents with my newfound wisdom they were able to pretend they were hearing it for the first time.

We never heard the term "catch-and-release." Sure, we would release undersized fish, but larger fish were caught to be consumed by our family or the frequent visitors to my grandparents' cottage. And we certainly kept and ate largemouth and smallmouth bass.

This scenario and approach to fishing held for much (but not all) of the twentieth century. By the 1980s things had started to change, and the "catch-and-release" ethic began to come into play. Let us look in detail at this shift in orientation.

CHANGES IN FISHING PRACTICES

How did this shift in attitudes toward bass and catch-and-release come about? According to one longtime fisherman who works for the Wisconsin Department of Natural Resources, one key factor was the start of bass tournament contests in the early 1980s. In the early days of these contests, all the bass were weighed and eaten. But fifty to a hundred sportsmen targeting bass on a single lake constituted a lot of pressure and it didn't take agencies such as the WDNR long to start encouraging catch-and-release. Soon there were tournaments for other prized fish such as walleyes, northerns, and muskies, and their organizers soon switched to requiring contestants to place their fish in livewells and let them go after they were measured and weighed, and the idea of catch-and-release as a conservation strategy caught on.

But livewells did not turn out to be a panacea. The death rate from immediate catch-and-release is around 1 percent, but some studies suggest that this figure swells to 20 to 40 percent at tournaments, at least for walleyes (Goeman 1991; Fielder and Johnson 1994).[1]

At about the same time, the early to mid-1980s, musky tournaments also began to take place, and more of a trophy orientation gradually came into play. The WDNR reinforced both the trophy and catch-and-release orientation by instituting and gradually increasing the size of fish that must be released. Over time, the practice of eating rather than releasing bass and musky has become something of a taboo. Today very few local majority-culture people eat bass and musky. Large northerns are almost always released as well. Menominee practice with respect to these fish is just the practice that we all used to follow: they eat them.

Another Wisconsin Department of Natural Resources fisheries person, R.K., offers a complementary perspective. According to him, some of the changes in regulations are based on better research and modeling tools. Prior to the 1950s there were quite a few size limits in place to protect the fish populations. With the 1950s came the realization that it is very difficult for anglers to overharvest fish, and most size limits were dropped. Then, in the 1980s, the orientation shifted to larger fish and increasing the pounds of fish caught per hour of effort, which had as a side effect the legal institution of size limits and the reinforcement of a catch-and-release ethic.

One useful source of data to back up these observations is the Wisconsin state fishing regulations. Starting in 1881 the fishing season for walleyes was closed from February 1 to May 1, presumably because walleyes spawn during this period. In 1903 the first size limits for catching fish were established in Wisconsin. Musky had to weigh at least four pounds and sturgeon at least eight. In 1905 the first length limit was codified: trout had to be at least six inches long. A bag limit for trout, a total of ten pounds, was also created.

In 1909 Wisconsin for the first time established a license for nonresident adult males and the annual fee was set at one dollar, to be followed in 1933 by the first "rod and reel" (hook and line) license for the same dollar fee. In 1909 a minimum-length limit for walleyes was set at twelve inches, and in 1917 a daily bag limit of ten was set.

As of 1934,[2] size and bag limits for the prized larger fish were in effect: the size minimum for muskies was thirty inches; for northerns, 16 inches; for smallmouth and largemouth bass, ten inches; and for walleyes, thirteen inches. You could take one musky, six bass, eight northerns, and ten walleyes. By 1940 the limit on walleyes and northerns had been reduced to seven and the bass limit had actually increased to seven. The size limit on northerns had also increased to eighteen inches. By 1950 the bag limits had been reduced to five for walleyes, northerns, and bass, but the size limits remained the same.

The size limits were pretty much abandoned in the 1950s (except for muskies, which remained at thirty inches). In fact virtually nothing changed at all until the 1980s, except that in 1954 Wisconsin was divided into two conservation areas, divided north and south by highway 10.[3] But by 1990 size limits had been restored for everything but northerns.

The first change in size limits for muskies in half a century, to thirty-two inches, was instituted in 1983. By 2000 this had been raised to thirty-four inches. The 1990 size limit for walleyes was fifteen inches and for bass it was twelve inches in the north and fourteen inches in the south. In 1995 the size limit was restored for northerns in the southern half of Wisconsin and set at twenty-six inches and the bag limit was lowered to two. By 2000 the bass size limit was fourteen inches throughout Wisconsin.

With the reinstitution of size limits, the issue of fishing bass on spawning beds was also reexamined. A major policy change for bass fishing came in 1992. Opening day stayed in early May, but in the northern part of Wisconsin, the first six weeks or so was a "catch-and-release-only" season (the exact days vary slightly from year to year). Interestingly this change was not based on WDNR research but rather was mandated by the Wisconsin Natural Resource Board, which has civilians on its committee and constitutes an important policy link in the overall regulatory system.

The current regulatory picture is much more complicated, as statewide limits are increasingly being replaced by local regulations.[4] In part this reflects better WDNR research into not just numbers but also size distribution of fish, leading to modeling capabilities that allow it to set goals not just for numbers of fish but also local size limits. The goal is to increase the pounds caught per angler hour of effort. The size limits also impose de facto catch-and-release much of the time.

These seemingly small changes in size limits can have fairly large consequences. For example, it is hard to estimate the size distribution for muskies caught, because creel surveys only provide information on fish over the minimum size limit. But data over the last twenty to twenty-five years from creel surveys show an average size of 37.3 inches and a standard deviation (a measure of variability of size) of 4.7 inches. Thus, a rough estimate of the true mean of muskies caught might be 34 inches with the same standard deviation. The change from a size limit of 30 inches to one of 34 inches would mean that anglers would go from having 20 percent of the muskies they catch being below the legal size limit to 50 percent being below legal size.[5] That's a considerable shift, though quite likely much smaller than the shift toward practicing catch-and-release for muskies uniformly.

The same creel surveys conducted by the WDNR that yielded the mean of 37.3 inches reveals a dramatic shift between 1991 and the year 2002 in the number of muskies showing up in surveys. Breaking the data into four-year units reveals a sample size of 274, 61, and 25 for the first, second, and most recent period, respectively. Overall the correlation between year and sample size is −.88. The reason that the sample size is so dramatically reduced is not that muskies are not being caught but that they are not being kept. This is a clear marker of the success of the catch-and-release ethic in sportsmen's behavior.

The changes with respect to walleyes are the most complex of all. Where it is feasible the WDNR tries to manage both the numbers and size distributions at a lake-specific level. This involves a variety of strategies depending on sampling estimates for numbers and sizes, and related relevant information such as whether the lake needs to be stocked or has a naturally self-sustaining population.[6]

This history of the fifty-year period between 1934 and 1984—minus some local complications—provides no evidence to justify either catch-and-release or raising limits on fish size. Since 1934 bag limits have changed relatively little, but the size limits for these various game fish have increased substantially and catch-and-release has become standard. It is surprising how recently and abruptly the change in philosophy has come into play.

The preceding data reflect a clear shift in majority-culture attitudes toward fishing in Wisconsin, whereby larger fish are targeted and fish that people used to eat are caught and released. Fishing for food and enjoyment appears to be being replaced by fishing as a competitive, sporting activity. This sport-fishing focus constitutes a widening of a cultural gap between Indians and whites. Arguably, an unintended consequence of this shift is increased intergroup conflict and an increase in majority-culture fishermen applying negative stereotypes to Menominee fishermen specifically and probably Native Americans in general.

Our view is that the changing size limits and the increased focus on catch-and-release are actually markers for a series of related changes in values, conceptual organization, and even framework theories. If we could do time travel and do the studies fifty years ago that we describe in this volume, we predict that we would see less stereotyping and intergroup conflict over natural resources than is observed today.

FISH MANAGEMENT: RELATED CHANGES

Many anglers think that fishing for walleyes isn't as good as it was in times past. One might think that this is just nostalgia for the good old days, but the 1998 walleye report (WDNR 1988) cites data that support this perception. The number of walleyes per acre in lakes with natural reproduction has been decreasing since 1970. In the 1970s the average was 6.1 per acre. This figure fell to 5.8 walleyes per acre between 1980 and 1984, to 4.8 per acre between 1985 and 1989, and to 4.1 per acre for the 1990-to-1994 period. This may be the result of slow but consistent loss of habitat as more shoreline owners "improve" their properties. Fishing pressure may be another factor. Under some conditions, such as when the water temperature is above sixty degrees, even released walleyes may have up to a 20 percent mortality rate. In addition, although the Ojibwe always take substantially fewer walleyes than their quota allows, sports anglers have often exceeded the WDNR guidelines. Stocking is not a panacea; recent studies show that stocked lakes consistently support densities of walleyes a half to a third of the level of naturally reproducing lakes.

Are there just too many fishermen? The number of resident fishing licenses sold in Wisconsin increased by more than 30 percent between 1974 and 1984, but then these numbers fell again in the 1990s by almost 20 percent, leaving the total a little more than 10 percent higher over two decades. The number of nonresident licenses sold has shown considerable year-to-year fluctuation since 1965, but there has been no overall trend for these numbers to increase or decrease.[7] Maybe the presence of jet skis and large boats that go roaring around lakes has had something to do with a diminished interest in fishing.

The total angler catch of walleyes in the ceded territories has fluctuated dramatically over at least the past fifteen years. For example it was about 1,500,000 in 1990, fell to 590,000 in 1994, only to jump to 2,200,000 just two years later, but then another two years later was at 760,000. It reached a low point in 2002 at 530,000 but, as we noted, was back at about 1,200,000 in 2003. These large fluctuations make it difficult to determine long term fish population trends.

State Regulation

Regulatory processes may represent effects rather than causes (though they may feed back and thus become causes). The decisionmaking process for fish and game management in Wisconsin is fairly complicated and has a strong democratic flavor. The WDNR is responsible for the science, and its staff draft regulations that must be approved by the state legislature. The Wisconsin Natural Resources Board acts as an advisory body to the WDNR and can mandate certain changes. The WDNR also seeks advice from hunters, fishermen, and trappers, holding hearings in every county each spring to get feedback from sportsmen on proposed regulations and policies. Although the voting is advisory, it represents democracy at work. Counties also elect representatives to a state Conservation Congress, which serves in an advisory capacity to the Natural Resources Board and the WDNR. Despite frequent complaints about the WDNR's not being responsive, local input may create conflict when science and local opinion disagree.

Actually, there is room for conflict at all levels. For example, in 2004 the WDNR and the Wisconsin state legislature were deadlocked over regulations concerning feeding and baiting deer, which had been banned since 2003, a year after three deer had tested positive for chronic wasting disease. The WDNR wanted to continue a complete ban to protect the herd against the spread of the disease, WDNR biologist argued that feed piles concentrated deer and increased the rate of CWD infection. CWD is a transmissible spongiform encephalopathy. It attacks the brain of the infected animal, causing it to become emaciated and display abnormal behaviors. Eventually, they lose control of bodily functions and die. The state legislature mandated that the department come up with some compromise planning that would allow some baiting. The Department of Natural Resources board voted 4 to 3 to refuse to do so; later they agreed to a compromise.

More recently the legislature pushed the Natural Resources Board to fund a study of the consequences of the use of livewells and culling associated with bass tournaments. Culling has been illegal in Wisconsin, but some national bass tournaments such as the ESPN Elite 50 will not come into a state that does not allow culling; hence the idea of changing the law to attract such tournaments to Wisconsin. The publicity associated with nationally televised tournaments may provide a boost to the tourism industry, which illustrates the impact of the media on natural resource policy decisions.

This chain of advice and mandate also can make the Department of Natural Resources the instrument of morality and ethics. Under discussion in 2006 is a fifty-inch musky limit on thirty-four lakes in Vilas and Oneida counties, with the goal being to produce trophy-sized fish. There is even some debate about whether the stock used in Minnesota produces more trophy fish than the native Wisconsin gene pool. Depending on one's perspective this is either democracy at work or an attempt to legislate fishing morality. From another perspective, trophy-sized fish are bait to lure in tourists and tourist dollars, and that's important for the economy of the state of Wisconsin.

Bass Tournaments

A more direct cause of a decline in fish is tournaments. Opinions on tournaments are divided, with some of the fishing experts we interviewed participating in them and other experts loudly denouncing them on a variety of grounds.

One way to gauge changes over time is to follow the evolution of a specific organization. BASS, which stands for what Bass Anglers Sportsman's Society, first became known when it started publishing *Bassmaster* magazine in 1968. By 1971 more than 90,000 people in the United States belonged to BASS, and in 1972 the organization began promoting catch-and-release tournaments. In 1985 the Bassmaster TV show debuted on the Nashville Network. By 1992, 50,000 children were competing for scholarships in Bassmaster "Castingkids" competitions. In 1999 BASS could boast of more than 600,000 members and in 2000 the Bassmaster television show shifted to ESPN2. The year 2000 also featured a five-event "World Championship Fishing Series." In 2001 ESPN purchased BASS and now features it in the program *ESPN Outdoors*. Clearly, fishing as a sporting competition has taken hold in the United States. In the year 2004 there were more than four hundred fish tournaments in Wisconsin large enough to require a formal permit from the WDNR.

Overall, then, the various changes since the mid-1980s have been in the direction of encouraging fishermen to practice catch-and-release and increasingly to focus on catching larger fish (and in many cases on releasing them). The cumulative effect of these changes has been to tilt the balance from fishing for food and the enjoyment of the activity itself to fishing for sport in a more competitive sense of targeting larger, even trophy-sized, fish. Let's turn now to the corresponding history of regulation on the Menominee reservation.

NATURAL-RESOURCE REGULATION
BY THE MENOMINEE TRIBE

Throughout its history the Menominee Nation has been dependent on the vast natural resources of the Great Lakes region. Early French explorers documented the Menominee people as hunters, fishers, trappers, and gatherers. The Menominee are most known to the outside world for their harvest of wild rice.

The status of Indian hunting and fishing rights, both on and off the reservation, has been very extensively litigated in both state and federal courts (see Hobbs 1963, 1969 for an earlier overview). Off-reservation rights were at issue in Ojibwe spearfishing, discussed earlier.

Within the Menominee reservation, one early, persistent issue was the tribe's right to regulate whites coming onto the reservation to fish, especially fishing on the Wolf River, which runs through the reservation. Whites' argument was that anyone could fish on navigable waters, regardless of who owned the adjacent land, so anyone should be able to go up or down the river and enter the reservation to fish. The Menominees' view was that they had the sole right to enjoy the resources that their reservation provided.

Menominee complaints focused not only on the presence of outsiders but also on the methods the outsiders were using to take fish. In 1909 the Menominee forester in charge, E. A. Barnif, wrote a letter to the commissioner of Indian Affairs in Washington, D.C., complaining that "whites from the outside have used dynamite and seines" to get fish. Although the commissioner tended to discount such reports as unsubstantiated, there were corroborative letters from whites as well. The following is an excerpt from a letter dated July 7, 1909, written by E. E. Hemingway of Mattoon, Wisconsin: "On Sunday last the Indians drove some of our men away from the lake and broke their rafts, and upon further investigation we have been unable to learn the exact conditions but are of the opinion that the fellows asked not to fish any more are the fellows who have been there many times before and have used dynamite and nets and we believe that such people should be driven off."

Other concerns were that outsiders who were going onto the reservation to hunt and fish were also bringing liquor, became inebriated, and started fires that often got out of control. Ultimately, these complaints led the commissioner of Indian Affairs to set up a permitting process. Petitioners would have to write to T. B. Wilson, the superintendent of the Keshena Indian School, for a fishing permit.

The permitting process led to complaints on both sides. A. F. W. Zirbel sent a letter of protest, dated July 7, 1911, to the commissioner:

> I and my son in law . . . injoy an outing at a certain Lake in Oconto County Berry Lake in this lake there are only Black Bass, Pearch and Sunfish within three blocks along a country road from this Berry Lake there is a Lake called Meachaket Lake in this Lake there are quite a lot of Pickeral, last summer in July & August we took the boat on a two wheeled cart along the country road to Meachaket Lake, now this Lake is in the Indian Reservation, according to the report I got from there, the Indian Agent bard us white people out of the injoyment to go fishing for Pickeral.

Meanwhile, Menominees continued to complain about fires and over-fishing. In 1910 the tribe set up a commission on game laws and asked the superintendent to require that a permit be purchased, that trout be taken only by hook and line, that a fine of twenty-five dollars be levied on violators, and that outsiders must hire a guide from the reservation (for not less that two dollars a day) to see that the game laws are obeyed. The superintendent issued permits under these conditions for at least the next several years.

All in all, though, the permitting process was not a happy compromise and it continued in an on again, off again pattern over the next few decades. A meeting of the Menominee General Council in 1937 provides a good overview of the costs and benefits. The superintendent proposed that three hundred permits be issued to outsiders at a fee of ten dollars each. His argument was that many whites were working for the forestry department in Neopit (where the reservation's sawmill is located) and that they would benefit from this diversion. Some present at the meeting suggested that the permit fees and use of guides would provide needed revenue and employment on the reservation.

Opposition to this permit proposal came from, among others, James Frechette, a tribe member who cited a forestry report to the effect that the average annual value of timber the tribe lost to fires in the previous eight years was $9,264.44 and its annual cost for fire fighting was $5,131.15. The report also noted that in 1936, when the reservation was closed to outsiders, there were thirty-eight fires, compared with fifty-two fires in 1931, when fishing was open. Frechette suggested that the difference might represent the added fire hazard caused by outside fishermen. He went on to say, "I believe that a closed ordinance on the Menominee reservation for fishing and hunting to the outside public is a right we have been given by our forefathers and not by the government, state, or public. To me it is the last symbol of freedom and liberty that we rightfully inherited . . . " Frechette also suggested that any benefits of the state of Wisconsin stocking the lakes and rivers with fish may be illusory: "Do we need the planting of fish here? I'm no fisherman but I've read somewhere in a magazine that about the only good thing the transplanting of hatchery fish into wild waters accomplishes is that it makes good feed for the fish that are already in the streams."

Al Dodge, a tribe member, moved that the fishing season be closed and the motion was seconded by Jerome Beauprey. It passed by a vote of 85 to 0.

During this period, for tribe members the ethic continued to be "Do not waste," and there were no formal limits on the numbers or size of fish that they could take. In 1954 federal control of the Menominee tribe by the federal government was terminated, and the status of the natural resources the tribe had long protected came into immediate jeopardy. In 1966 the state of Wisconsin enacted legislation (Wisconsin State Law s.20.370(1), chapter 313) that preserved the Wolf River and granted free public access for fishing and camping.

When termination was formalized, the state regulations for hunting and fishing went into effect on the Menominee reservation. This continued until 1968, when the U.S. Court of Claims ruled that the Menominee had not relinquished their hunting and fishing rights when federal control of the tribe was terminated. It was a landmark case that helped other tribes, because later in 1968 the Supreme Court ruled that termination did not abrogate treaty rights. This decision helped force the federal government to abandon their termination plans.

In 1976 control of hunting and fishing rights was restored to the Menominee by the Wisconsin Supreme Court. In 1981 the tribe held a referendum vote to determine whether hunting and fishing privileges should be granted to other individuals other than tribe members. The vote came back in favor of allowing first- and second-generation descendants, spouses of enrolled tribe members, and resident clergy (permittees) to become eligible for permits to hunt and fish within the exterior boundaries of the Menominee reservation. The following year the Menominee Conservation Commission was formed to craft and pass laws that would regulate the use of the resources by permittees and tribe members. Until this point, the only regulation was that of the general provisions of the Menominee Constitution, which states that the natural resources of the tribe are to be governed by the tribe for the use of its members. Use of resources by anyone other than enrolled members is allowed only if it has been approved by the tribe membership in an election where a majority of eligible voters vote.

Ordinances that have been developed as a result of the referendum have covered a wide range of regulations pertaining to natural resources. Fishing and hunting have been the main focus, but there were also issues related to trapping and gathering that had gotten very little attention over the years. As the ordinances were amended and more attention was focused on broader resources, it became necessary to develop laws concerning additional issues such as trespassing and escort guiding regulations. All ordinances were created under the existing guidance of the tribe through its administrative and legislative procedures as part of the governmental operations dictated by the constitution. This process allowed for public involvement and comment as part of ordinance development, which included public meetings and public notification. Final approval authority resided in the Menominee Tribal Legislature acting as the governing body for the tribe.

The wanton destruction of any fish is prohibited. In general, the size limits are smaller for the Menominee reservation than the off-reservation limits. For example, the Menominee tribe currently has a ten-inch size limit for bass versus the state's fourteen inches, a thirty-two-inch limit for muskies versus the state's thirty-four inches and forty or fifty inches on many lakes, and a twelve-inch limit for northerns versus twenty-six inches or more. Conservation Commission meeting minutes reveal no expression of interest in shifting size limits in the direction of yielding trophy-sized fish. Catch-and-release does not appear in the tribal regulations. In short, the state and tribal regulations reflect the cultural difference in orientation toward fish and fishing that our studies reveal.

SUMMARY AND CONCLUSIONS

An evolution in attitudes and practices associated with fishing has both led to and been guided by changes in state fishing regulations. Size limits have been systematically increasing over the past twenty years, and these increases track with an increasing focus on the competitive aspects of fishing. Policies have been put into place that both adjust for and encourage fish tournaments, and probably this has been good for the economy of Wisconsin. Yet these changes have reflected and, more important, reinforced a shift in the framework theories and models that majority-culture fishermen bring to bear in understanding fish and fishing. Majority-culture orientation has moved away from fishing for food and as a result has become distanced from a Native American orientation.

Chapter Twelve | Hunting and Forest Ecology

"Hunters shouldn't be thinking that the more deer the better when it comes to surviving a severe winter. Look at it this way—if a farmer has forty cows but only has enough feed for twenty, he doesn't put twenty more in, hoping that forty will survive; he takes twenty out so that at least twenty will survive."

—Bruce Bacon, a WDNR wildlife manager

OUR STUDIES OF hunting very much parallel our research on fish and fishing. As with fishing, cultural differences in hunting orientation lead to misperceptions and intergroup conflict. Would we continue to find that majority-culture sportsmen misperceive Menominee values when we looked at hunting? Our informal observations suggested that we would, but there are two reasons for thinking that we might not observe stereotyping. One is that when it comes to hunting there is no clear counterpart to Native American off-reservation fishing rights and the surrounding publicity and controversy. The other reason for thinking we might not see stereotyping is the international and local reputation the Menominee have for sustainable forestry. It is well known that the Menominee "take care of their forest" and if taking care implies managing the forest as an ecosystem, then one would expect that Menominee also successfully manage the components of this system, such as deer, bear, and other game and one would expect others to expect this.

There is, however, controversy over practices. When it comes to hunting, the "shining" deer may be the analogue of spearfishing walleyes. Shining involves going out on country roads at night and shining a bright spotlight into the woods and clearings where deer may be found.

Deer often freeze when the spotlight blinds them and hunters then have time to shoot them. Hunting deer at night and shining is illegal in Wisconsin, and majority-culture hunters also consider shining immoral and unsporting. It may also provide an unfair opportunity to shoot an older buck with large antlers. European-American hunters also resent the fact that tribes are allowed to establish their own hunting regulations.

When we started our research, in 1997, the Menominee tribe had a shining season. But even then, the practice of shining was controversial on the reservation. Some Menominee hunters expressed the concern that deer were being wounded and since the current generation of hunters was not good at tracking deer at night, they were unable to track the wounded deer and consequently deer were being wasted. Others noted that dragging a deer across a clearing full of tree stumps at night was very difficult, and they wondered out loud whether people always took out the deer that they shot or whether they just left the carcasses where they fell. These arguments ultimately proved to be compelling when Don Reiter, the Menominee fish and wildlife biologist and the assistant director of the tribal Conservation Commission, reported on the number of carcasses found. Finally, population estimates suggested that the deer population, six to nine per square mile, was a bit below the carrying capacity. For all these reasons shining deer was banned on the Menominee reservation in 2000.

The deer populations in counties surrounding the Menominee reservation are much higher than in Menominee County itself. This is because the neighboring counties tend to have forty- to eighty-acre patches of forest surrounded by cornfields, where the deer can feed, whereas the Menominee reservation is pretty much pure forest. The carrying capacity for the reservation forest is roughly eight to twelve deer per square mile, though some have suggested that it could go as high as fifteen deer per square mile.[1] Forest patches and cornfields in surrounding counties can support a population density several times greater. Some majority-culture hunters mistake this difference in carrying capacity for a difference in successfully managing deer populations.

CURRENT POPULATIONS

The estimated deer population per square mile on the Menominee reservation for the years 2003, 2004, and 2005 was 10.2, 9.2, and 12.0, respectively. These figures are solidly in the range of the estimated carrying capacity.

In contrast, most of the other counties in Wisconsin are burdened with an overpopulation of deer, and many counties have overwintering populations almost twice the level that wildlife biologists think is proper. Shawano County is among the many counties with an overpopulation of deer.

Deer overpopulation poses the risks of rapid spread of disease and excessive damage to forest plant species. The Wisconsin Department of Natural Resources has tried to reduce the deer population to more reasonable levels, but has had mixed success. One problem is that hunters prefer to shoot bucks (and the bigger the better), yet to control the deer population, it is much more important to shoot does. To encourage deer hunters to take does, the WDNR has tried a variety of regulations such as having a special season for antlerless deer or requiring hunters to kill an antlerless deer before getting a tag entitling them to shoot a buck (the so-called "earn-a-buck" program).[2] Some conservationists have called for a plan where every fifth year becomes a "does only" season.

It seems straightforward to conclude that deer overpopulation means that deer hunting will be good. Surprisingly, however, many hunters complain that there are very few deer available. Although this may seem puzzling, it is not as strange as it seems. The hunters who are complaining mainly hunt on public lands, and over the past several decades there has been an increasing "privatization" of hunting lands. In times past farmers would often grant permission for sportsmen to hunt on their lands, and hunters usually reciprocated with some venison. Nowadays many hunters own forty-acre parcels or organize into small groups that pay a large part of a farmer's real estate taxes in exchange for the exclusive right to hunt on their land. Many of these hunters are practicing "quality deer management," aimed at producing large bucks.[3] Of course, they wouldn't want other hunters coming on to their land and taking their prize bucks. Hunters who own their own land often "bait" deer— put out piles of corn and other food—to keep them on their lands.[4]

The net effect of this shift toward privatization of hunting territory is that deer are sometimes scarce on public lands and concentrated on private lands. As a consequence, the WDNR has less and less control over its deer-management policy, including measures such as encouraging hunters to shoot does. Deer-management policy becomes more and more an emergent property of the collective practices of people who restrict access to their lands. The year 2002 saw the appearance of chronic wasting disease in a few Wisconsin counties. Even then, however, the WDNR was frustrated by the unwillingness of private landowners, including farmers, to greatly reduce the herd. All in all, the state of Wisconsin has not been able to deal effectively with the overpopulation of deer, in part because of a tendency for landowners to feel that they "own" the game on their lands and in part, because hunters much prefer shooting bucks to antlerless deer.

THE WISCONSIN DEER POPULATION: A CHRONOLOGY

What follows is a summary of the changes in the Wisconsin deer population and state regulation of hunting over the past century or so:

1851 First closed season for deer, February to June

1876 Hunting deer with dogs prohibited

1897 First bag limit for deer, two per season

1915 First buck-only season

1917 Shining deer made illegal

1919 Estimated gun kill of about 25,000

1925 Legislature passes law closing the deer season every other year

1934 First bow season

1941 Gun kill of deer around 40,000

1943 First antlerless deer season in twenty-four years

1958 Gun kill of deer about 95,000

1962 Deer population above 400,000

1978 Record gun kill of 150,845

1985 Fifth consecutive record kill of 274,302 deer

1990 Prehunt herd estimated at 1.3 million; and record kill of 350,040

1999 Prehunt herd estimated at more than 1.5 million; record harvest of 402,204 deer

2004 Fall population of deer estimated to be 1.7 million

These figures reveal that "there's no time like the present" when it comes to deer. The state population of deer has been growing steadily over the past forty years, and so has the deer harvest. The 1999 harvest is equal to the estimated total 1962 herd. Note that early in the twentieth century there was a concerted effort to increase the deer population by, for example, only allowing bucks to be shot. It is somewhat paradoxical that the current focus on shooting large bucks comes at a time when Wisconsin faces a serious overpopulation problem, and hunters have to be forced to shoot a doe in order to be allowed to shoot a buck. A 2004 online poll of hunters by *Wisconsin Outdoor News* indicated that 29 percent of hunters rated the opening weekend as average and 53 percent rated it as poor. This discontent may reflect both the consequences of privatization and high expectations for seeing deer.

These sorts of problems do not occur on the Menominee reservation. If we were giving out grades for conservation, the Menominees would get an A and the state of Wisconsin a C minus. The Menominee tribe manages deer as part of an overall forestry management plan that values biodiversity, including protecting species that are endangered elsewhere in Wisconsin. Of course, the state of Wisconsin has a more difficult challenge, so the poor grade is not a reflection on WDNR policies but results from the fact that conditions being what they are, no concerted policy can be enacted on the state or county level. The WDNR has to deal with many more hunters, closed access to private lands, and a set of practices such as quality deer management that exacerbate the population-control problem. The overcrowding of deer is partly responsible for the spread of chronic wasting disease in several Wisconsin counties, and though it receives little attention, it has harmful effects on forest ecology.[5] Deer hunting has a significant economic impact in many counties of Wisconsin and it is quite a challenge for the WDNR to address the various competing interests.

For many years a major issue of controversy was baiting deer. Until quite recently, the state allowed farmers to set out up to ten gallons of bait at once, usually corn. Some hunters consider baiting to be unethical because it doesn't constitute "fair chase." Other critics argue that it changes the normal movement patterns of deer. They also note that it tends to encourage deer to congregate and creates more chances for disease to spread. Advocates say that it allows for a cleaner shot and results in fewer wounded deer. Opponents say: "Shooting a deer over a pile of corn isn't hunting." Still others draw a line between gun hunting and bow and arrow hunting and only support baiting for bow and arrow hunts. The anti side won a temporary victory when the presence of chronic wasting disease led the Department of Natural Resources to ban the baiting and feeding of deer but the pro side has made at least a partial comeback more recently.

HUNTING PRACTICES AND INTERGROUP CONFLICT

By practices we mean the what, when, how, and how many of hunting. Overall, Menominee and European Americans do not differ in what they hunt for food (deer, bear, turkeys, rabbits, squirrels, ducks, geese, grouse) or for their pelts (beaver, mink, muskrat, fox, coyote, bobcat, otter, weasel). A fair number of Menominee who belong to the bear clan do not hunt bear; other bear clan members have been taught that they can hunt bear, as long as proper respect is shown and all the parts of the bear are used. Generally speaking, Menominee do not use just the hide and meat of bears, but also use the tallow and other parts that have medicinal uses. They are somewhat more likely than majority-culture hunters to eat the meat of other fur-bearing animals as well; those who don't eat, say, beaver meat will leave it out for other predators rather than put it in the garbage.

The concept of tribe membership is not entirely straightforward, and it needs to be understood, because the hunting and fishing regulations on the Menominee reservation are different for enrolled tribe members and "descendants," people with a Menominee parent but without enough Menominee blood to enroll. This is a controversial issue. One Menominee hunter has a son who is a descendant, who has blond hair. He gets teased for being an Indian off the reservation and for not being an Indian on the reservation. This hunter says, "Only the Menominee are prejudiced against their own people."

A Menominee elder has a different perspective. She is worried that if descendants are allowed to enroll, too many people would come to the reservation and want things. At the same time it is clear that she feels conflicted. The tribe is making strenuous efforts to keep the Menominee language alive, and later on in our conversation she suggests that anyone willing to learn the Menominee language and adopt Menominee values should be welcomed into the tribe.

There is some criticism by majority-culture hunters of Menominee shooting does and other antlerless deer; many of them do not see that the Menominee deer population is healthy. There is more criticism over the "hows" of hunting. Many majority-culture hunters mistakenly believe that shining deer is still allowed on the reservation. In addition there are two other differences. Both groups use dogs for hunting bear, but only Menominee are allowed to use dogs to drive deer. Furthermore, Menominees are allowed to hunt from their vehicles on backwoods roads with guns loaded and uncased and to shoot game from their trucks. There are also some differences in the "when" of hunting, but these do not seem to be a source of contention between the two groups. Menominees usually have a longer season for deer. Their bucks-only season goes from August to September, though the vast majority of reservation deer hunting takes place in the fall. The state of Wisconsin is also more precise than the tribe in specifying hunting hours. Each year a regional guide is published prescribing the exact hour and minute when hunting may begin and must end. Menominee regulations simply state that hunting begins at dawn and ends at dusk. We have never heard a complaint from majority-culture hunters about either aspect of these laws, though everyone has a story about how big bucks seem to wear a watch and come out only minutes after the official state of Wisconsin sunset has been declared.

The "how many" of hunting also produces few complaints. Enrolled tribe members are initially given three tags and if they fill them, can come back for two more, so they may take up to five deer each year. That may seem like a lot, but off the reservation the rules are, if anything, more liberal. There is a bow-and-arrow season, a gun season, and even a black powder (musket) season. In addition, in almost all parts of the state there are so-called T-zones where one can get a tag to shoot an antlerless deer, get one deer, and then get another tag for another antlerless deer, shoot another deer, and so on. In other areas an "earn-a-buck" program may be in place where one first has to kill an antlerless deer in order to get a tag allowing one to shoot a buck. Still, in areas that are hunter's choice, the majority of deer shot are bucks.

In summary, the strongest complaints by majority-culture hunters about Menominees' hunting practices center on shining, road hunting (mainly in the context of shining), using dogs for deer, and (in their eyes) depleting the deer population on the reservation. Menominees tend not to complain about whites, but when they do, it is about the apparent focus on getting a trophy-sized buck.

The similarities of practices in the two groups are greater than the differences. Both groups require that a person complete a hunting-safety class and pass a test before being issued a license.[6] The minimum age for taking the class is twelve in both communities. Both communities use the same curriculum, prepared by the state of Wisconsin, though the Menominee class also spends time talking about Menominee regulations, cultural values, and the "do not waste" ethic.

Interestingly, the most recent Wisconsin state curriculum has an expanded section on hunter ethics and also talks about the five stages of hunter development:

1. The shooting stage, where the priority is getting off a shot, sometimes leading to bad decisions

2. The limiting-out stage, where the goal is to bag one's limit

3. The trophy stage, where the focus is on bagging big game

4. The method stage, where the hunting process is more important than the outcomes

5. The sportsman's stage, where the focus is on the total experience of being outdoors, the appreciation of the game, the process and the companionship of other hunters (and, we will add, passing down the tradition to future generations)

The hunters in our study often talked about how their focus has changed over the years and this analysis rings true to their experience.

But one other aspect of the hunter-education instructional manual requires comment. Diagrams and drawings of deer appear ten times in the sections leading up to the discussion of hunter ethics, and all ten representations are of adult bucks with healthy racks. So there is at least the implicit message that bucks are what deer hunting is about. The drawings of hunters include women and minorities but apparently it is still not "politically correct" to shoot does, at least as judged by the artistic renditions.

WISCONSIN WOLVES

Majority-culture and Native American hunters have sharply contrasting views on the reintroduction of wolves to Wisconsin. Here is a sampling of comments.

Wolves are part of the ecology of Wisconsin—it's not called the Wolf River for nothing—and because wolves are predators of livestock as well as deer, emotions about them run high. Wolves had been hunted to virtual extinction, but the WDNR started a program of reintroduction. Opposition to the move was widespread. Over the past several years there have been about twenty letters written to the *Wisconsin Outdoor News* and all but one were negative. The sole exception was a letter from a hunter who noted that there are 1.7 million deer in Wisconsin and three or four hundred wolves. He pointed out that wolves strengthen the herd by culling out the weak, sick, and wounded, and that cars kill many thousands more deer than wolves do.

The current wolf population is about four hundred, and these interest groups are pushing to reduce that back to one hundred. Hunters who have had dogs killed by wolves and farmers complain that they are not being adequately compensated for livestock losses.

Peter David (2004), a wildlife biologist with the Great Lakes Indian Fish and Wildlife Commission, wrote:

In the Ojibwe creation story Ma'iingan (wolf) is a brother to original man. The two traveled together throughout the earth naming all that they saw. After this task was completed, the Creator said that the two had to take separate paths, but indicated that whatever happened to one would happen to the other. Each would be feared, respected and misunderstood by the people that would later join them on Earth.

Given this perspective, it is obvious why the Ojibwe have rejoiced in the recovery their brother has made in the ceded territory—and why they are greatly concerned that some livestock growers and individuals who hunt bears with dogs are pushing to set that recovery back.

It is important to keep these losses in perspective. While they can be very significant to individual ranchers, they are not a threat to the industry. From July 2003 to July 2004, there were 21 cases on 21 different farms, of verified wolf depredations on livestock in the state, involving five cows and 24 calves, two sheep and 17 lambs, and six game farm deer. This is about 1/10th of 1% of farms within wolf range. In restitution for those losses 21 wolves were trapped and killed, and about $24,000 will be paid out. This level of damage is on the order of magnitude of what Wisconsin dairy producers report losing in feed to starlings in a year, or the annual estimated cost to repair Wisconsin buildings damaged by woodpeckers.

And there remains the bigger question: will reducing the wolf population reduce livestock losses? The answer is likely not as straight forward as one would think, since natural systems tend to be more complex than we often acknowledge. Reducing the wolf population would likely reduce the number of livestock killed by wolves, but losses to coyotes may increase where the wolf population is suppressed—and ranchers have to absorb losses to coyotes without compensation from the state.

NARRATIVES AND OTHER OBSERVATIONS

Some informal anecdotes provide additional flavor to cultural perspectives on hunting.

Quality deer management focuses on shooting younger bucks, since the goal is to let the older bucks do the breeding. But this practice leads to overpopulation.

One aspect of quality deer management is that it has large social costs. Landowners lock up their land and privatize access to deer. People start to feel like the deer on their land are theirs and have a sense of entitlement.

Thirty years ago people hunted on private lands by permission but that option is largely unavailable now. So we have large numbers of hunters crowded into public lands because of closed access to private lands.

A WDNR biologist

Another hunter, L.M., expresses the worry that deer hunting is becoming a rich man's sport. Some hunters are spending hundreds of thousands of dollars to lease land to hunt on. He's also concerned that debates about issues such as whether deer baiting should be allowed just provide ammunition for the "anti-hunting" lobby.

The total number of hunters in the United States declined by 1 million, or 7.3 percent, between 1991 and 2001, according to the Census Bureau and the U.S. Fish and Wildlife Service. The privatization of hunting is likely a contributing factor. In addition, the shift in population from rural to urban areas has led to a focus on short hunting vacations, which have made hunting on "game farms" increasingly popular. It is even possible to do target practice from a website that allows remote control of a camera and gun on a private hunting ranch near San Antonio, Texas. The owner of this ranch and website recently created a large controversy when he proposed that hunters be allowed to shoot wild pigs and exotic game animals via this same remote control system. The Texas hunting community broadly condemned this form of hunting as unethical.

I am not an anti-hunting type of person, but after what I've seen on some "outdoor" TV shows, it's easy to see why some people are. It seems there is a new "breed" of hunter and a new form of hunting. These "sportsmen" do their hunting out in the "wilds" of the nearest game farm. A few hours before they arrive, a bunch of pen-raised pheasants are released in a hay field where there isn't enough cover to hide a chipmunk. When the "hunters" get there, they line up on the edge of the field a few yards apart. They have the best of guns and dogs.

They march across the field. When a dog points everyone moves in. The bird is flushed and the shooting begins. It's hard to believe that shooting a pheasant can generate that much excitement in a group of grown men.

As the bird tumbles to earth, there are congratulations and hand shakes, high fives and back slapping. A person would think they just shot a charging grizzly bear that was about to wipe out the whole gang. It was only a pheasant and a tame one at that.

If this is somebody's idea of hunting, they are welcome to it. I just wish they would have the common sense not to make it for TV. It looks bad.

Wisconsin Outdoor News, July 21, 2000, letter to the editor

Whatever happened to the quality of the hunt? With T-zones, unlimited antlerless tags and "anything goes" tribal hunting, the DNR has succeeded in convincing hunters that we must kill deer at any cost—the cost being the total destruction of quality deer hunting in Wisconsin.

Wisconsin Outdoor News, February 26, 2001, letter to the editor

From July 1, 1999, to June 30, 2000, a total of 47,555 car-killed deer were reported in the state. In fact, given the high numbers of deer killed in accidents state authorities decided that the state cannot afford any longer to pick up carcasses of dead deer.

WDNR figures on car-killed deer

Long before any Democrats take away our guns, Republicans will have turned the last duck marsh into a Wal-Mart parking lot. It may be just as well though. The present administration's parallel efforts to roll back efforts for clean water and clean air may eventually render our remaining fish and game inedible.

Wisconsin Outdoor News, March 14, 2003, letter to the editor

Sometimes after work I'll go with some of the guys to a bar. We'll have a drink or two and after a while the bartender will usually ask us what we do for a living. We always say, "What's the worst thing you can imagine?" and nine times out of ten they will guess Department of Natural Resources.

A WDNR field biologist from northern Wisconsin

When I was young we were very poor. My father had a musket. One day when we didn't have any shot left, my father loaded the musket with cherry pits. He saw a deer and shot at it but the deer got away. A year later my father shot a deer and we figured that it must have been the one he shot before, because it was sprouting a little cherry tree.

A Menominee elder

Some Menominee elders say that if you have any venison left in your freezer, then you can't hunt deer. If you have any bear meat left, then you can't hunt bear.

I.P., a Menominee elder, was raised by her grandmother. She gathered berries, fished a lot, and built snares to catch rabbits. She says, "We used to eat everything we caught: my grandmother could make skunk taste like rabbit. When we were hungry we would even eat porcupine. It tastes like pork."

We asked one expert Menominee hunter what he thinks about when he's out in the forest waiting for a deer to come by. He said, "I pray."

We were taught that deer meat will taste okay when you can see fireflies at night. We would also soak deer meat in tallow to take out the hemlock taste.

A Menominee elder

Recently a local business owner and friend received a letter and picture of me in the mail. The picture was of a buck I shot this year while gun-hunting. . . . On the photo were written the words "Bambi killer." The letter stated that we were Bambi killers and that we were making the trophy buck hunting in our county look bad. The buck was an 8-pointer with a 12-inch inside spread. . . . The farm I was on has been in Quality Deer Management for four years and this is not a buck that should have been shot. I made a mistake. I should have waited for a better look but I don't believe this to be a Bambi. If the buck had four more inches of spread I guess it would be a shooter to the person who wrote me the letter. . . . I have lost my privileges on that farm now and nobody is more sorry than me about what happened.

Wisconsin Outdoor News, March 3, 2000, letter to the editor

A common point of view is that people who own the land should have the right to have as many deer as they want on their land. . . . Take a landscape that is getting more and more fragmented by private ownership and allow all those new owners to maximize "their" deer populations and you have a recipe for ecological disaster and that includes humans. . . . Maybe we should make people responsible for damages to property caused by "their" deer when they leave the land. Maybe the threat of buying someone a new car would be enough of an incentive so that private landowners won't be so eager to maximize their deer numbers.

Wisconsin Outdoor News, April 8, 2005, letter to the editor

If a dog doesn't hunt what good is he? I don't want to feed him, I don't want to pet him, I don't want to take care of him.

A majority-culture neighbor along the Wolf River

This doesn't mean that majority-culture folks don't care about their dogs. Another neighbor, who is too disabled to walk any distance, uses his riding lawn mower and a long leash to take his husky for long walks along the roadside.

Whether you're a hunter using bait, hunter with dogs, bow hunter, or a gun hunter, we all carry a common thread—we are hunters. If we don't

band together and accept the choices of others, we will kill our sport ourselves.

Wisconsin Outdoor News, August 2, 2002, letter to the editor

One night I (Medin) had dinner with a Menominee hunter. He talked
about hunting as a cultural activity, as part of becoming an adult. Being
a respectful hunter demonstrates both skills and that one is becoming
ready to take on adult responsibilities. For this reason hunting is a very
important tradition to be passed down across generations.

The next day I interviewed a majority-culture fisherman. He talked at
length about the importance of introducing children to fishing and hunting as activities where they can both have fun and learn responsibilities.
His comments were almost an exact parallel to the remarks of the Menominee hunter; they are kindred spirits whether they know it or not.
Unfortunately, "or not" seems to be the case.

Chapter Thirteen | Ecological and Value Ratings

"One day when I was a little boy I made a slingshot. My mother told me to be careful with it and not to kill any animals. But it was a good slingshot and I couldn't keep myself from aiming at birds. My mother looked out the window and saw me just as I had my first success—killing a robin. She called to me and told me to bring the robin inside. Then she plucked its feathers, dressed it and put it into a soup she was making. We ate it and it didn't taste bad. I learned that we're not supposed to waste anything."

—A Menominee elder

OUR RESEARCH WITH hunters partially parallels the studies done with expert fishermen. Initially we asked a sample of Menominee and majority-culture hunters to name the most important plants and animals of the forest. We used these nominations to select twenty-nine animals and thirty-nine plants to be used in a series of rating tasks (see table 13.1). Next, we asked each hunter to indicate his familiarity with each kind by indicating whether he had heard of the kind, could recognize one if he saw it, and whether he had seen one. Informants were also asked to rate the importance of each kind to the forest and its importance to themselves. We also asked for justifications for the latter two ratings, though we didn't push if nothing came immediately to mind.

For the next task we asked hunters to rate the importance of various goals that might be associated with hunting and to give approval or disapproval ratings for twenty-one practices that hunters might engage in. Several weeks later we followed up this interview with another, similar, interview, during which we asked hunters to answer the same questions but this time from the perspective of equally expert hunters from their own community and equally expert hunters from the other community.

Table 13.1   The List of Plants and Animals Used for the Forest
Ecology Studies

Common Name	Scientific Name
Animals	
Bear (black)	Ursus americanus
Beaver	Castor canadensis
Blue jay	Cyanocitta cristata
Bobcat	Lynx rufus
Chipmunk	Tamias striatus
Coyote	Canis latrans
Deer	Ococoileus virginianus
Eagle (bald)	Haliaeetus leucocephalus
Finch (house)	Carpodacus purpureus
Fox (red)	Vulpes fulva
Grouse (ruffed)	Bonasa umbellus
Hawk (red-tailed)	Buteo jamaicensis
Junco (dark-eyed)	Junco hyemalis
Moose	Alces alces
Otter	Lutra canadensis
Owl (great horned)	Bubo virginianus
Partridge (gray)	Perdix perdix
Porcupine	Erethizon dorsatum
Possum (Virginia)	Didelphis marsupialis
Rabbit	Sylvilagus spp.
Raccoon	Procyon lotor
Robin (American)	Turdus migratorius
Skunk (striped)	Mephitis mephitis
Squirrel (red; pine; chikaree)	Sciurus carolinensis
Turkey	Meleagris gallopavo
Turtle (painted)	Chrysemys picta
Wolf (gray, timber)	Canis lupus
Wood duck	Aix sponsa
Woodpecker (downy)	Picoides spp.
Plants	
Alder (red)	Alnus rubra
Basswood	Tilia americana
Bitterroot	Lewisia rediviva
Black spruce	Picea mariana
Blackberry	Rubus spp.
Bloodroot	Sanguinaria canadensis
Blueberry	Vaccinium spp.
Butternut	Juglans cineraria
Cattail	Typha spp.

Table 13.1 Continued

Common Name	Scientific Name
Cedar (yellow)	Thuja spp.
Cherry tree	Prunus serotina
Chokecherry	Prunus virginiana
Cowslip	Caltha palustris
Cranberry	Vaccinium macrocarpum
Dogwood	Cornus spp.
Elderberry	Sambucus canadensis
Elm (American)	Ulmus americana
Fern	Filicineae family
Ginseng	Panax quincefolium
Gooseberry (American)	Ribes spp.
Hemlock (western)	Tsuga heterophylla
Hickory shagbark, true	Carya ovata
Prickly ash	Xanthoxylum americanum
Red maple	Acer rubrum
Red oak	Quercus rubra
Silver maple	Acer saccharinum
Silver poplar	Populus alba
Skunk cabbage	Symplocarpus foetidus
Solomon's seal	Polygonatum biflorum
Sumac (staghorn)	Rhus typhina
Thornapple	Datura stramonium
Trillium	Trillium spp.
White ash	Fraxinus americana
White birch	Betula papyrifera
White oak	Quercus alba
White Pine (whitebark)	Pinus strobus
Wild columbine	Aquilegia canadensis
Wild ginger	Asarum canadense
Witch hazel (American)	Hamamelis virginiana

Source: Authors' compilation.

The two communities were Menominees and majority-culture hunters from the Shawano-area.

Thus, the goals and practices part of the study was exactly analogous to the assessments we did with expert fishermen. Although our expectations were somewhat chastened by the (to us) surprising results with fishermen, we expected that the main outcome would be that majority-culture hunters would be surprised to find out that Menominees have mixed reactions to the practice of shining deer and to hear that the tribe had banned shining. Again we were guilty of underestimating the impact of differing cultural models on cross-group perception.

In addition to assessing familiarity of individuals with these plants and animals we also explored the importance given to these species by each participant. To evaluate familiarity, we asked participants for each of the species in the list to report whether they had "heard of it," whether they were "able to recognize it," or whether they actually "had seen one." Obviously, these responses were not mutually exclusive, since reporting having seen a species includes being able to recognize it and having heard of it as well. In a second step, each participant was asked to rate, on a seven-point scale, the importance of each of these kinds to the forest ("How important is X to the forest?") and to the participant himself ("How important is X to you?"). The questions were intentionally open-ended to avoid setting constraints on the rationales for individuals' importance ratings.

There are at least two good reasons for exploring our participants' familiarity with plants and animals. We were curious to see whether we would find differences in the degree of familiarity with and importance of the plants and nongame animals on the part of people who were avid hunters but not forest experts. Second, previous research (Medin et al. 1997; Ross 2002) has shown that expertise has an impact on how individuals organize their conceptual knowledge and we suspected that it also might influence evaluation of species' importance. Consequently, we have to make sure that any cross-cultural differences are not due to differences in familiarity with these species (see Medin et al. 2002).

We had some misgivings about asking our subjects to rate forest kinds, because we thought that some hunters would argue that every plant and every animal has a role to play and is important. Of course, these responses, too, are informative if there are group differences in their likelihood. Furthermore, we were interested in hearing informants' reasons for their evaluations. Finally, we wanted to examine the relationship between importance-to-self and importance-to-forest ratings. If importance to self is based on personal goals, it may conflict with or be uncorrelated with importance to forest. Alternatively, if a hunter values the health of the forest itself, then there may be a close correspondence between the ratings.

We also wished to see whether there is a consensus in these ratings both within and across groups. Between-group differences in notions of importance may fuel intergroup conflict. A study we did on goodness of example ratings with Menominee and majority-culture fishermen (Burnett et al. 2005) led us to expect that Menominee hunters would give higher ratings on average than majority-culture hunters and that they would be more likely to argue that every kind is important and has a role to play. Similarly, we expected majority-culture hunters to be more likely to take an evaluative stance and provide negative comments about particular kinds, though we thought that Menominee hunters might be likely to make negative comments about nonnative species.

We were more interested in understanding the meaning participants of each group give to these species than in numerical differences between Menominee and majority-culture hunters' values.

GENERAL RESULTS

Every expert interviewed reported having heard about all the animals in the list except for the junco. On average, majority-culture hunters were twice as likely (76 percent) to report having heard of the junco as Menominee (38 percent).[1] All the experts also reported being able to recognize all the animal kinds. In addition, all hunters reported having seen most of the animals of the list except for the junco, which more majority-culture hunters (64 percent) report to having seen than Menominee hunters (33 percent).[2] It is possible that some Menominee are familiar with the junco but have a different name for it (we recently learned that it is also known as the snowbird), but we suspect that this difference arises because the junco is more likely to be found along forest edges and in more open spaces. The Menominee reservation has less of this sort of habitat than do the surrounding counties, including Shawano County.

As we expected, most of our informants also reported having heard of most of the plants (more than 75 percent of the plants across groups) in our set. For most of the remaining plants, lack of familiarity is more or less equally spread across members of the two groups. The only exception is cowslip. Significantly more majority-culture hunters (86 percent) reported having heard of the cowslip than Menominee (53 percent).[3] Menominee hunters might well know cowslip by a different name, since it is also known as marsh marigold and subsequent to this study we have heard some Menominee use this term.

Hunters found the plants to be more difficult to recognize than the animals. We found group differences for only three plants: Majority-culture hunters were more likely (86 percent) to recognize cowslip than Menominee hunters (53 percent).[4] Menominee hunters were more likely (84 percent) than majority-culture hunters (40 percent) to recognize bitterroot, and basswood (Menominee: 100 percent; majority-culture: 73 percent).[5] While Menominee and majority-culture hunters were equally likely to report having heard of these two plants, Menominee were more likely to report recognizing them. Menominee reported using bitterroot for medi-

cal purposes, whereas majority-culture hunters did not report any specific use for it. With respect to basswood, hunters from both groups described the tree as a lumber of medium value that can be used for wood-
carving. Menominee have additional traditional uses: they use the bark
of this tree to make baskets and the shell of their wigwams. Although
basket making is still alive on the reservation, wigwams are mainly built
to instruct the youth in Menominee traditions. Thus these species appear
to be culturally more salient for Menominee than for majority-culture
hunters.

Finally, all and only individuals who reported being able to recognize
a plant reported having seen the plant.

PLANTS: RESULTS OF IMPORTANCE RATING

We decided to focus on the plants and animals for which at least 65 percent of the hunters in each group indicated familiarity. Overall there
were no reliable group differences in familiarity with the kinds that we
employed.

We excluded several Menominee from the analyses for the lack of
variance within their ratings. All of them gave the highest possible importance ratings to everything.[6] Although we cannot include these responses in our analyses, these data should be considered as informative.
This response pattern marks a worldview in which all things are interdependent and consequently, equally important. This is also reflected in
the justifications these participants gave for their ratings. Another motivation for high ratings is the presence of multiple goals that are widely
distributed across kinds. Such a perspective has often been described for
Native Americans, yet so far little experimental evidence has been provided linking this perspective to actual value judgments (see Atran et al.
2005 for an exception).[7]

By way of contrast, approaching nature from a goal-orientation perspective should lead to a clear ranking of species with respect to their importance. No majority-culture hunters reported the same importance ratings for all species, plants and animals. Our research in Mesoamerica has
revealed parallel findings. Older Lacandón Maya subscribe to a worldview in which each species has a designated place and role, a perspective
that differs significantly from that of younger adults in the community
(Ross 2002). Similarly, in Guatemala only the native Itza' Maya seem to
subscribe to multiple value systems with respect to plants, compared to
migrant Maya and Ladinos, who seem to evaluate plants with the measuring stick of cash value and utility (Atran et al. 2002).

The mean ratings for importance of various plants to the forest and to self for each group are summarized in tables 13.2 and 13.3. For all consensus analyses we excluded the responses of the Menominee hunters who gave uniformly high ratings to everything, since they will show zero correlation with other raters. With respect to plants, we found neither within- nor cross-group consensus either on ratings of importance to the forest or for importance to self. Being an expert hunter does not necessarily lead to coherent value judgments of plants, although the situation might be different for animals. This view is somewhat supported by the fact that participants were less familiar with plants than animals.

The lack of consensus does not allow us to aggregate the data within or across groups and one should be cautious about generalizations concerning group differences. Nevertheless, some specific cross-group differences are of interest. Menominee hunters gave higher ratings for plants that they saw as important to the forest. This overall difference is significant (means of 5.3 and 4.5, respectively).[8] Since these analyses do not include the Menominee who gave the highest ratings for every plant, the actual difference is even larger. This main effect was accompanied by a moderately high correlation between Menominee and majority-culture ratings of plants ($Rxy = 0.66$, $p < .01$). Both groups tended to give trees higher ratings than other plants.

Essentially the same pattern was observed for ratings of importance to the self (though in one case there was a slight reversal and in a few other cases the difference in rating was quite small). Again, this main effect on ratings is statistically reliable (means of 5.2 versus 4.1).[9] The correlation between overall Menominee and majority-culture ratings was again moderately high ($Rxy = .74$, $p < .01$), and once again trees tended to receive higher ratings than other plants.

One challenge in this sort of research is to determine whether the differences observed in ratings reflect genuine differences in value or merely different interpretations of the scale—if, say, a majority-culture 5 corresponds to a level that Menominee hunters call 6. One way to address this question is to look at the justifications for answers. Two observations suggest that the differences are likely real. First of all, nine of the seventeen Menominee hunters justified their choices with general statements such as that every plant has some role or part to play, something like "I don't know what it does but everything has a job to do." None of the majority-culture hunters provided this type of justification.[10]

A second difference arose from justifications for importance-to-self ratings. Menominee hunters mentioned more uses or sources of value for both plants and animals than did the majority-culture hunters. There was a reliable difference (by a chi-square test) for use of plant material, including medicinal uses of plants, and for justifications in terms of reli-

Table 13.2   Ratings of the Importance of Plants to the Forest

	Menominee	Majority Culture
White oak	6.5	6.1
Cedar	6.3	5.5
White pine	6.3	4.6
Fern	5.3	4.4
Hemlock	5.8	4.2
Cherry tree	5.7	4.3
Witch hazel[a]	4.7	4.0
Ginseng	5.8	3.3
Thornapple	5.4	4.6
Chokecherry	6.0	4.7
Elm	5.6	3.3
White birch	5.7	3.8
Popple or Poplar	5.6	4.8
Gooseberry[a]	4.1	3.9
Blackberry	6.3	5.0
Bitterroot[a]	5.8	1.0
Skunk cabbage[a]	4.8	2.4
Solomon's seal[a]	4.7	1.5
Blueberry	5.3	4.7
Cranberry	5.6	4.3
Alder	4.8	4.3
Hickory	5.6	4.2
Butternut	5.7	4.5
Sumac	4.5	2.8
Wild ginger[a]	5.5	1.7
White ash	6.0	3.9
Black spruce[a]	5.1	4.3
Dogwood[a]	5.0	2.6
Red maple	5.6	4.2
Elderberry[a]	5.6	3.9
Basswood	5.6	3.6
Cowslip	4.4	2.5
Bloodroot[a]	5.4	2.0
Trillium	4.9	4.1
Prickly ash[a]	4.9	3.6
Wild columbine[a]	3.0	2.8
Cattail	5.6	4.4
Silver maple	5.3	4.1
Red oak	6.1	6.0

Source: Authors' compilation.
[a]Fewer than 75 percent of hunters knew these plants.

Table 13.3   Ratings of the Importance of Plants to Self

	Menominee	Majority Culture
White oak	6.0	6.0
Cedar	6.2	4.9
White pine	6.6	5.1
Fern	4.6	3.6
Hemlock	5.4	3.9
Cherry tree	5.5	4.3
Witch hazel[a]	4.8	3.8
Ginseng	5.8	4.4
Thornapple	4.4	2.9
Chokecherry	5.0	3.2
Elm	5.4	3.1
White birch	5.8	4.2
Popple or Poplar	5.5	4.4
Gooseberry[a]	4.0	2.9
Blackberry	6.4	5.2
Bitterroot[a]	6.1	2.7
Skunk cabbage[a]	3.7	2.7
Solomon's seal[a]	4.7	1.5
Blueberry	5.4	4.7
Cranberry	5.3	5.3
Alder	4.0	2.6
Hickory	5.6	4.7
Butternut	5.6	4.6
Sumac	4.3	2.1
Wild ginger[a]	4.6	2.2
White ash	5.6	4.4
Black spruce[a]	4.6	3.6
Dogwood[a]	2.9	2.1
Red maple	6.0	4.6
Elderberry[a]	3.9	3.8
Basswood	4.9	3.3
Cowslip	3.7	2.8
Bloodroot[a]	4.8	2.0
Trillium	4.5	4.0
Prickly ash[a]	4.1	2.0
Wild columbine[a]	2.7	2.5
Cattail	3.7	3.4
Silver maple	4.6	4.2
Red oak	5.7	5.5

Source: Authors' compilation.
[a]Fewer than 75 percent of hunters knew these plants.

gious, cultural, or symbolic value, including clan relevance of animals. A third difference in the importance-to-self ratings was that several Menominee hunters mentioned that if something is important to the forest then it is important to them.

Looking in closer detail at the importance to the forest ratings, the differences in ratings for white pine, hemlock, ginseng, elm, white birch and blackberry were all reliable, with Menominee hunters giving higher rating in every case. For importance-to-self ratings, cedar, white pine, hemlock, chokecherry, elm, white birch, blackberry, sumac and red maple all yielded reliably higher ratings for Menominee than for majority-culture hunters.

One guess is that these differences are mediated by particular cultural and ecological factors. For example, hemlock is culturally significant, is abundant on the reservation, and makes a good perch for birds. White pine is an economically important species and is historically significant for the Menominee. Cedar is culturally significant and provides habitat for deer. Elm dies readily and serves both as a nurse log for animals and as firewood for Menominee. Blackberries are an important source of food for people and animals alike, and the reservation has lots of them. White birch was used in the past for canoes and is still used in basketry. Ginseng is collected as a medicinal plant and is either used or sold. Sumac is used by Menominees in pipes, for fishing poles, and as a medicine. Chokecherries are used in jams. Red maple is an excellent wood for furniture and floors and the tree is also a source for maple syrup and sugar candy. Overall, the forest provides much more to Menominee than just a background habitat for game.

In contrast, majority-culture hunters were more likely than Menominee hunters to justify their lower ratings by saying that a plant either has little use or that they can't think of a use to themselves (for bitterroot, skunk cabbage, black spruce, and chokecherry) or to the forest (for ginseng, bitterroot, cranberry, hickory, white ash, and basswood). It is not clear whether this reflects a lack of knowledge or a more narrow definition of utility, and we suspect that both factors are operating. Majority-culture hunters were also almost twice as likely as Menominee to describe a plant in negative terms, but this difference fell short of statistical significance.

Guided by the above examples, our impression is that the Menominee perspective on the forest is broader and more personal than the majority-culture perspective. In other work (partially described earlier), where we have interviewed Menominee and majority-culture parents, we also find that Menominee take a more personal perspective in the sense that they tend to say "I [we] use X" rather than "X is used for" and are more likely to use concrete rather than abstract descriptors in talking about activities and goals associated with nature (see Bang et al. 2005 for details).

Importance-to-Self versus Importance-to-Forest Ratings

Are the same plants that are important to the forest also important to the self? For this analysis we correlated the two ratings given by each individual. As the comparison is done on an individual level no consensus is needed as formal justification for this procedure. On average the same correlation is found for both Menominee and majority-culture hunters (r = .63), indicating that for both groups the ratings are closely related. This does not come as a surprise. We often heard justifications such as, "Plant X is important to me because it offers food to animals."

IMPORTANCE OF ANIMALS RATINGS

The mean ratings of the importance of various animals to the forest and to the self are given in tables 13.4 and 13.5, respectively. They show the same pattern as rating of plants: Menominee hunters consistently give higher ratings for both importance to the self (mean = 4.5 versus 3.7 for majority-culture hunters) and importance to the forest (mean = 4.9 versus 3.7 for majority-culture hunters).[11]

Importance-to-Self Ratings

We conducted a consensus analysis to examine within- and across-group similarities and differences in detail. There was overall cross-group consensus in importance-to-self ratings.[12] The majority-culture hunters showed higher first-factor scores than did Menominee hunters, suggesting that majority-culture hunters were less variable in their ratings and thus had a greater influence on the overall consensus. Evaluation schemes that involved multiple uses, such as the Menominee hunters', should lead to lower agreement. Separate analyses for each group confirm this pattern,[13] and residual analysis of the overall data show that Menominee hunters have reliably greater within-group than cross-group residual agreement.[14]

On average game animals receive higher ratings than nongame animals from both Menominee (5.1 and 4.1 respectively)[15] and majority-culture hunters (4.7 and 3.2, respectively).[16] Menominee hunters rated nongame animals significantly higher than majority-culture hunters.[17] These data support the hypotheses that, in contrast to majority-culture hunters, Menominee use multiple perspectives to evaluate animals.

Table 13.4   Ratings of the Importance of Animals to the Self

	Menominee	Majority Culture
Coyote	4.8	3.2
Fox	4.5	3.5
Deer	6.6	6.6
Bobcat	4.9	3.5
Wolf	5.0	3.3
Bear	6.3	5.1
Raccoon	3.9	2.4
Opossum	2.6	1.3
Mouse	3.0	1.8
Partridge	5.6	5.5
Rabbit	4.9	4.3
Squirrel	4.3	3.8
Grouse	5.6	5.3
Beaver	4.9	2.9
Eagle	6.4	5.7
Hawk	5.3	4.3
Turkey	5.0	5.8
Chipmunk	3.6	2.9
Otter	5.1	3.7
Porcupine	4.0	1.8
Woodpecker	4.6	3.4
Owl	4.6	3.9
Turtle	4.9	2.6
Bluejay	4.2	3.2
Robin	4.1	4.6
Skunk	2.8	1.8
Wood duck	4.6	5.3
Finch	4.4	3.8
Junco	4.7	3.1

Source: Authors' compilation.

Menominee hunters gave reliably higher ratings than majority-culture hunters for coyote, wolf, bear, raccoon, opossum, beaver, otter, porcupine, and turtle. These differences appear to derive from a pattern of not strongly discounting any species—again, everything has a role to play—and using broad concepts of significance and utility. The only two kinds that got ratings from the Menominee lower than 3.0 were skunk and opossum, the latter being a nonnative species that many consider to be a nuisance. Some elders say that the meat of skunks is tasty and that at one

Table 13.5   Ratings of the Importance of Animals to the Forest

	Menominee	Majority Culture
Coyote	5.6	4.3
Fox	5.1	4.4
Deer	6.1	4.8
Bobcat	5.7	3.8
Wolf	5.6	4.2
Bear	5.8	4.6
Raccoon	4.8	3.3
Opossum	3.1	1.8
Mouse	4.6	3.5
Partridge	5.5	4.6
Rabbit	5.5	4.1
Squirrel	5.4	4.6
Grouse	5.5	4.6
Beaver	4.7	3.7
Eagle	6.1	5.0
Hawk	5.6	4.6
Turkey	4.4	4.2
Chipmunk	4.2	3.4
Otter	5.2	3.1
Porcupine	4.1	2.2
Woodpecker	5.4	4.0
Owl	5.1	4.6
Turtle	4.4	2.8
Bluejay	4.5	2.7
Robin	4.6	3.2
Skunk	3.8	2.6
Wood duck	4.5	4.0
Finch	4.4	3.5
Junco[a]	5.25	2.9

Source: Authors' compilation.
[a]Fewer than 75 percent of hunters recognized these animals.

time oil from the skunk was used to treat earaches in babies. This aspect of Menominee tradition appears to have been lost.

Majority-culture hunters gave low ratings for skunk and opossum and also for raccoon, beaver, porcupine, turtle, woodpecker, chipmunk, and mouse. The higher Menominee ratings also appear to have been influenced by utility and cultural significance. Wolf and bear are Menominee clans and turtle is a major subclan. Porcupines' quills are still used for ornamental quillwork and parts of otter and beaver are used in making tribal regalia. Turtles and bears are a source of food and bear parts have a number of uses, including medicinal. In earlier times every mammal whose pelt was taken was also a source of food.

Importance-to-Forest Ratings

If every animal is important to the forest, then it is not clear that we should expect to see a consensus on ratings of relative importance. Indeed, we failed to find either cross-group or within-group consensus.[18] As a result, any group differences must be interpreted with caution as not reflecting a broad consensus.

At a finer level of detail Menominee hunters gave a somewhat low rating only for the nonnative opossum. Majority-culture hunters gave as low or lower ratings to opossum, otter, porcupine, turtle, junco, robin, and skunk. Menominee hunters gave reliably higher ratings to coyote, deer, bobcat, wolf, bear, raccoon, rabbit, otter, porcupine, turtle, and bluejay. There may be a variety of reasons underlying these differences and we will only offer an illustration. A common response among almost all majority-culture hunters and more than a few Menominee was to rate the porcupine as not being important to the forest and to note that they mainly are destructive because of their habit of girdling trees. But some Menominee gave the porcupine a higher rating and suggested that they have a positive impact. For example, one hunter said that porcupines help because they open up the forest and allow smaller plants to grow, which in turn provides ground cover that helps the forest trees maintain moisture.

Comparison of Importance-to-Self and Importance-to-Forest Ratings

Both Menominee and majority-culture hunters show significant correlations between importance ratings for animals with respect to the self and to the forest. For the Menominee individuals these correlations range from .26 up to .92, with an average of .65. For majority-culture people the range is from .19 to .86, with an average of .55. The average difference between the two groups is not significant.

There are three distinct potential reasons for this correlation between importance-to-self and importance-to-forest ratings. First, individuals draw on the importance for the self when evaluating the importance of a species for the forest. Second, individuals draw on the importance for forest when evaluating the importance for the self, and third, the animals that are important for the forest are also important for individuals. We don't know of any way to distinguish between these explanations on the basis of importance ratings per se. Ecosystems are so complicated that it's not straightforward to determine what the "correct answers" are. Therefore, our best source of information consists of justifications. Here we find that Menominee hunters often explain their ratings for an animal's importance to self in terms of the importance of these animals within the wider system. If majority-culture hunters entertained similar thoughts for animals, they certainly did not appear in their justifications.

SUMMARY AND CONCLUSIONS

In many respects our findings on importance ratings are striking. Although members of both groups are more or less equally familiar with the plants and animals used in the tasks, there is a large main effect of cultural group in all of the ratings. Menominee hunters consistently give higher overall ratings. There are also some interactions of kinds with groups. For example, in the case of the importance of animals to the self, the cultural differences only reach statistical reliability for nongame animals as a group, but not for game animals. This is consistent with majority-culture hunters' focusing on and valuing game animals.

The differences are strikingly large and persistent. It appears that they derive from both an important abstract principle and a variety of species-specific considerations. The abstract principle that many Menominee expressed is that every kind has a functional role in the life of the forest. Hence, their default assumption was that a plant or animal was important to the forest. This orientation toward the forest also carried over into importance-to-self ratings where a fair number of Menominee mentioned that if some plant or animal is important to the forest, then it is important to them.

The species-specific considerations derive from the fact that the forest means much more to Menominee hunters than the game that is part of it. Many biological kinds have significance for Menominee because of their cultural significance (animals that correspond to clans), religious significance (cedar), medicinal value (ginseng), food value (blackberry) or other forms of utility and meaning (materials used for tying flies, for creating regalia, and so forth).

Do these observations tell us anything about intergroup conflict? Both groups seemed to be more focused on animals than on plants, and majority-culture hunters seem to be more focused on game than nongame animals. This difference could potentially lead to conflict over forest management, as Menominee hunters are engaged with a wider range of uses and broader valuation in general. We suspect, however, that these modest differences pale by comparison with nonhunters who spend much less time in the woods and who may be much more focused on single species.

Overall, both groups have a rich understanding of the forest, but their overall similarities also help highlight the differences. Although we do not see factors that lead inevitably to intergroup conflict, the broader orientation of Menominee hunters at both an abstract and concrete level suggests that Menominees would be more likely to seek out a holistic forest-management plan that focuses on the overall health of the forest rather than a plan that focuses on the management of one or two important species, such as "quality deer management," which reduces attention to just a few or even a single species for the specific goal of generating trophy bucks.

There is a clear parallel between the shift from fishing for food to fishing as a competitive sport and from hunting for food to hunting for the biggest bucks. Even if there had not been a shift in hunting orientation for majority-culture hunters, there would be an increasing mismatch between their traditional goals and proper forest management. A half century ago, when deer were much less plentiful, a "bucks only" season made perfect sense as a means to maintain or increase the herd. But at present, where carrying capacity is pushed to the limit and beyond, this same strategy is completely counterproductive, as does need to be taken to control herd size. Overpopulation leads deer to be destructive of forest plants and provides opportunities for disease to spread.

The tendency to focus on trophies or the adoption of a competitive orientation may be symptomatic of broader changes in our society, but these broader changes are beyond the scope of this book. Our current focus is on whether these shifts have resulted in changes in goals, values, and attitudes and whether these changes have in turn been associated with intergroup conflict over resource management. The majority-culture focus on big bucks includes the potential for group conflict, as it calls for focused attention not just on one species but on a specific subpopulation of this species.

Chapter Fourteen | Reported
and Perceived
Hunting Values

"If it's brown, take it down."
—A majority-culture hunter

IN THE PREVIOUS chapter we looked at the ways Menominee and major-ity-culture hunters rate the importance to themselves and to the forest of certain species. We found general agreement coupled with modest group differences. This is essentially the same result as we reported for the fish experts. As with the fish experts, however, we were not only interested in how individuals value specific practices, but also the values they pre-dict for members of their own group and members of the other group.

In this chapter we shall examine the extent to which the two groups' orientations are reflected in goals, values, and attitudes toward various hunting practices. We expected that different values and meanings attached to specific species and practices, along with general differences in episte-mological frameworks (overall approaches to nature and the relation of humans to it), would lead to differences in how each group perceived the other group.

MENOMINEE AND MAJORITY-CULTURE VALUES
AND GOALS

To test this idea, we carried out two sets of interviews with our hunter informants, separated by a minimum of several weeks. In the first inter-view we asked participants to answer a set of questions about the hunt-ing behaviors listed here.

161

Hunt for biggest buck

Hunting deer by "shining"

Hunting deer with bow and arrow

Baiting deer for gun hunting

Baiting deer for bow hunting

Hunting deer for food

Hunting bear for food

Baiting bear

Hunting with dogs for bear

Hunting with dogs for deer

Shooting wolves

Hunting turkey for food

Shooting raccoons or squirrels for fun

Exceeding deer limit in order to feed family

Giving away game

Selling deer

Borrowing deer tag

Leave beaver meat and take only the pelt

Leave a downed doe

Leave bear meat and take only the pelt

Take only the tenderloin from a downed deer

The questions targeted topics that were relevant to both Menominee and majority-culture hunters. In the second interview we posed the same questions again but asked hunters how equally expert hunters in their own community would answer them and then how equally expert hunters in the other community would answer them. Finally, we showed each person the average ratings from the initial interview for each of the two groups.

When we designed this pair of studies we thought the big news for white hunters would be that Menominees disapproved of shining and

Table 14.1   Average of Individual Goal Rankings of Menominee (M) and Majority-Culture (MC) Hunters (Lower Numbers Indicate Greater Importance)

	M	MC
Close to nature	4.3	3.0
Outsmart game	4.1	4.0
Source of food	3.4	5.6
Trophy	4.9	4.8
Get away from it all	4.8	3.1
Pass on to future	4.1	3.2
Doing as ancestors did	4.4	4.3

Source: Authors' compilation.

had banned the practice. Of course, with the fishing-attitude results in hand, we were prepared to see additional stereotyping. We did. First, however, let's look at some overall numbers.

Goals

Importance ratings for seven potential goals associated with hunting were based on responses of fourteen majority-culture and thirteen Menominee hunters. These goals and the mean rankings for both groups of hunters are shown in table 14.1 (lower numbers correspond to greater importance). For both groups the most important goal was hunting as a means of being close to nature. For Menominees, hunting to get a trophy-sized buck was the least important goal (their ratings are close to neutral). For majority-culture hunters the least important goal was hunting as a source of food.

Across-group differences were statistically reliable for two of the goals. Hunting as a source of food is more important for Menominee hunters than for majority-culture hunters, as we had anticipated.[1] The other main difference is that majority-culture hunters gave higher priority to hunting as a way to "get away from it all."[2] A common response among Menominee hunters was that they don't need to get away from it all, because they already are away from it all by virtue of living in the Menominee forest. The difference in orientation toward trophy hunting was in the predicted direction but it was not reliable.

Values and Attitudes Toward Hunting Practices

In this part of the study we asked the same participants for their approval or disapproval rating of the twenty-one practices associated with

Table 14.2   Mean Approval Ratings of Menominee
and Majority-Culture Hunters for the Hunting Practices
(Larger Numbers Indicate Greater Approval)

	Menominee	Majority Culture
Biggest buck	3.3	4.2
"Shining" deer	2.3	1.2
Bow for deer	6.5	6.7
Bait deer for gun	3.7	3.6
Bait deer for bow	4.7	4.0
Deer for food	6.7	5.9
Bear for food	5.2	4.6
Bait bear	4.0	5.9
Dogs for bear	4.5	4.0
Dogs for deer	5.4	1.7
Shoot wolves	1.8	3.6
Turkey for food	6.4	5.8
Raccoons or squirrels for fun	1.5	3.4
Exceed limit for family	3.8	4.5
Give away game	4.3	4.1
Selling deer	1.4	1.9
Borrow tag	2.7	3.6
Leave beaver meat	4.3	4.4
Leave downed doe	1.1	1.1
Leave bear meat	1.1	1.3
Tenderloin only	1.0	1.0

Source: Authors' compilation.

hunting and listed earlier (the results are summarized in table 14.2). Generally, if members of one group approve or disapprove of a practice so does the other group, and mean ratings of the two groups correlate +.77, indicating substantial agreement.

A consensus analysis revealed strong consensus[3] coupled with residual group differences represented in reliable differences on the second factor.[4] In short, there is an overall consensus coupled with clear group differences. The largest difference is that Menominees approve of using dogs for hunting deer and majority-culture hunters disapprove of it; this practice is illegal off the reservation. Another difference is that Menominee disapprove of shooting raccoons and squirrels for fun or shooting wolves, an issue on which majority-culture hunters are relatively neutral. Finally, Menominee hunters have more mixed feelings about using bait for hunting bear than do majority-culture hunters. Several of our Menominee informants belong to the bear clan, and for some of them this means that they cannot kill a bear. (As noted earlier, other members of the bear clan have been taught that they can hunt bear if they use all the parts.) Statistical tests support essentially all of these observations.[5]

The overall picture with respect to both goals and attitudes toward practices is one of substantial overall agreement, coupled with some modest group differences. Both groups condemn shining deer, leaving a doe that has been shot, taking a bear hide and leaving the meat, selling deer, and shooting a deer and taking only the tenderloin. They are in general agreement on methods of hunting, though Menominee are less approving of using bait for bears and more approving of using dogs in deer hunting. Menominee hunt for food and they strongly disapprove of shooting something just for the fun of it. Majority-culture hunters are divided on the status of wolves but Menominee disapprove of killing wolves (wolf is one of the five main Menominee clans).

PREDICTING OWN-GROUP AND OTHER-GROUP PERCEPTIONS

Does this broad agreement between the groups carry over into the perceptions each person has of his own group and members of the other group? The prediction data are based on fifteen Menominee and fourteen majority-culture hunters. There was less than a 50 percent overlap between the participants who did the individual ratings and the sample that made predictions about their own and the other group. In part this reflected our strategy of having a broad sample and in part it reflected the practical challenge of fitting interviews into people's schedules—especially during hunting season.

In the first set of analyses we asked how well members of each group perceive their own group and in a second we ask how well members of one group perceive the values of the other group. Our standard of accuracy is the mean ratings by individual group members that we just covered in the first part of this chapter.

How Accurate Are Predictions?

One could argue that individual ratings are self-serving and do not reflect true values or behaviors. Ideally, there would be some way of "groundtruthing," where we follow each hunter to see if they practice what they preach. In the present case this isn't practical and we have to fall back on a somewhat weaker argument. Partial groundtruthing is achieved by comparing the health of the Menominee and the Shawano County forests and assuming that the collective behavior of hunters in

Menominee versus Shawano County is a proxy for the behavior of our sample. Obviously this is unfair, since our experienced hunters might behave according to their values but other hunters might undermine the resources.

The Menominee are world-famous for their sustainable-forestry practices, but for now we'll just focus on the game animal receiving the greatest attention by hunters, deer. As we mentioned earlier, the Menominee forest has a carrying capacity of eight to twelve deer—perhaps up to fifteen—per square mile, and recent Menominee Conservation Department estimates are right in this range. For 2001 to 2002 the overwintering goal for Shawano County set by WDNR was twenty-five deer per square mile compared to an estimated actual population of forty deer per square mile. So there is no evidence that the Menominee "kill all their deer," and there is some evidence of a deer overpopulation problem in Shawano County.

Furthermore, there is no particular reason for hunters to distort their values, and given the seriousness with which they took the task, if they were deliberately lying, they deserve an acting award. In almost every case the expressed values appeared to be heartfelt and often were accompanied by stories about their own and others' behaviors. Similarly, several experts reported values and behaviors for themselves that are even illegal, indicating their sincerity and their assumption of our sincerity— our long-term commitment in the area provided us with good rapport in the communities. As a further check, if individual ratings agree with ratings that hunters make for other members of their group, we at least have evidence of reliability.

There is some literature that we mentioned before, suggesting that people may see their own group as more extreme (or with stronger or weaker values) than they themselves are. So people stereotyping their own group may lead to some disagreement between individual and own-group ratings. The main focus of the analyses, however, was on the question of how well each group's predictions of the other group correspond to reality. Reality is defined as the average of the individual ratings of each group.

Goal Predictions

Since we did not find a consensus on individually reported goals, we thought it unlikely that we would find a consensus on predictions of goals. We were right. Setting aside the fact that there is no combined consensus, there nonetheless are some patterns of differences that are statistically reliable. The overall goal-prediction data are summarized in table

Table 14.3   Goal Rankings Predicted by the Two Samples of Hunters for One's Own Community (Lower Numbers Correspond to Greater Importance)

	M-Mª	Miᵉ	MC-Mᵇ	MC-MCᶜ	MCiᵉ	M-MCᵈ
Close to nature	3.7	2.3	3.7	3.2	3.0	4.7
Outsmart game	4.3	4.1	4.1	3.8	4.0	4.1
Source of food	1.9	3.4	3.3	4.8	5.6	3.7
Trophy	5.1	4.9	4.0	4.7	4.8	3.1
Get away from it all	5.3	4.8	4.3	2.6	3.1	3.1
Pass on to future	3.6	4.1	3.9	3.2	3.2	5.0
Doing as ancestors did	4.1	4.4	3.6	4.6	4.3	5.3

Source: Authors' compilation.
ªMenominee hunters' predictions of own-group responses.
ᵇMajority-culture hunters' predictions of Menominee responses.
ᶜMajority-culture hunters' predictions of own-group responses.
ᵈMenominee hunters' predictions of majority-hunters' responses.
ᵉMi and MCi = mean individual rankings from table 14.2.

14.3 (individual mean rankings are repeated for ease of comparison; lower numbers represent greater importance). Comparing Menominee individual ratings with Menominee predictions we find that Menominee hunters think that being close to nature is less important for their peers (higher rank) than it actually is (average: 3.7 versus 2.3).[6] Majority-culture hunter predictions of Menominee rankings show this same underestimation.[7] There is also a modest tendency for Menominees to think that food as a goal is more important to their peers than it actually is (average: 1.9 versus 3.4).[8] Note, however, that individual Menominee ratings of the importance of hunting for food are substantially higher than individual majority-culture ratings of hunting for food.

We also did the corresponding combined analysis of majority-culture-hunter self-reports, majority-culture predictions for majority-culture hunters, and Menominee-hunter predictions for majority-culture hunters. In neither the overall analysis nor for any pair of ratings do we find evidence of a consensus. We then compared rankings of specific goals across data sets. There were no significant differences between majority-culture individual ratings and majority-culture predictions. Menominee predictions departed reliably from majority-culture individual ratings in several respects. First, Menominees predict that hunting as a way of being close to nature is a less important (higher number) goal for majority hunters than majority-culture hunters actually report (average: 4.7 versus 3.0).[9] Second, Menominees predict that hunting for food is more important than individual majority-culture hunter ratings reveal (average: 3.7 versus 5.6).[10] Third, Menominees assign a higher importance to hunting for a trophy buck to majority-culture hunters than majority-culture hunters report (average: 3.1 versus 4.8).[11] The first and third items give evidence of negative stereotyping but the second item suggests a type of positive stereotyping.

Thus, we find some modest signs of stereotyping. However, predictions on goal rankings should not be given too much weight in the face of an overall lack of consensus. The specific values and attitudes toward practices are considerably more informative.

Value Predictions

Table 14.4 shows the mean estimates for one's own group and for the other group (individual means from table 14.2 are included for ease of comparison). To the extent that each group accurately perceives its own group's values, the estimates for one's group should agree with the individual means. In the same way, cross-group accuracy is measured by, first, the agreement between majority-culture hunters' predictions for Menominee hunters and the Menominees individual ratings and, second, the agreement between Menominee hunters' predictions for majority-culture hunters and the majority-culture hunters' individual means.

The first thing to note is that members of each group are remarkably accurate at perceiving the values of their own group. For Menominee participants there are only two questions that lead to a difference between predictions and individual means of more than one rating point. Menominee hunters thought that individual hunters would be more approving of borrowing or using another person's deer tag than they actually are and they thought their fellow hunters would be more disapproving of taking a beaver pelt and leaving the meat than individual ratings suggest. Thus, there is little evidence of Menominee participants' self-stereotyping or any tendency to see their own group as more extreme or more or less moral than they themselves are.

Majority-culture hunters are at least as accurate at predicting their own-group individual ratings. The largest discrepancy was .90 of a rating point, revealing a tendency to think that other hunters would be more disapproving of someone's taking more than his limit to feed his family than the individual ratings reveal. Even taking smaller differences seriously reveals no pattern of seeing one's own group as more extreme than oneself.

By chance alone one would expect that forty-two comparisons should

Table 14.4   Approval Ratings Predicted by the Menominee (M) and Majority-Culture (MC) Hunters for Twenty-One Hunting Practices (Larger Numbers Indicate Greater Approval)

Hunting Practice	M-M[a]	Mi[e]	MC-M[b]	MC-MC[c]	MCi[e]	M-MC[d]
Biggest buck	3.2	3.3	4.7	4.6	4.2	5.9
Shining deer	2.7	2.3	5.6	1.1	1.2	1.7
Bow for deer	6.3	6.5	4.5	6.3	6.7	6.7
Bait deer for gun	4.2	3.7	5.2	3.8	3.6	5.5
Bait deer for bow	4.7	4.7	5.4	4.7	4.0	5.8
Deer for food	6.9	6.7	6.3	5.9	5.9	5.1
Bear for food	5.3	5.2	5.6	4.1	4.6	4.0
Bait bear	4.3	4.0	6.1	6.5	5.9	4.8
Dogs for bear	3.8	4.5	6.6	4.4	4.0	4.7
Dogs for deer	4.9	5.4	6.4	1.5	1.7	1.7
Shoot wolves	1.5	1.8	4.6	3.4	3.6	2.5
Turkey for food	6.3	6.4	5.5	6.0	5.8	6.0
Raccoons or squirrels for fun	2.3	1.5	4.4	3.2	3.4	4.1
Exceed limit for family	4.2	3.8	6.3	3.6	4.5	3.7
Give away game	4.1	4.3	4.2	3.8	4.1	3.5
Selling deer	1.8	1.4	4.6	1.4	1.9	2.3
Borrow tag	4.0	2.7	5.6	4.1	3.6	4.9
Leave beaver meat	2.9	4.3	4.4	4.6	4.4	5.0
Leave downed doe	1.1	1.1	3.4	1.1	1.1	3.1
Leave bear meat	1.0	1.1	2.7	1.4	1.3	2.9
Tenderloin only	1.1	1.0	2.5	1.1	1.0	2.7

Source: Authors' compilation.
[a]Menominee hunters' predictions of own-group responses.
[b]Majority-culture hunters' predictions of Menominee responses.
[c]Majority-culture hunters' predictions of own-group responses.
[d]Menominee hunters' predictions of majority-culture hunters' responses.
[e]Mi and MCi = mean individual ratings from table 14.2.

yield roughly two statistically reliable differences. Hunters seem to have a very accurate view of the values of their own group.

The same cannot be said for predictions concerning the values of members of the other group. First consider majority-culture hunters' predictions of Menominee values. The predictions and individual means differ by at least one rating point for no less than fifteen of the twenty-one items and differ by two or more rating points for ten of the probes. Menominee predictions of majority-culture individual ratings differ by at least one rating point for nine items and by two or more points for one question. Although neither group is very accurate, Menominee hunters estimate majority-culture hunters' values considerably more accurately than majority-culture hunters estimate Menominee values.

Let's turn to more specific differences. We start with perceptions of majority-culture hunters. There are six cases where Menominee hunters show stereotyping with respect to their majority-culture peers: going for the biggest buck, baiting deer for gun hunting, baiting deer for bow hunting, shooting a doe and leaving it on the ground, shooting a bear for its fur and leaving the meat, and taking only the tenderloin from a deer and leaving the rest of the meat.[12] Each of these mispredictions is in the direction of Menominee hunters' stereotyping majority-culture hunters as being trophy-oriented, being willing to use bait to get these game animals, and not being interested in the meat per se.

How do majority-culture hunters perceive Menominee hunters' values? We find quite a few probes for which majority-culture hunters' predictions of Menominees' values differ significantly from Menominees' individual self-ratings: shining deer, hunting deer with bow and arrow, using bait for hunting deer with guns, baiting bear, using dogs to hunt bear, shooting wolves, shooting raccoons and squirrels for fun, taking more than one's limit to feed one's family, selling deer, filling out someone else's tag, shooting a doe and leaving it, taking a bear hide and leaving the meat, and shooting a deer and taking only the tenderloin.[13] That's a long list! Furthermore, in most cases these misperceptions involve attributing negative values to Menominee hunters—none of them are positive.

Our results again fit with a more systematic stereotyping of Native Americans in other domains of action.[14] We hasten to add that we only find marginal consensus with respect to majority-culture hunters talking about Menominee attitudes, indicating that not all majority-culture hunters stereotype Menominee hunters.

Our prediction that majority-culture hunters think that Menominee strongly endorse shining deer, when in fact they generally disapprove of shining, was confirmed. But we failed to predict many other systematic misperceptions. Majority-culture hunters incorrectly think that Menominee hunters are less approving of hunting deer with bow and arrow and more approving of baiting deer, using dogs for bear hunting, taking more than their limit of deer to feed their family, and shooting raccoons and squirrels for fun. They think that Menominee hunters show greater approval for shooting wolves, shooting raccoons and squirrels for fun, and filling out someone else's tags than they actually do. Menominee hunters disapprove of each of these practices. It is almost as if majority-culture hunters expect Menominee hunters to be following the "if it's brown, take it down" principle with the amendment of "take it down in the easiest way possible."[15]

Finally, majority-culture hunters expect Menominee to be less disapproving of leaving does, taking just the tenderloin and leaving bear meat than they are. For these last three items apparently there is mutual suspicion and to some extent stereotyping, although the means are at least on the correct side of neutral on the scale. To be honest, in a few cases Menominee hunters answered these last questions almost gleefully. It was as if they had taken so much flak about shining deer or using dogs to hunt deer that they were "returning the favor" by intentionally overestimating majority-culture approval of these roundly condemned practices.

Individual Differences

There are significant individual differences in the magnitude of stereotyping, with several hunters in each group showing no tendency to do so. Our studies with hunters focused more on generating a broad sample of expert hunters rather than on examining the responses of a smaller group across tasks. Consequently, we are handicapped in looking for correlates of stereotyping. Nonetheless we did develop an index of stereotyping for each group to look for patterns internal to the ranking and rating tasks. For Menominee hunters our index was based on predicted majority-culture ratings minus Menominee ratings for going for the biggest buck, baiting deer, leaving a downed doe, taking a bear pelt only, and taking only the tenderloin of a deer. For majority-culture hunters our index was based on predicted Menominee ratings minus majority ratings for going for the biggest buck, shining deer, shooting wolves, shooting raccoons and squirrels for fun, selling deer, using someone else's tag, leaving a downed doe, taking a bear pelt and leaving the meat, and taking only the tenderloin of a deer. One could add or delete one or another item, but the general picture would not change.

For Menominees we could not detect any meaningful correlates that would predict stereotyping of majority-culture hunters. For majority-culture hunters we found that individuals who predicted that their fellow majority-culture hunters would endorse the goal of hunting for food showed less stereotyping of Menominee hunters.[16] This −.52 correlation fits the pattern that we observed with majority-culture fishing experts: the closer a majority-culture hunter's goals are to Menominee goals, the less his tendency to stereotype.

SUMMARY AND CONCLUSIONS

Overall, the results with respect to intergroup perceptions are not wildly encouraging. Menominee hunters show moderate stereotyping of majority-culture values and majority-culture hunters show much stronger stereotyping of Menominee values. Just as in the case of fishing, actual values for the two groups are substantially more similar than the way the groups perceive each other's values. The attention given to trophy game in sporting magazines makes it perhaps unsurprising that Menominee hunters think that majority-culture hunters are focused on getting a trophy buck, a goal that is analogous to the majority-culture's practice of fishing as a sport.

The majority-culture misperception of Menominee seems to be driven mainly by differences in attitudes toward practices such as shining deer and using dogs to hunt. A further factor may be majority-culture hunters' lack of appreciation of factors determining carrying capacity. In other words, majority-culture people deduce from their beliefs that if Menominee shine and use dogs to hunt deer, then deer must be really scarce on the reservation. This belief is reinforced by the fact that fewer deer are to be observed on the reservation than on off-reservation land. In fact, however, this genuine difference in density of deer population is due to limits imposed by the differences in ecological conditions and carrying capacity.

Another source of misperceptions is that majority-culture hunters clearly are unaware of Menominee hunters' broad use of and respect for the plants and animals of the forest. They are also presumably unaware of the Menominee belief that humans are a part of nature and that everything has a role to play. Instead, they interpret practices such as using dogs to hunt deer or shining deer from a majority-culture perspective, in which the practice would be considered unsporting. If majority-culture hunters were acquainted with Menominee values it would be much harder to make these sorts of negative inferences.

The positive element is that there is a lot of variability—some majority-culture hunters show no stereotyping whatsoever. As was the case of majority-culture fishing experts, stereotyping of Menominees decreases as alignment between an individual majority-culture person's goals and Menominee goals increases. It appears that the present results are driven by the fact that similar understandings of the environment lead to similar evaluation of specific activities and vice versa. Together these data underline the main thesis of the book: a failure to understand differences in mental models of nature is important in generating intergroup misperception and conflict.

Chapter Fifteen | Why Meanings Matter

Dear Amy:

My boyfriend and I are in our early 50s, so we're not kids. We get along great and are even speaking of marriage.

Here's the problem: I am a true-blue animal advocate. Frank absolutely loves to hunt.

He hunts deer, turkey and bear—anything he can. He wants for nothing and says it's the "thrill" of the hunt. This is something I cannot comprehend. I'm not compulsive about it; I do eat hamburger and wear leather, but why kill an innocent animal, just for the thrill?

Please help. We both agreed we'd abide by your ruling.

—Animal Lover

Dear Animal Lover:

Temperamentally I come down on your side of the issue. As someone who grew up in a rural area, I've eaten and enjoyed my share of venison. I know and love hunters. Hunting isn't the problem; actually, it's the killing I object to.

If "Frank" is truly bringing home the bacon and would like to stock his freezer with turkey, venison and bear; or if he is donating the meat he kills to a shelter or food bank (as some hunters do) he has some leverage on this issue. If he is helping to cull overabundant animal populations under the direction of your state's Department of Fish and Game, that is also somewhat defensible, in my mind.

If he is stalking and killing game and leaving the woods littered with carcasses, that is just killing for the sake of killing. That is unconscionable, no matter how much he enjoys it.

I'd like to suggest a few activities that Frank might enjoy as much as hunting. Since he sounds willing to entertain options, I hope he finds a less violent pastime.

Frank could try: fly-fishing (catch-and-release, of course), skeet shooting, paintball, competitive bird watching, "shrooming" (mushroom hunting), or orienting. I'm sure readers have additional suggestions.

—*Chicago Tribune*, November 15, 2004,
Amy Dickinson advice column

THIS STORY NICELY illustrates our main point: meanings matter. For both women, hunting in and of itself is not a problem, but it matters a great deal why the boyfriend wants to hunt. But it goes further than that; the suggested compromise presumes that catch-and-release is the needed ethical compromise and that a competitive orientation toward nature is reasonable.

These same sorts of presumptions underlie Menominee and majority-culture worldviews and mental models. The preceding chapters have illustrated how Menominee and European American hunters and fishermen construct different worldviews by attaching different meanings to seemingly similar events. Menominees approach fishing and hunting from a very different epistemological framework, which is associated with a "do not waste" ethic and the ecological notion that everything in nature is connected and has a role to play. Majority-culture fishermen and hunters are more likely to see nature through the eye of an outsider who is apart from nature, not a part of it. These different models of the world relate to interpretations of behaviors and lead as a consequence to stereotyping and conflict.

In this chapter we draw out the implications of our research for three areas of inquiry:

1. Theories of concepts and conceptual organization

2. Models of decisionmaking

3. The relationship between conceptual understanding and intergroup perception and conflict

Since within-culture variation is a critical component of our thesis, we shall review our approach to studying culture, which is to bring different approaches and questions together.

CAN GOALS AND VALUES ALONE EXPLAIN INTERGROUP CONFLICT?

It is important to explain why we think one particular way of organizing our findings is incorrect: treating cultural differences in goals and values

as the key causal factor, in other words, assuming that cultural differences in values affect knowledge organization and also lead to intergroup conflict and stereotyping. In this theory, the only relation between
stereotyping and knowledge organization is that they are both effects of
a common cause, cultural differences in goals and values. This interpretation has the virtue of being simple and straightforward, but we think it
is wrong.

First, values alone do not make sense in the absence of concepts and
associated conceptual knowledge. That is, they will not do the work one
might want them to do in isolation. The practices of catch-and-release,
spearfishing, or keeping fish for food are not in themselves sources of
conflict. Majority-culture fishermen are happy to spear carp and suckers
and to keep panfish and smaller walleyes for food. Conflict arises only
when muskies and bass are kept for food or when game fish are speared.
Similarly, conflict does not arise from differences in utility or value associated with particular species of fish. Both groups value bass about the
same, but Menominee fishermen value them as food and majority-culture
fishermen value them as sport fish. In short, values and practices in isolation do not provide the basis for the intergroup conflict we have been
studying.

Second, concepts mediate between framework theories and specific
values. To understand the conflict between the Menominee and the majority culture, one needs to know the relationship among practices and
values as they are manifest for particular species of fish or game. One's
concept of largemouth bass must include that they are good fighters
when they are hooked and that they are good to eat. In addition, one
needs to know that majority-culture fishermen see trophy-sized fish as a
limited resource that is threatened by people who see these same fish as
a food source and that Menominee may see releasing fish who may well
die after being hooked as a waste. It is this system of conceptual knowledge, framework theories, and associated values that gives meaning to
practices.

Third, the presence of cultural differences in worldviews or framework theories places important constraints on both conceptual organization and values. Consider, for example, the Menominee beliefs that everything has a role to play and that humans are a part of nature. A focus
on roles is, at a minimum, consonant with and perhaps equivalent to an
ecological perspective. At the same time, this orientation affects values. If
humans play their appropriate role (for example, do not waste), the ecosystem will remain healthy. A role orientation also undermines the idea
that some kinds are worthless or without value. Compare this perspective with the majority-culture worldview that humans are outside of na-

ture and that people must take care of it in order to enjoy its fruits. The latter view implies a ranking of utility or value of different kinds for humans and is also compatible with categorizing in relation to human goals, leading to categories such as sport fish versus panfish versus garbage fish. In short, worldviews blur the very distinction between conceptual knowledge and values.

We see worldviews, conceptual knowledge, values, and specific practices as interwoven, working together as the carriers of meanings. Overall then, a major implication of our studies is that, in order to understand natural resource use and associated conflicts, one cannot focus on practices or even practices and values in isolation; instead one needs also to include worldview and conceptual knowledge.

IMPLICATIONS OF THEORIES OF COGNITION FOR ENVIRONMENTAL DECISIONMAKING

As emphasized throughout the book, there's more to environmental decisionmaking than how much value, importance, or utility is attached to some resource. Critically important are the deeper and more detailed understandings of resources and their interrelationships with people that we have described under the umbrella term "mental models." In the present case study we have seen that different groups living in the same area and interacting with nature in more or less the same ways nonetheless differ substantially in mental models of fish and game. These different frameworks are a major factor in intergroup misperceptions and conflict over natural resources.

Meanings, Values, and Content

Attempts to describe environmental decisionmaking in terms of abstract considerations of utility miss out on many of the dynamics and meanings that are relevant to how people see and act on nature and how they perceive the actions of others. Insights into meanings and values is unlikely to be gained by one-shot surveys asking people about how and how often they use particular resources. In this respect the present case study reinforces our findings from Guatemala, where we were studying three cultural groups living in the same area and engaging in the same practices, but differing strikingly in both the sustainability of their agroforestry practices and in their mental models of rain-forest ecology (Atran, Medin, and Ross 2005).

More broadly, there is increasing evidence that the field of decisionmaking will need to focus on the contents and meanings that people attach to decisions (see, for example, Goldstein and Weber 1995; Rettinger and Hastie 2001, 2003; Medin et al. 1999) and that this will require systematic ethnographic analysis (Henrich et al. 2003, 2005; see also Weber and Hsee 1999). There is also accumulating evidence that moral, value-laden decisionmaking differs from the more commonly studied value-neutral decisionmaking (see Baron and Spranca 1997; Tanner and Medin 2004). Content matters.

Categorization and Reasoning

A great deal of work on categorization and reasoning has been undertaken with undergraduates as participants and using stimulus materials that the students don't particularly have knowledge of or care about. This work has led to theories of categorization and reasoning that are limited in scope and applicability (see also Medin and Atran 2004). Consider categorization. The widely accepted view is that the way people organize categories is extrinsically driven by the real-world structure of things. Little attention has been directed to the role of goals or values or other more intrinsic factors in how people may organize categories.

Our studies show that goals and values are important in category organization. If category examples relevant to goals and values tend to be learned first, they will have an important role in the formation of categories. The recent Mark Steyvers and Josh Tenenbaum (2005) paper showing that order of learning matters and that new concepts build on existing ones is a welcome sign that cognitive scientists are beginning to shift to this more active view of learning (see also Love et al. 2004). We think that the same conclusion holds for how people use categories in reasoning (Medin and Atran 2004). In short, our data favor a more intrinsic approach to category learning, with values and goals as important pieces in the development of conceptual organization.

Our most direct data on category organization (Medin et al. 2006) came from our experiments on sorting and probes of ecological knowledge. We found that Menominee fishermen are more likely to spontaneously sort ecologically and that they could quickly access relevant ecological knowledge when we probed for beliefs concerning fish-to-fish interactions. Majority-culture experts had the same knowledge base, but since their knowledge was organized in a different way, this fact only emerged in an unspeeded task. In short, the two groups apparently have the same knowledge of ecological relations, but this knowledge is organized differently in the two groups. These observations are important for theories of categorization in pointing to a role for intrinsic factors such as goals and values in concept formation and knowledge organization.

They also underline the point that cultural differences may lie not only in differences in actual knowledge but also in how that knowledge is organized (see Ross and Medin 2005). In this framework, knowledge organization influences what will be easy to think and what will take more effort to access.

Intra- and Intergroup Perception and Stereotyping

Our research has highlighted an important source of stereotyping: intergroup differences in the meanings attached to acts. The same behavior that is ethical and coherent within one framework, fishing for food (spearfishing walleyes, eating smallmouth bass) is transparently unethical and not sporting according to a different framework, fishing for sport. The majority-culture ethic of practicing catch-and-release can be seen by Native Americans as transparently disrespectful and wasteful, since the released fish may well die. Other research has shown that groups of "others" are usually described and perceived as much more homogeneous than in-group members, which means that observations of single instances are sufficient to create stereotypes.

It is important to bear in mind that the differences we observed didn't create the groups. That is to say, if the differences in understandings we have been studying were associated with two rural Wisconsin towns where there were no ethnic differences, they might never have been noticed. Although there likely is some stereotyping on the part of local majority-culture people of hunters and fishermen who come from cities or from out of state, this is probably tiny compared with that the same group attaches to ethnic groups such as Native Americans in Wisconsin. Unfortunately, racial and ethnic categories are easy for people to think with (Hirschfeld 1996).

CONCEPTIONS OF CULTURE

Although we have used Menominee and majority-culture as convenient descriptors, we explicitly disavow treating them as homogeneous. Instead, we suggest that cultures should be studied as a causal distribution of ideas in a given ecological context. Communities and cultural groups are dynamic and it is important to try to understand the processes by which knowledge, beliefs, and values are transmitted both within and across groups, and how they change.

Within-Culture Variation

We believe that our observations on within-culture variations in stereotyping provide our strongest evidence that meanings matter. Perhaps most strikingly, in the case of fishermen we could predict majority-culture stereotyping from the kinds of categories majority-culture experts created on a sorting task run years earlier. Specifically, ecological sorting tended to be correlated with less stereotyping, and creating a "sport-fish" category tended to be associated with increased stereotyping of Native American fishermen. In addition, the greater number of goals mentioned by a majority-culture fisherman in the sorting, the less the tendency to stereotype the other group. This latter trend was statistically reliable.

We also found that both individual fish rankings and predicted community differences in fish were linked to stereotyping. The more majority-culture fishermen valued bass, or the more they thought members of their own community preferentially valued the "big five" sport fish (walleye, northern, musky, largemouth bass, smallmouth bass), the greater the tendency to stereotype Menominees. And the more they thought that Menominee experts would value the big five for food, the greater the stereotyping. It was also the case that majority-culture fishermen who knew that Menominees place a premium on trout showed essentially no stereotyping. With the hunters, we found that the more a majority-culture informant ranked hunting for food as an important goal, the less tendency to stereotype he displayed.

Why are these within-group variations in stereotyping important? Aside from the encouraging news that not everyone shows stereotypes, these data show that stereotyping is linked to specific patterns of conceptual organization and framework theories. In the absence of these correlations, one might claim that stereotyping was driven by culture-wide beliefs about Native Americans propagated by media reports such as those concerning Ojibwe off-reservation spearing rights. The correlations we did observe form a coherent pattern, showing that stereotyping is positively correlated with a sports focus and negatively correlated with hunting and fishing for food or an approach that takes several goals into account. In short, the details of one's understanding of nature matter, as does the meaning attributed to fishing. These differences have behavioral consequences, where the creation of stereotypes and consequent intergroup conflict.

Historical Changes

Finally, we uncovered some evidence suggesting that important historical changes in majority-culture hunting and fishing orientation may be taking place, such phenomena as the apparently increasing privatization of hunting and perhaps a growing tendency to see oneself as competing with other sportsmen. As we noted earlier, in the 1960s everyone ate bass, but now many majority-culture fishermen only employ catch-and-release with bass. In fact the Wisconsin Department of Natural Resources plays an active role in this process by recommending catch-and-release for bass in order to increase access to trophy fish. Regardless of what one thinks of these trends, they do underline the dynamic nature of cultural ideas and, likely, the associated mental models.

MEANING AND CULTURAL CHANGE: THE SPECIAL CASE OF DEVOLUTION

It is so easy to focus on the differences between our two populations of hunters and fishermen that we may lose sight of their deep similarities. The similarities are even more striking when the hunters and fishermen are compared to those who live in or near cities and whose ideal for being outdoors consists of activities such as lounging on the beach, hiking on trails that wind through a state or national park, or downhill skiing. If nature is nothing more than a scenic background for our activities, then our relationship with Mother Earth may be breaking up. Many people may be at serious risk for disconnecting with nature.

The loss of detailed knowledge about and concepts of particular species can be expected to lead to the loss of the meanings attached to them. In this section we follow this line of thought and provide some information suggesting that, in many populations, biological kinds are receding in their significance or salience. We refer to this as devolution.

Anthropologists studying traditional societies often note with concern the loss of indigenous language and a lessening of knowledge about the natural world (Diamond and Bishop 1999; Nabhan and St. Antoine, 1993; Wester and Yongvanit 1995). In technology-oriented cultures, such as the United States and Japan, contact with biological kinds appears to be so minimal that researchers can demonstrate significant differences in children's reasoning about biological kinds as a function of whether they do or do not have goldfish as pets (Inagaki 1990; Hatano and Inagaki 1987).

A survey we conducted at Northwestern University a number of years ago provided some index of what the typical undergraduate knows about one domain of biology, trees. We provided the names of eighty trees and asked the students to circle the trees that they had heard of before, regardless of whether they knew anything about them. More than 90 percent said they had heard of birch, cedar, chestnut, fig, hickory, maple, oak, pine, and spruce. But fewer than half indicated any familiarity with alder, buckeye, catalpa, hackberry, hawthorn, honey locust, horse chestnut, larch, linden, mountain ash, sweetgum, and tulip tree—all of which are common to the Evanston area where Northwestern University is located.

Historical Changes

Of course, these observations by themselves do not imply a loss of knowledge. It may be that Northwestern undergraduates from a hundred years ago would have proved to be equally unfamiliar with biological kinds. Nevertheless, such low levels of knowledge are consistent with the possibility that knowledge about trees is declining.

Phillip Wolff, Douglas Medin, and Connie Pankratz (1999) reported a historical analysis bearing on the devolution hypothesis. They looked at the life form, tree. Trees are of special interest because they could represent a particularly strong test of the devolution hypothesis, because although people in urban environments may have limited exposure to all but a few mammals—cats, dogs, squirrels—they are likely to have seen many different kinds of trees. And trees, because of their size, are not likely to be ignored. As noted by Eugene Hunn (1999), size is a key factor in determining which natural kinds in a culture attract attention and get named.

Wolff, Medin, and Pankratz decided to focus on what people write about. Are people writing about plants and animals as much as they used to? When they do so, are they writing at the life-form level (for example, bird, tree) or at what Brent Berlin (1992) refers to as the folkgeneric (sparrow, oak) level? Not only are written records available, but these records are accessible in on-line databases that permit automated search.

Because their interest was in a longer time span than U.S. written history affords in terms of accessible databases, they selected a database from England for study: the *Oxford English Dictionary*, a historical dictionary. The editors of the *Oxford English Dictionary* seek to capture the evolution of all words in the English language except those that became obsolete before 1150 or are intelligible to only the specialist.

The dictionary contains approximately 616,500 word forms (Berg 1993; Murray 1989). Definitions for these words are illustrated with quotations from each century of use with extra quotations provided for significant changes in meaning. The quotations are drawn from a wide range of books and other literary materials. The total number of quotations in the most recent edition of the *Oxford English Dictionary*, roughly 2.5 million, was drawn from a sample of 5 million to 6 million quotations. The on-line corpus may be searched for any key words (for example, "tree," "maple tree," "maple," and so forth) and search codes may be written such that the date, source, and full quotation context will be returned. Given the breadth of the inquiry, we have no reason to expect that the quotations represent a biased sample with respect to the questions we are asking.

Wolff, Medin, and Pankrantz looked at quotations mentioning "tree" or specific kinds of trees from 1975 back to 1475 in hundred-year intervals. The proportions for quotations and sources were fairly constant through the sixteenth, seventeenth, and eighteenth centuries. In the nineteenth century, the relative number of quotations and sources increased, suggesting that knowledge of tree terms evolved during this period. However, the gains of the nineteenth century were completely lost in the twentieth century, which witnessed a striking decline in both quotations and sources using tree terms. The start of the decline corresponds closely with the start of the industrial revolution. According to this analysis, the incidence of writing about trees is lower now than in any other time in the history of the English language.

The same set of quotations was also coded according to level of organization or specificity. Three levels of organization were coded. The life-form level was indicated by use of the word "tree," the generic level by quotations containing one of twenty-two chosen generic tree terms (such as "pine"), and the specific level by a modification or specification of one of the twenty-two generic tree terms (for example, "red pine").

The findings from this analysis provide further evidence for the devolution hypothesis: The twentieth century is the only century where frequency counts for all levels of organization declined. The overall drop in tree terms cannot be explained as a drop in the life-form level alone ("tree") and masking increases at more specific levels of organization. In fact, Wolff, Medin, and Pankrantz found a crossover whereby the use of generic terms such as "oak" fell more rapidly than the use of the life-form term "tree." So even when people are talking about trees they are tending to use the most abstract term.

We see this decline paralleled by a corresponding lack of knowledge about biological kinds in Northwestern University undergraduates. One reason for conducting our research on folkbiology in Guatemala and rural Wisconsin is that people in these settings might be much more familiar with local flora and fauna. Maya children just four to five years old may be familiar with well over a hundred plants (Stross 1973), in contrast with the handful that a young suburban child might know (Dougherty 1979).

Of course, there also have been changes in Wisconsin, even over the past fifty years. For example, in the 1950s farmers grew a wider range of crops and had a greater variety of farm animals than is common today.

Some farmers have had to move toward mono-cropping or shift to managing specialized pig or cattle feedlots. In addition, farmers used to leave space at the end of each row in their field that some animals could use as a habitat. Now economics dictates that they plow right up to the fence line, pick corn down to tiny stubble, and mow the ditches along their roads to get additional grass for their livestock. The result of all three changes is a very considerable loss of habitat for game and fewer opportunities for farm children to learn about these animals.

Our view is that hunting, fishing, bird watching, and berry gathering are important activities with respect to passing on knowledge about the biological world. It is very likely the case that both Menominee and majority-culture fishermen and hunters know less about nature than their nineteenth-century counterparts did, but it is even more likely that they know substantially more than their twenty-first-century urban counterparts.

Devolution and Caring About Nature

Does it matter that people are living in less intimate contact with nature? We offer an anecdote and a research study that suggests it might.

An editorial in the *Chicago Sun Times* by Raymond Coffey ("Smoking Out the County's Tree-Burning Plan," February 20, 1998) strongly criticizes the Cook County Forest Preserve District Board for doing controlled burns to keep down invasive species. The writer suggested that the board's president, John Stroger, strained credulity when he stated, "Native plants withstand and adapt to fire while most invasive plants are destroyed." Coffey wrote, "Fire kills foreign plant life brought by European immigrants, but selectively spares native plants? Will only foreign logs burn in an American fireplace? Are these `restoration' people to be believed?"

According to a study by Anna Gunnthorsdottir (2001), people show more willingness to donate money to protect apes if the appeal is accompanied by an attractive picture of gorillas than if by an unattractive one.

Both of these observations are disturbing. Obviously, fires can't tell a difference between species, but different species are differentially affected by fires. Burr oaks are well adapted to a savannah environment, and their thick bark protects them from prairie fires. Some species of pine and other plants actually require a forest fire to trigger seed germination. Buckthorn, a very invasive species, is affected by fire.

When people are alienated from nature, they use other frameworks for understanding and interacting with it as the donation scenario suggests. We can't just protect species that are cute, only so-called "charismatic megafauna."

We are also examining cross-group and cross-generation changes in values and ecological models of the forest among Itza' Maya and Ladino agroforesters in Guatemala. Our early observations suggest that framework theories are more resilient to loss than is knowledge of specific ecological relationships. For example, we found that younger Itza' nominated as many relations involving animals helping plants as older Itza' but that about half of these nominated relations involve plausible but incorrect overgeneralizations. It remains to be seen whether and how this change in knowledge affects forestry practice.

SUMMARY

Different frameworks lead groups to attach different meanings and interpretations to observed activities and practices. For example, majority-culture fishermen interpret eating a bass as a waste of an important fish that is most suitable for sport fishing. We have argued that meanings matter and that to understand how people act on the environment and perceive the actions of others requires a holistic analysis of how framework theories, conceptual knowledge, and values shape each other. This orientation has implications for basic research on conceptual understanding and decisionmaking. It also has methodological and policy implications, which we take up in the next and final chapter.

Chapter Sixteen | Summary and Implications

"A group of Indians went out deer hunting. The custom was for a person to let out a whoop when they hit a deer and the others would come to help. As it happened, two braves saw the same deer between them and both shot at the same time. Both hit the deer and each let out a whoop. When they got to the deer they immediately started arguing. One said, 'My arrow is closer to the heart and it killed the deer.' The other said, 'My arrow came first and the deer was already dead when your arrow hit it.' The argument grew violent and one brave ended up killing the other. This led to very bad feelings amongst clan members. Finally the Great Spirit decided he must intervene. He brought flint and kindling to the tribe and showed them how to make fire in order to rekindle warmth."

—A Potawatomi tale recounted by a Menominee elder

IT IS TIME to address ourselves to the potential implications of our research for policy. Along the way, we'll discuss possible misconceptions concerning our goals and orientation.

POLICY

What would we like policymakers in the general area of natural resources to understand? In this section our focus is local, but most of our recommendations likely have generality.

Meanings Matter

We have argued that Native American and European American hunters and fishermen have differing approaches, different mental models, with

185

respect to fish and game, and these differences lead to misunderstanding, stereotyping, and intergroup conflict. The more majority-culture sportsmen move away from seeking fish and game as a source for food, the greater the potential for conflict between groups.

There may be some grounds for optimism. We noted earlier that the hunter-education manual for the State of Wisconsin has trophy hunting as the third stage of a five-stage development process that shifts to a focus on enjoyment of the process and the social dimensions of hunting. When passing up a buck in order to shoot a doe is commended as much by sporting magazines as releasing a trophy-sized musky, then the State of Wisconsin should be well on its way to being able to manage its deer herd.

The Whys Are at Least as Important as the Whats

If mental models determine the meanings of different hunting and fishing practices, then it is critical for policymakers to pay attention to the motivations and understandings associated with behaviors. This is especially true for the media. As we mentioned earlier, in the case of the controversy surrounding Ojibwe off-reservation spearing rights, the media covered the fact of the conflict but essentially nothing about the underlying motivations of the Ojibwe and their associated conservation behaviors. When the Menominees seek to have fish ladders installed on the Wolf River dams, one potential interpretation of majority-culture fishermen is that they'd like to spear them or wrestle with one on their fishing line, for sturgeons put up a great fight. Responsible media owe the public an analysis of the role of the sturgeon in Menominee culture.

Keep Your Eyes on the Prize

Menominee and majority-culture hunters and fishermen generally are so similar in their practices that it is easy to focus on comparing the two and to interpret any differences as reflecting inappropriate values, privileges, and practices. What makes this most striking is that the two groups share the superordinate goal of wanting to preserve fish and game for future generations and both see hunting and fishing as deeply meaningful activities that both reflect and instill deeply held values. Groups with such strongly shared goals and values should not be in conflict.

Even more striking is the fact that there are genuine serious threats to this way of life that demand attention. Important factors in maintaining fish and game include loss of habitat, invasive species, practices that facilitate the spread of disease, and different sources of pollution. Presumably majority-culture and Menominee hunters and fishermen should be allies, speaking with a united voice on these critical issues.

Don't Treat Cultural Groups as if They Were Stable and Unvarying Natural Kinds

Even in the small samples in our studies we found striking within-group variability. Although pretty much all of our participants condemn certain practices, Menominees are sharply divided on the issue of spearfishing walleyes or shining deer. Majority-culture hunters are equally divided on whether or not baiting deer is acceptable. In short, cultural groups are dynamic and many ideas and practices may be as contested within cultures as they are across cultures. When a disgruntled majority-culture fisherman suggests boycotting all tribal casinos, he is acting as if not only a particular tribe but all Native Americans in general are completely homogeneous. They are not.

At the same time it is important to understand the reality of culture in people's lives. Circumstances constantly remind Menominees of their ethnicity, and cultural values play an important role in their day-to-day lives. Majority-culture members should be aware that culture is not something that "other people have" and that what appears to them to be an objective reality often is reality as perceived through their own cultural lens. It is critical to avoid essentializing culture. This does not mean that cultural processes are not of great significance.

Besides cross-cultural differences, one should also be alert to historical changes within and between cultural groups. In just the past handful of years Menominees have shifted away from shining deer and have introduced large changes in their forest-management system that are reflected in tribal regulations. Yet other changes are perhaps more subtle and as a result more difficult to trace. As we noted earlier, in the 1960s everyone ate bass, but now many majority-culture fishermen only employ catch-and-release. Another apparent trend is toward the privatization of deer hunting with a corresponding tendency to act as if one "owns" the deer on one's land. These sorts of historical changes in practices may be accompanied by changes on how resources are conceptualized, so it is important to be alert to them (and in some cases, to try to counteract them).

PERSPECTIVE TAKING AND ALLIANCES

Anyone exposed to scientific research knows how important it is to remain objective. It's also easy to equate "objective" with "neutral." We think objectivity is more likely to emerge from taking multiple perspectives than from trying to take no perspective. This does not come as news to anthropologists because the central idea underlying participant observation is taking someone else's point of view. To try to be "neutral" is like trying to pretend that one doesn't have culture.

In our research in Wisconsin, perspective taking has been our goal. In a sense this means that at some points we take one side and at other points, the other. One nice virtue of a team of researchers is that one gets multiple perspectives. Medin grew up in a majority-culture hunting and fishing environment; Cox grew up on the Menominee reservation; and Ross grew up in Germany. This fostered multiple insider-outsider perspectives in a way that really helped us. Insiders have critically important knowledge, but they may take for granted something that requires an outsider to see.

Equally important, we do not see cultural research as a one-way enterprise where we administer some interview or test and the participant gets paid with cash and that's all there is to the exchange. This "extractive" approach to research presumes on the goodwill of the communities being studied. More balance is needed. We think that the research enterprise is more collaborative and some of our studies are based on suggestions made by participants.

We also think that there are some formal obligations when one is working with groups that historically have been underserved (Hermes 1999; Guyette 1983; Mihesuah 1998; Smith 1999). This includes community input and working with the appropriate tribal committees. Finally, attention to and respect for cultural groups that have been neglected or oppressed may have some intrinsically beneficial aspects. To the extent that the research fosters cultural identification and dignity, it may support cultural survival and help people maintain their bearings in difficult circumstances. Count us in on this.

CONCLUSIONS

Conflicts over resources when different value systems are involved are often straightforward to understand. The confrontation between conservationists and business interests over oil drilling in Alaska is no mystery. It is much less obvious why different groups living close to one another and sharing essential values and attitudes are in conflict over natural resources.

Menominee and majority-culture fishing and hunting experts show a high level of agreement in values and attitudes, yet differ remarkably with respect to their perceptions of each other. This was especially true for majority-culture perceptions of Menominees. These findings are both surprising and troublesome, but they also create some space for hope.

We have argued that different frameworks lead groups of individuals to attach different meanings and interpretations to activities observed. Majority-culture fishermen may interpret eating a bass as a waste of an important fish species that is most suitable for sport fishing. Where do these different evaluations of activities come from? Our analyses indicate that it is actually fairly recently that majority-culture hunters and fishers have shifted away from an emphasis on fishing and hunting for food in favor of an emphasis on sport. Although this shift may encourage re-source conservation, it has also had the consequence of giving rise to negative value judgments of Native American hunting and fishing practices.

Shifts in attitudes may also accompany and be accompanied by pro-cesses we described as "knowledge devolution," a development that is equally troublesome, if not more so. First, the intensity of conflicts over resources is increasing, yet individuals seem to be more and more de-tached from their natural environment. Second, decisionmakers in the area of natural resources are rarely local people embedded within a socio-cultural environment, having the kind of experience with the outdoors we found among our experts. Decisionmakers may be more like univer-sity biology majors who name Christmas tree in a free listing task of all the trees they can think of. Tree huggers may have a role to play, but we would be more optimistic if we could be sure that they knew whether they were hugging a maple or an oak.

Studying how people think about and act on nature is central to a wide range of theoretical and applied issues. For mainstream cognitive science, we see our work as an invitation to venture into field research as a means of increasing the validity and general applicability of theories. For cognitive anthropology, our suggestion is that ethnography can go hand in hand with systematic probes that constitute, rather than contrast with, experiments. For decisionmaking, the message is that meanings are centrally involved in the choices people make and the ways they under-stand the behavior of others. Finally, for the hunters and fishermen of Wisconsin as well as other policymakers, we urge them to strive to go beyond the whats of others' behaviors in order to understand the whys from a new perspective.

Sustainability and intergenerational fairness are related concepts that all of us support. We do want to leave the world a better place to live than when we entered—certainly no worse. But as Jared Diamond's Col-lapse (2005) vividly illustrates, there are both sociocultural success stories and failures, and the distinction between the two may only emerge after many generations. So we are left with the puzzle illustrated on the cover of this book: Who is the Protector?

Notes |

CHAPTER 1

1. This type of study is normally done "between participants," where one group of people is asked about one quantity and another group is asked about some other quantity. This avoids the demand characteristic to give higher numbers for greater quantities but presumably still allows people to express meaningful values. If one asked one group of people how much they would pay for a fourteen-day stay at some resort they would presumably give a higher number than a group asked how much they would pay for a three-day stay.

2. We use "sportsmen" and other gendered terms in this monograph because our participants were men. There are many women in Wisconsin who hunt and fish, but none emerged in response to our request for nominations of the most expert hunters and fishers. We don't know whether this is a true reflection of expertise levels or only of perceived social roles.

3. It may seem presumptuous to equate having somewhat different goals with having different "models" or understandings of nature. As we will see, however, the various similarities and differences form a pattern in which a fundamental difference in approaches to the biological world can be seen. Majority-culture people tend to see nature as an externality that they have responsibility to care for, whereas Native Americans tend to see themselves as a part of nature, being cared for by Mother Earth.

4. Similarly, when students of one of the authors asked individuals in Nashville about what comes to mind first when they think about the word "Cherokee," people were more likely to think of a common SUV brand than of a Native American tribe that had lived in the southeast until their removal to Oklahoma in the infamous "Trail of Tears."

5. It is also easy to come up with local examples. People who oppose shooting deer on ethical grounds seem not to have any viable solutions for the deer

overpopulation problems that plague many suburban areas, and large swaths of Wisconsin.

CHAPTER 2

1. It may be worth mentioning here that the critical issue in whaling is not subsistence practices by indigenous communities but rather an economic or marketing perspective whereby whales are seen as a financial resource to be harvested.
2. This summary is based on a paper by Scott Atran et al. (2002) and details can be found there (see also Atran, Medin, and Ross 2005).
3. Protecting a plant often means clearing the ground around it before the spring burning of the agricultural field so it won't be burned.
4. Note that in these instances we combine informal research with statistical tools. Individual stories confirm our interpretations and flesh out the statistical results, which then become only secondary to the actual story told.

CHAPTER 3

1. It could also be the case that the measuring tools are just not powerful enough to capture an existing difference, in which case the study would have generated a false positive.
2. People familiar with research design might claim that these two groups form a "two-by-two factorial design" but that is not quite accurate. Although we took pains to establish that our two groups of experts were equally expert, we did not feel constrained to match the less expert fishermen so precisely. Still, we have no problem viewing two-by-two designs as allowing for various triangular comparisons.
3. See Lawrence Hirschfeld (2002) for a nice analysis of cultural processes associated with children underlining the point that learning is much more complicated than taking in information from parents and other adult figures.
4. In more formal terms the cultural-consensus model consists of a principal-components analysis (essentially, factor analysis) over the inter-informant-agreement matrix. A cultural consensus is found to the extent that the data overall conform to a single-factor solution. In this case each informant's first-factor score represents her participation in the consensus, the extent to which he or she agrees with everyone else.
5. On the basis of each individual's participation in the consensus (the first-factor score) we are able to test whether pairs of individuals agree more with each other in reality (raw-agreement score) than what would be predicted by their participation in the consensus (the product of their first-factor scores). This analysis of "residual agreement" allows us to test for systematic differences within a consensus.

6. We may be guilty of exaggerating the difference between intuitive and scientific notions of species. For many purposes they may be roughly equivalent. The most serious discrepancies arise at more abstract levels. For example, the concept tree has no status in scientific taxonomy because the same genus may encompass vine, a shrub, and tree species.

7. At the same time, individual perceptions "feed back" into their concepts of culture in that individuals often tend to act in specific ways based on their assumption of being part of a cultural group. That is, beliefs about the nature of culture help create culture.

8. Arguably these context effects would never be detected by traditional ethnographic methodologies.

CHAPTER 5

1. Actually there were and are two colleges in the Menominee reservation, and our research team has worked with both of them.

2. Although many people such as loggers, game wardens, and others make a living doing forest-related work, no one makes a living from fishing or hunting.

3. There is some evidence that fish stocking may reduce biodiversity (see Radomski and Goeman 1995).

4. Of course, one should also take into account that money saved by subsistence hunting, fishing, and cutting firewood for heating is not reflected in these income figures.

5. We describe a number of these efforts in chapter 6.

6. Restoration is discussed in greater detail in the next chapter.

7. Logging contracts can be a source of discontent. Where investment in heavy machinery is required, small groups of Menominee loggers find themselves at a competitive disadvantage vis-à-vis off-reservation logging businesses. Recently, Menominee loggers were successful at winning only four of fourteen contracts being let. Given that the forest is supposed to provide for the people, many Menominees think that the point system is not working very well.

8. One exception to this rule is the short spearing season for sturgeon in the Lake Winnebago system.

CHAPTER 6

1. Available at www.beloitdailynews.com/1097/4wis23.htm.

CHAPTER 7

1. For the record we also obtained pictures of all these different fish, mostly from the Internet, and asked some of our experts to identify them. This just

didn't work well. Some of our pictures were better than others and there are also some local variations in the appearance of some of the smaller fish. The experts identified the fish in our good pictures instantly, but had more trouble with the bad-quality pictures.

2. In some cases pictures are taken of a trophy fish and the taxidermist constructs the representation from the pictures.

3. Sign seen posted by the Wisconsin Department of Natural Resources at various boat landings: "Today's release could be tomorrow's trophy."

4. Pike, musky, and walleye: ($t = 2.21$, $p < .05$); trout: ($t = 2.28$, $p < .05$).

5. Majority-culture: average number left out, 3.3; Menominee: average left out, 4.7.

6. The first three eigenvalues were 18.4, 2.4, and 1.6. The first latent root was large relative to the second (7.6 to 1) and accounted for just over 57 percent of the variance. Furthermore, every informant had a positive loading on the first factor.

7. In order to look at patterns of residual agreement, an informant-by-informant residual agreement matrix was prepared (see Nakao and Romney 1984 for details). This residual agreement matrix first was standardized and then we compared within- and between-group residual agreement for the two groups.

8. This percentage can range from 0 to 100 percent, so when we get close to 100 we know that the spatial representation is doing a very good job of capturing similarities.

9. For completeness we mention correlation with scientific taxonomy. We used conventional evolutionary taxonomy as our scientific standard in this study, rather than cladistic classifications over which there is less historical consensus. Overall, there was fair agreement between taxonomic distance and distance in each group's consensual sorting. The correlation was +.62 for the majority culture experts and +.60 for the Menominee experts. This is in the same range reported for Itza' Maya and undergraduates sorting mammals (López et al. 1997) and for different types of tree experts (Medin et al. 1997, eigenvalues were 18.4, 2.4, and 1.6) and almost the same as bird experts sorting birds of the Chicago area (Bailenson et al. 2002). Note that although the correlation is strongly positive, it accounts for less than half the variance (to determine the variance accounted for, square the correlation; a correlation of +.60 corresponds to 36 percent of the variance). That is, there is probably more to the story than converging on natural clusters which nature provides. Several factors work to reduce the correlation. For example, folkgenerics usually correspond to genera, but there are notable exceptions—the American eel and the lamprey eel belong to different classes and the mudminnow and the bluntnose minnow belong to different orders. Folk classifications tend to underdifferentiate small organisms (Hunn 1999), and that appears to be borne out

in our data. Another difference between science and folk sorts is that science gives little weight to size, but folk sorts do. For example, the darter, which is quite small, belongs to the perch family, yet rarely is sorted together with its larger cousins, the walleye and yellow perch. Similarly, the carp, which grows to be quite large, is a member of the minnow family, yet almost never is grouped with minnows by our fish experts.

CHAPTER 8

1. Here are the details. For each expert, a fish-by-fish distance matrix was calculated. For example, two species were scored as having distance 0 if they shared a habitat at the lowest level of the informants' sorting. Of course, a given fish might appear in more than one group. In the event that a fish appeared in more than one pile, the shortest distance to the other species was entered into the matrix. Then the analyses were performed just as in study 1 (in other words, the distance matrices were used to compute a correlation between the sortings of each pair of experts).

2. The ratio of the first- to the second-factor scores was 9.52, with the first factor explaining 72 percent of the variance.

3. Study 2 indicated that the two fish in these pairs tended to be placed in different habitat categories.

4. We also looked for more specialized ecological knowledge. Recall that walleyes and northerns appear to be relatively more salient and trout relatively less salient for majority-culture fishermen than for Menominee experts. Are there corresponding differences in reported relations involving trout versus walleyes and northerns? The data are only weakly consistent with this idea. Menominee informants report more relations, twenty-five on average, involving trout than do majority-culture fishermen, at sixteen on average. But Menominees also report more relations involving walleyes and northerns, thirty-six on average, than do majority-culture fishermen, at thirty on average. It is also the case that many of the relations reported for brook trout and brown trout are reciprocal or involve eating spawn. Thus, we do not see the clear interaction that one would expect if one group were expert with respect to one subset of fish and the other group were expert with respect to another subset of fish.

5. If this analysis is correct, then there should be a different set of probes that majority-culture experts would be able to answer quickly because the questions fit with the way their knowledge is organized. If one assumed that this organizational framework was not compatible with an ecological organization, one would expect that Menominee experts would be the ones to benefit from having extra time.

CHAPTER 9

1. Chi-square = 14.9, p < 0.01.
2. Expressed in significant differences with respect to the second factor loadings (F = 22.9; MSe = 1.2; p = 0.000).
3. F = 21.6; MSe = 164; p = 0.000.
4. Only the difference for musky is significant: F = 8.2; MSe = 86; p = .007.
5. F = 11.8; MSe = 26; p = .002.
6. Marginally significant: F = 3.6; MSe = 7.5; p = .06.
7. Ratio of first to second eigenvalue = 2.6; first factor = 44 percent of variance; mean first factor = .63.
8. Data to be reviewed in chapter 11, on Ojibwe spearfishing, suggest that about ten males are speared for every female walleye speared.
9. Fish finders are machines that provide information about the depth of water and the presence of fish. More expensive machines provide considerable resolution and one may be able to identify the presence of particular species.
10. The Wisconsin Department of Natural Resources and tribal limits are bag limits, specifying the numbers of different species of fish (and in some cases, the size restrictions) one can take in a day. Culling means continuing to fish after you have reached your limit for a particular species, and each time another fish is caught, throwing out the smallest fish so as to reach your limit with the largest possible fish.

CHAPTER 10

1. Menominees who oppose spearfishing don't do so on grounds that it isn't sporting—their concern is with the waste associated with spearing females full of spawn.
2. For convenience in making comparisons we have repeated the data on individual rankings from chapter 9. Again, smaller numbers refer to higher priorities.
3. For purposes of this analysis it would have been nice to have a larger sample size, particularly when there was only partial overlap of informants across tasks, but we were constrained by the fact that only eight majority-culture participants from the value-prediction study had done the original sorting task described in chapter 7. This means that we will only be able to detect differences that are quite large.
4. We are currently gathering social-network data as a converging source of evidence. Data collected so far are consistent with the idea that knowing specific Menominee who fish is negatively correlated with stereotyping.
5. Another common response was, "Well, I know Menominees really take care of their forest, so it makes sense that they also take care of their fish."

6. A federal district court judge, Barbara Crabb, ruled in 1991 that Stop Treaty Abuse was motivated by racism in its antitreaty protests against the Ojibwe and issued an injunction against physical anti-Indian harassment by the group. The S.T.A. leader, Dean Crist, appealed the judgment in the Chicago Circuit Court, but it was upheld. As part of the ruling Crist was ordered to pay $270,000, mainly in legal fees and court costs.

7. Even for the small percentage of specific lakes in the ceded territory that are declared, tribal harvest represents only 20 to 30 percent of the total harvest on lakes where there is a fifteen-inch minimum size limit and about 10 percent on lakes with no size limit.

8. For information on 2003 walleye limits in lakes where Native Americans have off-reservation spearfishing rights, go to http://www.dnr.state.wi.us/org/water/fhp/fish/ceded/walley.htm.

CHAPTER 11

1. A more recent problem in Wisconsin is contestants moving into different bodies of water without cleaning their boats, which may be responsible for the spread of a virus that is affecting bass. It is also presumably responsible for the recent introduction of zebra mussels into Shawano Lake.

2. We were able to examine copies of the regulations as far back as 1934, with the assistance of the staff of the Wisconsin Department of Natural Resources.

3. The only important change over this period concerned the timing of the bass season. Bass are late spawners and in the 1930s, 1940s, and 1950s, opening day was late in June, after the bass were finished spawning. In the mid- to late 1950s, when size limits were eliminated, the opening day was moved up to the first week of June in northern Wisconsin and to the beginning of May in southern Wisconsin (1954 was the first year of a north-south separation). In the 1970s and '80s this division was dropped and was not restored until after size limits for bass were reinstituted in 1989.

4. For example, in 1990 when the statewide size limit on muskies was thirty-two inches, there were ten inland waters that had a thirty-six-inch limit. By 2003 to 2004, when the statewide size limit was thirty-four inches, there were ninety-five inland waters with a forty-inch limit, two with a forty-five-inch limit, and three with a fifty-inch limit. For northern pike the twenty-six-inch limit instituted in the southern half of Wisconsin in 1995 has spread to thirty-two lakes in the north half, and seventeen lakes have a thirty-two-inch limit and three have a forty-inch limit. The state's fourteen-inch bass size limit now coexists with a sixteen-inch limit in a few lakes and fifty-six lakes with an eighteen-inch limit. Clearly, the trend for muskies, northerns, and bass is for size limits to be increasing at the state level and for local regulations to amplify this trend.

5. And where the legal size limit is forty inches this figure would shrink to less than 20 percent.

6. The most common modification of the statewide rule, which applies to 115 water bodies, is to have no size limits, but only one walleye larger than fourteen inches may be kept. Another forty-two bodies of water have no size limits at all. A third strategy, practiced in about thirty lakes, is to have a "slotted" limit, which fine-tunes what fish may be kept. For example, even with a minimum size fifteen inches, fish in the "slot" from twenty to twenty-eight inches in length may not be kept, and only one fish larger than twenty-eight inches may be kept. About thirty lakes have imposed a minimum length of eighteen inches and a bag limit of three fish. These special regulations are far more common in the ceded territories in the northern part of Wisconsin, very likely because more data are available to serve as a basis for policy setting.

7. Of course, resort owners blame the Ojibwe for "ruining the fishing."

CHAPTER 12

1. Carrying capacity varies somewhat as a function of forest subtypes, with aspen stands supporting more deer and hardwoods supporting fewer deer.

2. It would be more sensible for Menominee hunters to focus on bucks since they do not face an overpopulation problem.

3. Quality Deer Management (QDM) takes a variety of forms but typically involves shooting some number of does and young bucks with the goal of achieving a population distribution that includes a higher number of older bucks.

4. There is also evidence that baiting deer leads them to be nocturnal, so that hunters may be much less likely to see deer moving around in the day.

5. The overpopulation of deer is also one reason for the nearly fifty thousand car-deer collisions and other accidents that occur each year.

6. Recently a subcommittee of the Wisconsin Conservation Congress made the suggestion that supervised hunters be allowed to hunt for a year before having to pass the course. This suggestion has not been welcomed, in part because of the demonstrable evidence that these classes reduce hunting accidents.

CHAPTER 13

1. $F = 5.5$; $Mse = 1.23$; $p = .025$.
2. $F = 3.6$; $Mse = .86$; $p = .06$.
3. $F = 3.92$; $Mse = .75$; $p = .058$.
4. $F = 3.92$; $Mse = .75$; $p = .058$.
5. $F = 6.8$; $Mse = 1.3$; $p = .015$ and $F = 4.3$; $Mse = .49$; $p = .046$, respectively.

6. One Menominee gave the highest rating for all animals with respect to the self; two Menominee gave the highest rating for all animals with respect to the forest; three Menominee gave the highest ratings for all plants with respect to the forest and finally two Menominee gave the highest rating for all plants with respect to the self.

7. Note that we were not able to observe these same overall differences for the fish valuation task since that involved rankings rather than ratings. But when we gave fishermen a goodness of example rating task we did see the pattern of Menominee fishermen overall giving higher ratings to all fish and providing the same sorts of justifications (Burnett et al. 2005).

8. $F = 18.5$, Mse $= 8.7$, $p < .001$.

9. $F = 17.3$, Mse $= 13.1$, $p < .001$.

10. This group difference is highly reliable by a chi-square test.

11. $F = 5.88$, Mse $= 8.3$, $p < 0.05$; $F = 35.4$; Mse $= 21.6$; $p = 0.000$).

12. First-to-second-factor ratio $= 3.6$ to 1; first factor explains 44 percent of the variance; average first-factor score $= .63$.

13. We find higher agreement for majority-culture hunters alone (first-to-second-factor ratio $= 4.35$; variance explained by first factor $= 54$ percent; average first-factor score $= .73$) than for Menominee hunters among themselves (first-to-second-factor ratio $= 3.2$; variance explained by first factor $= 40.4$ percent; average first-factor score $= .61$).

14. $F = 8.1$, Mse $= 1.61$, $p < 0.01$. The residual analysis means that Menominee hunters agreed with one another more than one would expect on the basis of the overall consensus.

15. $F = 7.6$; Mse $= 6.4$, $p = .01$.

16. $F = 10.9$; Mse $= 14.6$, $p = .003$.

17. $F = 7.7$; Mse $= 8.2$; $p = .008$.

18. For the combined analysis: first-to-second-factor ratio $= 2.3$; first-factor variance explained $= 52$ percent; average first-factor score $= 0.56$. Two Menominee and two majority-culture hunters had negative-factor scores. For majority-culture hunters alone, ratio $= 1.8$, variance $= 50.3$ percent, average score $= .54$, two hunters with negative loadings. For Menominee: ratio $= 1.7$; variance $= 30$ percent; average $= .48$, one negative score.

CHAPTER 14

1. Average: 3.4 versus 5.6; $F = 10.8$; Mse $= 33.2$; $p = .003$.

2. Average: 5.8 versus 4.1; $F = 5.0$; Mse $= 19.5$; $p = .034$.

3. First-to-second-factor ratio $= 4.5$; first-factor variance accounted for $= 52.3$ percent; average first-factor score $= .71$.

4. $F = 28.4$; Mse $= 1.6$; $p = 0.000$.

5. Menominee hunters are reliably more approving of hunting deer as a

source of food and using dogs to hunt deer. Majority-culture hunters give higher ratings to using bait for hunting bear, shooting wolves (wolves are a protected species in Wisconsin), and shooting raccoons and squirrels for fun.

6. $F = 4.8$; Mse = 13.4; $p = .036$.
7. $F = 10.3$; Mse = 33.4; $p = .004$.
8. $F = 4.7$; Mse = 15.4; $p = .039$.
9. $F = 4.7$; Mse = 13.5; $p = .038$.
10. $F = 6.2$; Mse = 20.5; $p = .019$.
11. $F = 5.1$; Mse = 18.8; $p = .031$.
12. The respective statistical results are as follows:

$F = 7.8$, Mse = 20.6, $p = .009$

$F = 13.6$, Mse = 27.8, $p = .001$

$F = 11.4$, Mse = 24.2, $p = .002$

$F = 14.4$, Mse = 28.6, $p = .001$

$F = 6.6$, Mse = 19.6, $p = .016$

$F = 12.2$, Mse = 20.0, $p = .002$

13. The respective statistical results are as follows:

Shining: $F = 23.4$, Mse = 74.9, $p = 0.000$

Bow hunting: $F = 12.1$, Mse = 25.0, $p = .002$

Baiting for deer for hunting with guns: $F = 5.2$, Mse = 14.8, $p = .03$

Baiting bear: $F = 12.0$, Mse = 30.9, $p = .002$

Using dogs for bear: $F = 14.7$, Mse = 32.0, $p = .001$

Shooting wolves: $F = 18.9$, Mse = 55.6, $p = 0.000$

Shooting raccoons, squirrels for fun: $F = 21.6$, Mse = 59.3, $p = 0.000$

Taking more than limit for family: $F = 13.1$, Mse = 40.1, $p = .001$

Selling deer: $F = 25.5$, Mse = 66.8, $p = 0.000$

Using someone else's tags: $F = 19.8$, Mse = 58.6, $p = 0.000$

Shooting a doe and leaving it: $F = 12.5$, Mse = 34.6, $p = 0.002$

Taking a bear hide and leaving the meat: $F = 7.8$, Mse = 18.0, $p = .01$

Taking only the tenderloin of a deer: $F = 6.2$, Mse = 14.5, $p = .019$

14. We are reminded of a majority-culture friend's telling how his former boss during a summer job in a store had him watch Menominees especially closely, in order to prevent them from stealing. The story has two sides, however. The obvious one is about ongoing prejudice enacted on a daily basis, but the other one is equally important: our friend was just as disgusted with this practice as we were, which underlines the fact that stereotyping is far from universal.

15. One individual justified his evaluations of Menominee by commenting, "Well, this is bad, so they will probably do it."

16. $R_{xy} = -0.52$, $p < .05$ by a directional test. We see this same trend in individual ratings of the importance of food, but the sample size is small because of the partial overlap between participants on the individual versus group rating task.

References

Anonymous. "Tribal Claims Were Too Much." *Milwaukee Journal-Sentinel*, April 25, 1999. Available at: www.jsonline.com/news/editorials/apr99/0425tribal.asp.

Atran, Scott. 1990. *Cognitive Foundations of Natural History*. Cambridge: Cambridge University Press.

———. 1998. "Folkbiology and the Anthropology of Science: Cognitive Universals and Cultural Particulars." *Behavioral and Brain Sciences* 21(4): 547–609.

———. 1999. "The Universal Primacy of Generic Species in Folkbiology: Implications for Biological, Cultural and Scientific Evolution." In *Species: New Interdisciplinary Essays*, edited by Robert Wilson. Cambridge, Mass.: MIT Press.

Atran, Scott, Douglas Medin, Elizabeth Lynch, Valentina Vapnarsky, Edilberto Ucan Ek', John Coley, Christopher Timura, and Michael Baran. 2002. "Folkecology, Cultural Epidemiology, and the Spirit of the Commons: A Garden Experiment in the Maya Lowlands, 1991–2001." *Current Anthropology* 43(3): 421–50.

Atran, Scott, Douglas L. Medin, Norbert O. Ross. 2005. "The Cultural Mind: Environmental Decision Making and Cultural Modeling Within and Across Populations." *Psychological Review* 112(4): 744–76.

Atran, Scott, Douglas Medin, Norbert O. Ross, Beth Lynch, John Coley, Edilberto Ucan Ek', and Valentina Vapnarsky. 1999. "Folkecology and Commons Management in the Maya Lowlands." *Proceedings of the National Academy of Sciences* 96(13): 7598–603.

Aunger, Robert, ed. 2000. *Darwinizing Culture: The Status of Memetics as a Science*. Oxford: Oxford University Press.

Aunger, Robert. 2002. "Exposure Versus Susceptibility in the Epidemiology of Everyday Beliefs." *Journal of Cognition and Culture* 2(2): 113–54.

Axelrod, Robert. 1997. *The Complexity of Cooperation: Agent-Based Models of Competition and Collaboration*. Princeton: Princeton University Press.

Bailenson, Jeremy N., Michael S. Shum, Scott Atran, Douglas Medin, and John

Coley. 2002. "A Bird's Eye View: Biological Categorization and Reasoning Within and Across Cultures." *Cognition* 84(1): 1–53.

Bang, Megan, Janae Townsend, Sara U. Holyk, and Douglas L. Medin. 2005. "Cultural Models of Nature and Their Relevance to Science Education." Paper presented at American Educational Research Association Conference. Montreal (April).

Baron, Jonathan, and Mark Spranca. 1997. "Protected Values." *Organizational Behavior and Human Decision Processes* 70: 1–16.

Barsalou, Lawrence W. 1985. "Ideals, Central Tendency, and Frequency of Instantiation as Determinants of Graded Structure in Categories." *Journal of Experimental Psychology: Learning, Memory, and Cognition* 11(1–4): 629–54.

Basso, Kenneth. 1996. *Wisdom Sits in Places: Landscape and Language Among the Western Apache.* Albuquerque: University of New Mexico Press.

Beck, David R. M. 1995. "The Importance of Sturgeon in Menominee Indian History." *Wisconsin Magazine of History* 79: 32–48.

———. 2002. *Siege and Survival: History of the Menominee Indians, 1634–1856.* Lincoln: University of Nebraska Press.

Berg, Donna Lee. 1993. *A Guide to the Oxford English Dictionary.* Oxford, New York: Oxford University Press.

Berlin, Brent. 1972. "Speculations on the Growth of Ethnobotanical Nomenclature." *Journal of Language and Society* 1(1): 63–98.

———. 1978. "Ethnobiological Classification." In *Cognition and Categorization*, edited by E. Rosch and B. B. Lloyd. Hillsdale, N.J.: Erlbaum.

———. 1992. *Ethnobiological Classification: Principles of Categorization of Plants and Animals in Traditional Societies.* Princeton, N.J.: Princeton University Press.

Berlin, Brent, Dan Breedlove, and Peter Raven. 1973. "General Principles of Classification and Nomenclature in Folk Biology." *American Anthropologist* 75(1): 214–42.

———. 1974. *Principles of Tzeltal Plant Classification.* New York: Academic Press.

Blackmore, Susan. 1999. *The Meme Machine.* Oxford and New York: Oxford University Press.

Boster, James S. 1987. "Agreement Between Biological Classification Systems Is Not Dependent on Cultural Transmission." *American Anthropologist* 89(4): 914–20.

———. 1988. "Natural Sources of Internal Category Structure: Typicality, Familiarity, and Similarity of Birds." *Memory and Cognition* 16(3): 258–70.

Boster, James, Brent Berlin, and John O'Neill. 1986. "The Correspondence of Jivoroan to Scientific Ornithology." *American Anthropologist* 88(3): 569–83.

Boster, James S., and J. Johnson. 1989. "Form or Function: A Comparison of Expert and Novice Judgments of Similarity Among Fish." *American Anthropologist* 91(4): 866–89.

Brown, Cecil H. 1984. *Language and Living Things: Uniformities in Folk Classification*. Camden, N.J.: Rutgers University Press.

Bruman, Christopher. 1999. "Why a Successful Concept Should Not Be Discarded." *Current Anthropology* (special issue : *Culture—A Second Chance?*) 40: S1–S14.

Bulmer, Martin G. 1974. "A Statistical Analysis of the 10-Year Cycle in Canada." *Journal of Animal Ecology* 43: 701–18.

Burnett, Russ, Douglas Medin, Norbert O. Ross, and Serge Blok. 2004. "Ideal Is Typical." *Canadian Journal of Experimental Psychology* (special issue: *In Honor of Lee Brooks*) 59(1): 3–11.

———. 2005. "Ideal is Typical." *Canadian Journal of Psychology* 159: 5–10.

Carey, Susan. 1985. *Conceptual Change in Childhood*. Cambridge, Mass.: Bradford Books.

Cohen, Dov. 2001. "Cultural Variation: Considerations and Implications." *Psychological Bulletin* 127: 451–71.

Coley, John D., Douglas L. Medin, Julia B. Proffitt, Elizabeth Lynch, and Scott Atran. 1999. "Inductive Reasoning in Folkbiological Thought." In *Folk Biology*, edited by Douglas L. Medin and Scott Atran. Cambridge, Mass.: MIT Press.

David, Peter. 2004. "WI Wolf Recovery Threatened." *Mazana'igan* (Winter 2004–5): 10.

Davis, Thomas. 2000. *Sustaining the Forest, the People, and the Spirit*. Albany: State University of New York Press.

Dawkins, Richard. 1976. *The Selfish Gene*. Oxford: Oxford University Press.

Diamond, Jared. 2005. *Collapse: How Societies Choose to Fail or Succeed*. New York: Penguin.

Diamond, Jared, and D. Bishop. 1999. "Ethno-Ornithology of the Ketengban People, Indonesian New Guinea." In *Folkbiology*, edited by Douglas L. Medin and S. Atran. Cambridge, Mass.: MIT Press.

Dougherty, Janet. 1979. "Learning Names for Plants and Plants for Names." *Anthropological Linguistics* 21: 298–315.

Eagly, Alice, and Shelly Chaiken. 1993. *The Psychology of Attitudes*. Fort Worth: Harcourt Brace Jovanovich.

Ellen, Roy. 1993. *The Cultural Relations of Classification: An Analysis of Nuaulu Animal Categories from Central Seram*. Cambridge: Cambridge University Press.

Fielder, David G., and Bruce Johnson. 1994. "Walleye Mortality During Live-Release Tournaments on Lake Oahe, South Dakota." *North American Journal of Fisheries Management* 14(5): 776–80.

Fisher, J. D. 1988. "Possible Effects of Reference Group–Based Social Influence on AIDS-Risk Behavior and AIDS Prevention." *American Psychologist* 43: 914–20.

Frank, Robert H. 1989. "Honesty as an Evolutionarily Stable Strategy." *Behavioral and Brain Sciences* 12(4): 705.

Fukuyama, Francis. 1995. *Trust.* New York: Free Press.

Gardner, Wendi L., Shira Gabriel, and Angela Y. Lee. 1999. "'I' Value Freedom, but 'We' Value Relationships: Self-Construal Priming Mirrors Cultural Differences in Judgment." *Psychological Science* 10: 321–26.

Gelman, Susan. 2003. *The Essential Child: Origins of Essentialism in Everyday Thought.* New York: Oxford University Press.

Ghiselin, Michael. 1981. "Categories, Life, and Thinking." *Behavioral and Brain Sciences* 4: 269–313.

Gilens, Martin. 1996. "Race and Poverty in America: Public Misperceptions and the American News Media." *Public Opinion Quarterly* 60(4): 513–35.

Gilliam, F. D., and S. Iyenger. 2000. "Prime Suspects: The Influence of Local Television News on the Viewing Public." *American Journal of Political Science* 44(3): 560–73.

Goeman, Timothy J. 1991. "Walleye Mortality During a Live-Release Tournament on Mille Lacs, Minnesota." *North American Journal of Fisheries Management* 11: 57–61.

Goldstein, William M., and Elke U. Weber. 1995. "Content and Discontent: Indications and Implications of Domain Specificity in Preferential Decision Making." In *Decision Making from a Cognitive Perspective,* edited by Jerome R. Busemeyer, Reid Hastie, and Douglas L. Medin. New York: Academic Press.

Goldstone, Robert L. 1998. "Perceptual Learning." *Annual Review of Psychology* 49: 585–612.

Goodman, Nelson. 1972. "Seven Strictures on Similarity." *Problems and Projects.* New York: Bobbs-Merrill.

Graunke, G. 2003. "American Rights Guardian Update." *Protect American Rights and Resources Newsletter* 5(7). Available at: www.parr1.com/ARGU7–5W2003 .html.

Grignon, David, R. Alegria, C. Dodge, G. Lyons, C. Waukechon, C. Warrington, C. Caldwell, C. LaChapelle, and K. Waupoose. 1998. *Menominee Tribal History Guide: Commemorating Wisconsin Sesquicentennial 1848–1998.* Keshena, Wis.: Menominee Indian Tribe of Wisconsin.

Gunnthorsdottir, Anna. 2001. *Determinants of Cooperation and Competition in Single-Level and Multilevel Interactive Decision Making.* Unpublished doctoral dissertation. Tucson: University of Arizona.

Guyette, Susan. 1983. "Community-Based Research: A Handbook for Native Americans." Los Angeles: University of California Press.

Hardin, Garrett. 1968. "The Tragedy of the Commons." *Science* 162(3859): 1243–48.

Hatano, Giyoo, and Kayoko Inagaki. 1987. "Everyday Biology and School Biology: How Do They Interact?" *Quarterly Newsletter of the Laboratory of Comparative Human Cognition* 9: 120–28.

Hays, Terence E. 1983. "Ndumba Folk Biology and General Principles of Ethnobotanical Classification and Nomenclature." *American Anthropologist* 85(3): 592–611.

Heider, Eleanor R. 1971. "'Focal' Color Areas and the Development of Color Names." *Developmental Psychology* 4: 447–55.

———. 1972. "Universals in Color Naming and Memory." *Journal of Experimental Psychology* 93: 10–20.

Henrich, Joseph, Robert Boyd, Samuel Bowles, Colin Camerer, Ernst Fehr, Herbert Gintis, Richard McElreath, Michael Alvard, Abigail Barr, Jean Ensminger, Natalie Smith Henrich, Kim Hill, Francisco Gil-White, Michael Gurven, Frank W. Marlowe, John Q. Patton, and David Tracer. 2005. "'Economic Man' in Cross Cultural Perspective: Behavioral Experiments in 15 Small-Scale Societies." *Behavioral and Brain Sciences* 28(6): 795–855.

Henrich, Joseph, Peyton Young, Eric Smith, Samuel Bowles, Peter Richerson, Astrid Hopfensitz, Karl Sigmund, and Franz Weissing. 2003. "The Cultural and Genetic Origins of Human Cooperation." In *Genetic and Culture Evolution of Cooperation*, edited by Peter Hammerstein. Cambridge, Mass.: MIT Press.

Hermes, Mary. 1999. "Research Methods as a Situated Response: Toward a First Nations' Methodology." In *Race Is . . . Race Isn't: Critical Race Theory and Qualitative Studies in Education*, edited by L. Parker, D. Deyhle, and S. Villenas. Boulder, Colo.: Westview Press.

Hirschfeld, Lawrence. 1996. *Race in the Making*. Cambridge, Mass.: MIT Press.

———. 2002. "Why Don't Anthropologists Like Children?" *American Anthropologist* 102(2): 611–27.

Hobbs, Charles. 1963. "Indian Hunting and Fishing Rights." *George Washington University Law Review* 32: 504–32.

———. 1969. "Indian Hunting and Fishing Rights II." *George Washington Law Review* 37: 1251–1272.

Hoffmann, Walter J. 1896/1970. "The Menomini Indians." In *Fourteenth Annual Report of the U.S. Bureau of Ethnology, 1892–93*. New York: Johnson Reprints.

Huff, Paula, and Marshall Pecore. 1995. "Case Study: Menominee Tribal Enterprises." Paper presented at "Forestry in the Americas: Community-Based Management and Sustainability." University of Wisconsin—Madison (February 3–4).

Hummel, Richard. 1994. *Hunting and Fishing for Sport: Commerce, Controversy, and Popular Culture*. Bowling Green, Ky.: Bowling Green State University Press.

Hunn, Eugene. 1977. *Tzeltal Folk Zoology: The Classification of Discontinuities in Nature*. New York: Academic.

———. 1999. "Size as Limiting the Recognition of Biodiversity in Folkbiological Classifications: One of Four Factors Governing the Cultural Recognition of Biological Taxa." In *Folkbiology*, edited by Douglas L. Medin and S. Atran. Cambridge, Mass.: MIT Press.

Huntington, Samuel. 1996. *The Clash of Civilizations and the Remaking of the World Order*. New York: Simon & Schuster.

Inagaki, Kayoko. 1990 "The Effects of Raising Animals on Children's Biological Knowledge." *British Journal of Developmental Psychology* 8: 119–29.

Johnson, Karen E., and Carolyn B. Mervis. 1998. "Impact of Intuitive Theories on Feature Recruitment Throughout the Continuum of Expertise." *Memory and Cognition* 26:382–401.

Keesing, Felix M. 1939/1987. *The Menomini Indians of Wisconsin: A Study of Three Centuries of Contact*. Madison, Wis.: University of Wisconsin Press.

Keesing, Robert. 1972. "Paradigms Lost: The New Anthropology and the New Linguistics." *Southwest Journal of Anthropology* 28(4): 299–332.

Keil, Frank C. 1995. "The Growth of Causal Understanding of Natural Kinds: Modes of Construal and the Emergence of Biological Thought." In *Causal Cognition*, edited by A. Premack and D. Sperber. Oxford: Oxford University Press.

Keil, Frank C., Daniel T. Levin, B. A. Richman, and Grant Gutheil. 1999. "Mechanism and Explanation in the Development of Biological Thought." In *Folkbiology*, edited by Douglas L. Medin and S. Atran. Cambridge, Mass.: MIT Press.

Kellert, Stephen R. 1980. *Public Attitudes Toward Critical Wildlife and Habitat Issues: Phase 1*. Washington, D.C.: U.S. Fish and Wildlife Service.

Kempton, W., J. Boster, and J. Hartley. 1995. *Environmental Values in American Culture*. Cambridge, Mass.: MIT Press.

Krech, S. 1999. *The Ecological Indian: Myth and History*. New York: Norton.

Krueger, J. 2004. "Open Water Spearing by Chippewa Indians During 2003." Great Lakes Indian Fish and Wildlife Commission GLIFWC administrative report 2004–01. Odanah, Wis.: Great Lakes Indian Fish and Wildlife Commission.

Laland, K., F. John Olding-Smee, and Marcus Feldman. 2000. "Niche Construction, Biological Evolution and Cultural Change." *Behavioral and Brain Sciences* 23: 131–46.

Leopold, Aldo. 1948. *A Sand County Almanac, and Sketches Here and There*. Oxford: Oxford University Press.

Lloyd, William F. 1833. *Two Lectures on the Checks to Population*. Oxford: Oxford University Press.

López, Alejandro, Scott Atran, John D. Coley, Douglas L. Medin, and Edward E. Smith. 1997. "The Tree of Life: Universal and Cultural Features of Folkbiological Taxonomies and Inductions." *Cognitive Psychology* 32: 251–95.

Love, Bradley C., Douglas L. Medin, and T. M. Gureckis. 2004. "SUSTAIN: A Network Model of Category Learning." *Psychological Review* 111: 309–32.

Malt, Barbara. 1995. "Category Coherence in Cross-Cultural Perspective." *Cognitive Psychology* 29: 85–148.

McNutt, Dorene, and Zachary Grossman. 2003. "Crandon Mine Victory Won by a Historic Alliance." Available at: http://www.nocrandonmine.org/crandon_mine_victory.html (accessed April 11, 2006).

Medin, Douglas L., and Scott Atran. 2004. "The Native Mind: Biological Categorization, Reasoning and Decision Making in Development Across Cultures." *Psychological Review* 111: 960–83.

Medin, Douglas L., Elizabeth B. Lynch, John D. Coley, and Scott Atran. 1997. "Categorization and Reasoning Among Tree Experts: Do All Roads Lead to Rome?" *Cognitive Psychology* 32: 49–96.

Medin, Douglas, Norbert O. Ross, Scott Atran, Russ Burnett, and Sergey Blok. 2002. "Categorization and Reasoning in Relation to Culture and Expertise." In *The Psychology of Learning and Motivation*, edited by B. Ross. Volume 41. New York: Academic Press.

Medin, Douglas, Norbert Ross, Scott Atran, and Douglas G. Cox. Forthcoming. "Why Folkbiology Matters: Resource Conflict Despite Shared Goals and Knowledge." *Human Ecology.*

Medin, Douglas, Norbert Ross, Scott Atran, Douglas Cox, John Coley, Julia B. Proffitt, and Sergey Blok. 2006. "Folkbiology of Freshwater Fish." *Cognition* 99(3): 237–73.

Medin, Douglas, Hillarie Schwartz, Sergey Blok, and Lawrence Birnbaum. 1999. "The Semantic Side of Decision Making." *Psychonomic Bulletin and Review* 6(4): 562–69.

Mihesuah, Devon A. 1998. *Natives and Academics: Research and Writing About American Indians.* Lincoln: University of Nebraska Press.

Miller, Dale T., and Catherine McFarland. 1987. "Pluralistic Ignorance: When Similarity Is Interpreted as Dissimilarity." *Journal of Personality and Social Psychology* 53(2): 298–305.

Murphy, Gregory L. 2002. *The Big Book of Concepts.* Cambridge, Mass.: MIT Press.

Murphy, Gregory L., and Douglas L. Medin. 1985. "The Role of Theories in Conceptual Coherence." *Psychological Review* 92: 289–316.

Murray, J. A. H. 1989. "O.E.D. Preface and General Explanations." In *The Oxford English Dictionary.* 2nd ed. New York: Oxford University Press.

Nabhan, Gary P., and Sara St. Antoine. 1993. "The Loss of Floral and Faunal Story: The Extinction of Experience." In *The Biophilia Hypothesis*, edited by S. R. Kellert and E. O. Wilson. Washington, D.C.: Island Press.

Nakao, Keiko, and A. Kimball Romney. 1984. "A Method for Testing Alternative Theories: An Example from English Kinship." *American Anthropologist* 86: 668–73

Neale, Margaret, and Max Bazerman. 1991. "Cognition and Rationality in Negotiation." New York: Free Press.

Nesper, Larry. 2002. *The Walleye War: The Struggle for Ojibwe Spearfishing and Treaty Rights.* Lincoln: University of Nebraska Press.

Newman, James G. 1967. *The Menominee Forest of Wisconsin: A Case History*. Unpublished doctoral thesis. Michigan State University.

Nisbett, Richard E. 2003. *The Geography of Thought: How Asians and Westerners Think Differently . . . And Why*. New York: Free Press.

Osherson, Daniel, Edward Smith, Ormond Wilkie, Alejandro López, and Eldar Shafir. 1990. "Category-Based Induction." *Psychological Review* 97(2): 185–200.

Ostrom, Elinor, Roy Gardner, and James Walker. 1990. "The Nature of Common-Pool Resource Problems." *Rationality and Society* 2(3): 335–58.

Ostrom, Elinor, and Vincent Ostrom. 1997. "Cultures: Frameworks, Theories, and Models." In *Culture Matters: Essays in Memory of Aaron Wildavsky*, edited by Richard J. Ellis and Michael Thompson. Boulder, Colo.: Westview Press.

Pecore, Marshall. 1992. "Menominee Sustained Yield Management." *Journal of Forestry* 90(5): 12–16.

Peroff, Nicholas C. 1982. *Menominee Drums: Tribal Termination and Restoration, 1945–1974*. Norman: University of Oklahoma Press.

Prentice, Deborah A., and Dale T. Miller. 1993. "Pluralistic Ignorance and Alcohol Use on Campus: Some Consequences of Misperceiving the Social Norm." *Journal of Personality and Social Psychology* 64(2): 243–56.

Proffitt, Julia B., John B. Coley, and Douglas L. Medin. 2000. "Expertise and Category-Based Induction." *Journal of Experimental Psychology: Learning, Memory and Cognition* 26: 811–28.

Radomski, Paul J., and Timothy J. Goeman. 1995. "The Homogenizing of Minnesota Lakefish Assemblages." *Fisheries* 20: 20–23.

Rappaport, Roy. 1993. "The Anthropology of Trouble." *American Anthropologist* 95(2): 295–303.

———. 1999. *Ritual and Religion in the Making of Humanity*. Cambridge: Cambridge University Press.

Rettinger, David A., and Reid Hastie. 2001. "Content Effects on Decision Making." *Organizational Behavior and Human Decision Processes* 85: 336–59.

———. 2003. "Comprehension and Decision Making." In *Emerging Perspectives on Judgment and Decision Research*, edited by S. L. Schneider and J. Shanteau. New York: Cambridge University Press.

Ricciuti, Edward R. 1997. *The Menominee*. Vero Beach, Fla.: Rourke Publications.

Ritov, Ilana, and Daniel Kahneman. 1997. "How People Value Information: Attitudes Versus Economic Values." In *Environment, Ethics, and Behavior: The Psychology of Environmental Valuation and Degradation*, edited by M. Bazerman, D. Messick, A. Tenbrunsel, and K. Wade-Benzoni. San Francisco: The New Lexington Press.

Rokeach, Milton. 1973. *The Nature of Human Values*. New York: Free Press.

Romney, A. Kimball, Susan C. Weller, and William H. Batchelder. 1986. "Culture as Consensus: A Theory of Culture and Informant Accuracy." *American Anthropologist* 88(2): 318–38.

Rosch, Eleanor. 1977. "Human Categorization." In *Studies in Cross-Linguistic Psychology*, edited by by Neil Warren. New York: Academic Press.

Ross, Lee, and Connie Stillinger. 1991. "Psychological Barriers to Conflict Resolution." *Negotiation Journal* 7(4): 389–404.

Ross, Norbert. 2002. "Cognitive Aspects of Intergenerational Change: Mental Models, Cultural Change, and Environmental Behavior Among the Lacandon Maya of Southern Mexico." *Human Organization* 61: 125–38.

Ross, Norbert, and Douglas Medin. 2005. "Ethnography and Experiments: Cultural Models and Expertise Effects Elicited with Experimental Research Techniques." *Field Methods* 17(2): 131–49.

Schmidt, Steven H. 1995. "A Survey of Lakes on the Menominee Reservation, Wisconsin." Master's thesis, University of Wisconsin, Stevens Point.

Shafto, Patrick, and John D. Coley. 2003. "Development of Categorization and Reasoning in the Natural World: Novices to Expert, Naöve Similarity to Ecological Knowledge." *Journal of Experimental Psychology: Learning, Memory and Cognition* 29(4): 641–49.

Smith, Adam. 1776/1904. *An Inquiry into the Nature and Causes of the Wealth of Nations*. 2 volumes. Reprint. New York: Knopf.

Smith, Linda Tuhiwai. 1999. *Decolonizing Methodologies: Research and Indigenous Peoples*. New York: Zed Books.

Spindler, George, and Louise S. Spindler. 1971. *Dreamers with Power: The Menomini Indians*. New York: Holt, Rinehart, and Winston.

Steyvers, Mark, and Josh B. Tenenbaum. 2005. "The Large-Scale Structure of Semantic Networks: Statistical Analyses and a Model of Semantic Growth." *Cognitive Science* 29(1): 41–78.

Stross, Brian. 1973. "Acquisition of Botanical Terminology by Tzeltal Children." In *Meaning in Mayan Languages*, edited by M. Edmonson. The Hague: Mouton.

Tanner, Carmen, and Douglas L. Medin. Forthcoming. "Examples of Deontological Activism: The Case of Environmentalism." *Memory and Cognition*.

———. 2004. "Protected Values: No Omission Bias and No Framing Effects." *Psychonomic Bulletin and Review* 11(1): 185–91.

Tenbrunsel, Ann, and David E. Messick. 1999. "Sanctioning Systems, Decision Frames, and Cooperation." *Administrative Science Quarterly* 44(4): 684–707.

Tetlock, Phillip. 2003. "Thinking the Unthinkable: Sacred Values and Taboo Cognitions." *Trends in Cognitive Sciences* 7: 320–24.

Thompson, Leigh, and Richard Gonzales. 1997. "Environmental Disputes: Competition for Scarce Resources and Clashing of Values." In *Environment, Ethics and Behavior: The Psychology of Environmental Evaluation and Degradation*, edited by Max Bazerman, David Messick, Ann Tenbrunsel, and Karen Wade-Benzoni. San Francisco: New Lexington.

Tracy, L. 1998. "State Trends." *Council of State Governments Newsletter*, Summer 1998. Available at: stars.csg.org/trends/1999/summer/su99st7.pdf.

Voelker, John. 1964. *Anatomy of a Fisherman*. New York: McGraw-Hill.

Wallace, Alfred. 1889. *Darwinism*. New York: Macmillan.

WDNR. 1998. *An Assessment of the Impact of Stocked Walleye on Stocked Salmonids in the Milwaukee Estuary*. Milwaukee, Wis.: Bureau of Fisheries Management and Habitat Protection.

Weber, Elke U., and Christopher K. Hsee. 1999. "Models and Mosaics: Investigation of Cultural Differences in Risk Perception and Risk Preference." *Psychonomic Bulletin and Review* 6(4): 611–17.

Wester, Lyndon, and Sekson Yongvanit. 1995. "Biological Diversity and Community Love in Northwestern Thailand." *Journal of Ethnobiology* 15(1): 71–87.

Wilson, David S. 2002. *Darwin's Cathedral*. Chicago: University of Chicago Press.

Wisconsin Department of Natural Resources. 2000. *Wisconsin's Lake Sturgeon Management Plan*. Milwaukee, Wis.: Bureau of Fisheries Management and Habitat Protection.

———. 2002. "Open Water Spearing and Netting in Northern Wisconsin by Chippewa Indians During 2001." Great Lakes Indian Fish and Wildlife Commission administrative report Wisc2002–01. Odanah, Wis.: Wisconsin Department of Natural Resources.

Wolff, Phillip, Douglas L. Medin, and Connie Pankratz. 1999. "Evolution and Devolution of Folkbiological Knowledge." *Cognition* 73(2): 177–204.

Index |

213